The Best
Family Ski Vacations
in North America

Also by Laura Sutherland
Great Caribbean Family Vacations

By Laura Sutherland and Valerie Wolf Deutsch
The Best Bargain Family Vacations in the U.S.A.
Innocents Abroad: Traveling with Kids in Europe

The Best
Family Ski Vacations
in North America

Laura Sutherland

St. Martin's Griffin ✖ New York

THE BEST FAMILY SKI VACATIONS IN NORTH AMERICA.
Copyright © 1997 by Laura Sutherland. All rights reserved.
Printed in the United States of America. No part of this book
may be used or reproduced in any manner whatsoever without
written permission except in the case of brief quotations embod-
ied in critical articles or reviews. For information, address St.
Martin's Press, 175 Fifth Avenue, New York, N.Y. 10010.

Design by *Maureen Troy*

Library of Congress Cataloging-in-Publication Data

Sutherland, Laura.
    The best family ski vacations in North America / Laura Sutherland.
        p.   cm.
    ISBN 0–312–16780–6
    1. Ski resorts—United States—Directories. 2. Ski resorts—
Canada—Directories. I. Title.
    GV854.4.S88   1997
    796.93'025'73—DC21   97–24854
                                                              CIP

First St. Martin's Griffin Edition: November 1997

10 9 8 7 6 5 4 3 2 1

Contents

Acknowledgments

To my dependable and amusing travel companions, Madeleine and Walker, whose willingness to strap on a pair of skis and test dozens of children's ski schools in blizzards, white outs, rain storms, and gloriously sunny weather demonstrates their love of the sport and easy-going travel styles.

To my good-natured husband, Lance Linares, my favorite chairlift companion.

I am especially grateful to my sister, Jani Sutherland, for her experienced opinions and sage advice on children's ski instruction.

Special thanks go to Robin Seaman for her assistance, to "Taking the Kids" travel columnist and author Eileen Ogintz for her help and insight, and to my agent, Vicky Bijur, and editor, Anne Savarese. The assistance and advice offered by the ski resorts and their staff was extremely useful and greatly appreciated.

Introduction

The first time my kids barreled past me on the ski slopes and stayed out of sight no matter how hard I tried to catch up to them, I was elated. Finally I could glide down a long cruiser without stopping every few hundred yards to look up and wait for them. But my elation quickly turned to a lump in my throat as I realized they'd be leaving me in the cold white dust for the rest of my skiable future. Not to worry, though; I held the keys to the lunch locker, so I knew I'd see them as soon as they got hungry. Back at the condo that night, we sipped hot chocolate around the fire together while they told master-of-the-mountain stories and my husband and I massaged our legs.

From the time our kids were able to step into a pair of boots, ski vacations have been one of our favorite family holidays. When the kids were young we took advantage of the wonderful children's ski schools now found across the continent. My husband and I enjoyed riding the chairlifts together almost as much as skiing; it seemed like the longest stretch of time we'd spent talking since the kids were born.

As our youngsters grew and their skiing progressed from the snowplow stage, we skied together as a family until the tables turned and the kids got tired of waiting for us. That's when the advantage of a family ski vacation really became clear.

As children hit the preteen and teenage years, skiing offers families a chance to do things together but also offers the kids a growing degree of independence. Families can ski together part of the day and then go their separate ways. Since it's a vacation everyone is more relaxed, and just having the chance to chat leisurely on the chairlift with your teen can allow subjects to come up that ordinarily are off limits.

❄

"Parents should visit the children's facility the day before with their child and tell the child that they will be returning the next day."

—*Chi Chi Gustavson, Director of Snowmass Snowcubs, Snowmass Ski and Summer Resort, Colorado*

❄

Even if you don't travel down the same paths on the ski slopes, back at the condo in the evening you'll have your exhausted kids to yourself. If they still have some get up and go, you can take them ice skating or night skiing while you sip a hot toddy at the lodge. Some families reunite for an annual ski vacation long after their children have left home for college, and some eventually include several generations of skiers in their annual winter trips.

Ski resorts regard families as a huge part of their current business, and since kids constitute the future of the sport, all sorts of family-friendly facilities and activities have been added. The best family resorts have something for everyone: day care for infants and toddlers, great daylong ski-school programs for school-age kids, protected slopes for nervous beginners, snowboarding, teen programs, terrain to suit all abilities, and plenty of off-slope activities.

CHOOSING A RESORT

A ski vacation can be a major expense, so it pays to shop around before you buy. Your family's ages, abilities, interests, and bank account are all part of the equation that will determine where you go.

Ski resorts are making great efforts to offer families an easy, user-friendly experience. One-stop children's centers housing a day care, a ski school, a ski-rental outlet, and even a small ski-accessories shop are becoming increasingly common. Features that were rare a decade ago—ski and snowboard lessons for kids with lively instructors who know how to impart a love of the sport, quality day care for toddlers through grade-school kids, special women-only lessons and clinics, child-size snowboard equipment available for rent, and teen programs—are becoming industry standards. More and more resorts are adding themed ski areas for kids and terrain parks for boarders and skiers.

A recent *Forbes* magazine article reported that skiing has practically turned into a division of the entertainment industry as ski areas make sure that every member of the family, from babies to grandparents, has something to do. Besides downhill and cross-country skiing and snowboarding, expect to find horse-drawn sleigh rides, shopping, ice-skating rinks, snowshoe tours, snowmobiling, and other non-skiing activities at most ski resorts. Some even offer hot-air balloon rides (Steamboat Ski Area, Colorado), bobsled rides (Whiteface Mountain Ski Area, New York; Park City Mountain Resort, Utah; Vail, Colorado), full-service spas (Snowbird Ski and Summer Resort, Utah; Telluride, Colorado), winter fly-fishing (Aspen Mountain, Colorado), paragliding (Sun Valley Resort, Idaho), dogsled tours (Jackson Hole Mountain Resort, Wyoming; Mont-Sainte-Anne, Québec), and other unusual activities. Resorts have found that offering well-rounded vacation experiences keeps families coming back, especially as parents find their ski legs might not support them for the full week of thigh-pounding, bone-rattling skiing that they enjoyed in their prime.

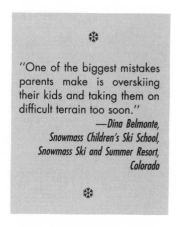

❄

"One of the biggest mistakes parents make is overskiing their kids and taking them on difficult terrain too soon."
—*Dina Belmonte,*
Snowmass Children's Ski School,
Snowmass Ski and Summer Resort,
Colorado

❄

Accommodating Varied Interests

If you are a family of both downhill and cross-country skiers, look for ski resorts that offer a strong cross-country program. Mont-Sainte-Anne, Québec, has the largest cross-country trail network in Canada, and its downhill skiing and off-slope activities are excellent. California's Northstar-at-Tahoe has cross-country trails that begin at the base of the ski lifts, and since both alpine and Nordic skiers share the same dining facilities, it's easy for everyone to meet for lunch. Lone Mountain Ranch near Big Sky Ski and Summer Resort, Montana, has spectacular cross-country skiing and lodging at the cross-country base. Stowe Mountain Resort, Vermont, has a number of interconnected cross-country ski centers, some with their own luxury lodging.

A number of resorts offer fine dining on the slopes, allowing parents with kids in ski school or day care to enjoy a leisurely gourmet lunch. Aspen Mountain and Vail, Colorado; Deer Valley Resort, Utah; Mont Tremblant, Québec; and Sun Valley Resort, Idaho, are particularly known for their high-altitude haute cuisine.

Child-Friendly Resorts

Parents of babies and toddlers will want to be on the lookout for high-quality, safe day-care facilities. Several resorts—Sugarloaf/USA, Maine; Northstar-at-Tahoe, California; Breckenridge, Colorado; and Deer Valley

Resort, Utah—offer electronic pagers to parents, and Mont Tremblant, Quebec, provides parents with cellular phones so they can check in easily on their little ones.

Preschool- and kindergarten-age beginners need kind and supportive ski instructors, a good selection of protected, gentle slopes, and a supervised children's lounge to relax in when they tire of skiing. As children age and gain experience on skis or snowboards, they need more intermediate runs and easy snowboard areas.

Teens need time with their peers and inventive snowboard parks. Some resorts, especially those in the East, have nonstop evening programs for teens. Mount Snow, Vermont, for example, devotes an entire section of their resort to evening activities such as ice skating, sledding, a nightlit half pipe (a popular on-mountain snowboard feature), and teen nightclubs.

What Do Parents Want?

❄

"Be sure to take the inner liner out of a boot when you fit your child. It's impossible to fit boots properly otherwise—you can't tell where the toe stops with the hard outer boot on."

—Robyn Christianson, Ski-School Director, Alta Ski Area, Utah

❄

And what about you, their parents? If you're a family of all abilities, you'll want a good variety of terrain spreading out over many acres and a full range of learn-to-ski programs. If you want to get in as much downhill skiing as you can in a day, look for resorts with the greatest number of gondolas and high-speed chairlifts and a lot of vertical drop. If you want to ski early or late in the season, pick a resort with a high elevation to ensure that the snowpack is adequate. If a member of your group doesn't ski, select a resort like Taos Ski Valley, New Mexico, where interesting activities await in town or in nearby Santa Fe, or Big Sky Ski and Summer Resort, Montana, where visitors can explore Yellowstone National Park.

Sophisticated or Homespun?

Think about the resort atmosphere you want. If you like glamour and sophistication, nothing beats Aspen Mountain and Vail, Colorado. For quieter, more homespun experiences, choose a resort like Alta Ski Area, Utah, or Attitash, Bear Peak, New Hampshire, that offers a lower key ski vacation. If you want a family-friendly and casual environment, pick a western resort like Crested Butte Mountain Resort, Colorado, or Jackson Hole

Mountain Resort, Wyoming, or a quintessential New England one like Stowe Mountain Resort, Vermont, but keep in mind that almost every ski area can be considered family-friendly these days. Thanks to the Winter Olympics, areas like Whiteface Mountain Ski Area, New York (1932 and 1980) and Park City Mountain Resort, Utah (2002) have such activities as bobsledding, luge, and ski-jumping lessons, which can be hard to find in other resorts.

Families on a budget who long to ski the famous resorts of Europe can get an international flavor at a lower price by choosing Mont-Sainte-Anne near Québec City or Mont Tremblant, near Montréal, where locals speak French and the cuisine tilts toward European-style rather than American-style food.

HOW TO GET THE MOST OUT OF YOUR FAMILY SKI VACATION
Timing: When Should You Travel?

Prices and crowds peak over Christmas, New Year's, and President's weekend, with March break and Easter coming in close behind. Plan your trip at times other than these to benefit from lower prices and shorter lift lines.

The weather can make or break any ski vacation; it's the part of your trip you can't control. January can be the coldest month throughout the continent, but it also can offer some great deals and awesome powder skiing. Nearly every ski area offers price cuts to lure skiers during the post-Christmas quiet season. Spring skiing may not guarantee powder snow, but you usually can count on plenty of sunshine and warm weather, cutting down on the number of layers you need to wear and sparing your family the cold-hands-and-feet syndrome.

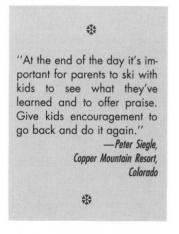

❄

"At the end of the day it's important for parents to ski with kids to see what they've learned and to offer praise. Give kids encouragement to go back and do it again."
—*Peter Siegle,*
Copper Mountain Resort,
Colorado

❄

Where to Stay

Families who stay at the base of the lifts usually enjoy one-stop vacationing, with restaurants, day care, a ski school, and shops just steps from their hotel room or condo. The convenience of a ski-in-and-out location will cost more than if you stay a short shuttle-bus or car ride away from the lifts, but you may get in more skiing and experience fewer hassles, making your lift tickets and transportation costs more worthwhile. If the weather gets bad, you can ski back to your accommodations for a break and head back to the slopes when the weather changes.

Condominiums offer more space and a kitchen, but weigh the advantages and disadvantages against your idea of family fun. Some parents don't consider a trip a real vacation unless they eat every meal out, while others find it simpler to cook family meals at "home." If you're on a budget, a condo will allow you to avoid the stiff prices of most on-mountain restaurants and cafeterias.

Hotels, motels, and inns range in price and amenities from budget chains to exclusive enclaves for the rich and famous. If your kids always seem to have energy to burn, no matter how hard they ski, look for lodging that has athletic facilities, which also are a bonus if you run into bad weather.

Some ski resorts have youth hostels with multifamily bunk rooms of three, four, five, or six beds. You'll share a kitchen and common living area, but you can save on overnight stays and will often have ski-in-and-out access to the slopes.

Do As Much in Advance As You Can

Many ski areas have a central reservations number so that with one call you can book accommodations, purchase lift tickets and ski-school lessons, reserve day-care slots, make restaurant reservations, and schedule après-ski or other recreational activities. If you plan on evenings out, ask about baby-sitting services and try to make reservations in advance.

✳

"If snow is a really new environment for a young child, they'll have a hard time concentrating in ski school. Give them the time to play in and experience the snow for a morning or day, and then put them in ski school. They'll be able to concentrate much better."

—Jani Sutherland,
SKIwee Western Regional Manager

✳

Some ski areas will send or fax you forms to fill out at home for ski school and day care, saving you valuable ski time when you arrive. Some lodging properties will even fill your refrigerator before you arrive so you don't have to stop at the store.

If you haven't been able to purchase lift tickets and lessons before you leave home, try to do so upon your arrival, the day before you plan to ski. Lift-ticket offices report that their least busy times are between 1 and 3 P.M. Since ski-school registration can often take 30 minutes, plan to start your morning early on your first day at a resort if you haven't been able to preregister.

IF YOU'RE ON A BUDGET

Skiing will never be cheap, but discounts are available at virtually every resort on the continent. Your goal is to find the resort whose discounts match your family's interests.

The two largest costs for most ski vacations are lodging and transportation. After you've created a short list of areas you'd like to visit, call each ski resort's central reservation number to see what kind of packages they offer and whether they have any airline partners. Look for tour operators and wholesalers that feature package deals in the Sunday section of your local newspaper. If you use a travel agent, find one that is experienced at creating ski vacations. Midweek rates for lodging and packages are always lower than weekend rates.

Keep your eye on a ski area's Web site for special packages and price deals. For example, as soon as Mount Snow, Vermont, found out that the New England Patriots were to play in the Super Bowl, they put together a special package to lure skiers away from their home TV sets and up to the snow. Their Web site carried the late-breaking details.

> ❄
>
> "Parents need to remember that their child's progress is individual, not based on age. Some little ones are not used to being in a group, making learning more difficult. . . . Also, two-piece snowsuits are easier than one-piece, as they're much faster to get on and off for an emergency bathroom break!"
>
> —*Susan Baca,*
> *Children's Ski-School Director,*
> *Beaver Creek Resort, Colorado*
>
> ❄

Travel During the Off-peak Season

The time of year you plan to ski can make a big difference in the price you pay. Christmas and Presidents' weekend, which are huge times for every ski area, have the highest prices of the season. When you shift your family ski vacation from February or March to early April, you can garner savings of up to 50 percent. Resorts in Colorado's Summit County, such as Keystone and Copper Mountain, still get ample snowfall in April and stay open until late in the month. Whistler Resort in British Columbia, Killington in Vermont, Mammoth Mountain in California, and Mt. Bachelor in Oregon all stay open through May and offer late-season packages that come with sunny days and low prices.

Early season (before Christmas), January, and early February can be slow times and ski resorts may put together price-reduced packages. But be aware that you run the risk of unpredictable snow early season, and excruciatingly cold weather in January, especially in the East.

Certain eastern resorts like Mount Snow and Killington in Vermont have special family-value weeks scattered throughout the year. Kids often ski free and lodging prices plummet.

Special Ticket Deals

Consider resorts with special kids' lift-ticket prices: Big Sky Ski and Summer Resort in Montana lets kids ten and under ski free; Squaw Valley USA charges $5 per day for all kids twelve and under; Snowbird Ski and Summer Resort and Solitude Ski Resort, Utah, sell kids' chairlift tickets for $10, and kids pay their age at Sugarbush Resort in Vermont. Crested Butte Mountain Resort, Colorado, offers free early-season lift tickets for children and adults staying in area hotels and condos. Steamboat Ski Area, Colorado, pioneered the "kids ski free" deal, and still offers a free child's ticket (12 and under) for each parent purchasing a five-day ticket.

> ❋
>
> "If it's your child's first time on skis, rent the equipment the night before and have them try on the boots and slip into the skis to see what they feel like."
>
> —Loopy Quinones,
> Junior Ski Program Manager,
> Sugarbush, Vermont
>
> ❋

If you are a family of beginners, choose a resort such as Copper Mountain Resort, Colorado, or Mont-Sainte-Anne, Québec, where you can ski beginner lifts for free. Invest in a lesson, and then practice what you learn at no charge. Smaller resorts often have good beginner and intermediate terrain and much lower lift prices; they're another good option for first-time skiing families.

Call a ski area and find out what kind of promotional deals they have: One year Squaw Valley USA, California, had a promotional deal with Kodak in which anyone who bought a one-use camera also could purchase two-for-one lift tickets. Many of the Colorado ski areas have discount coupons at major sports retailers, such as Christy Sports, or REI in the Denver area. If the reservation clerk can't tell you, ask for the marketing or sales department.

Lift ticket prices are listed as single-day prices in the guidebook. Note that nearly every ski area discounts multiple-day lift ticket purchases. The more days you buy, the lower the daily price drops.

Shop at Home

Load up on supplies such as lip balm, sunblock, and high-energy snacks before you leave home so you won't get stuck paying resort prices. Get used to carrying a lightweight daypack or fanny pack to hold snacks, water, sunblock, and extra layers of clothing. Encourage each member of the family to wear their own fanny pack. It will help cut down on replacement purchases of lip protection or sunblock, gloves, hats, and goggles. Make your own snacks and lunches and put them in a locker or carry them with you.

Evaluate Ski-Discount Cards

Ski-discount cards can offer substantial savings if you're willing to study various vendors' catalogs carefully and plan around what you read. Once you purchase a discount card, you receive discounts on lift tickets, lodging, dining, and equipment rentals in ski areas throughout the United States and Canada.

Lift-ticket discounts vary considerably. Many of the larger ski areas offer discounts only during early and late season while the smaller areas have standing discounts throughout the season. Discounts can range from $5 off a lift ticket to two-for-one lift tickets or free lessons. Restaurants generally offer 10 to 20 percent off a meal, and lodging discounts average around 10 percent.

❄

"Goggles can get too hot on a sunny day and kids will pull them off; if you are spring skiers, have kids wear dark glasses to protect their eyes on those days."

—*Glenn Goldstein,*
Children's Ski School Instructor,
Steamboat Ski Area,
Colorado

❄

The four most reliable businesses are: U.S. Passport Ski and Mountain Card, 800-754-8326; Ski Card International, 800-333-2754; National Lift Ticket, 800-318-7772; and World Ski Association, 800-525-SNOW.

TIPS FOR TAKING THE KIDS

Babies and Toddlers

Make sure the resort you want to visit has day care for a baby as young as yours. Most take children from eighteen months on, and growing numbers take infants as young as six weeks. All require advance reservations.

Day-care operators at ski resorts report that 70 to 80 percent of the little ones who come through their doors have never been left by their parents before. It is recommended that you visit the day-care center the afternoon before you plan to leave your child. (You can sign your child up at that time and avoid the morning rush.) While you tour the facility, prepare your child for the experience by talking about how you'll be leaving but will be back later to pick her up. Many day-care centers suggest bringing a special blanket or toy from home, and some require that you provide formula and diapers.

Parents are advised to call to check on their child every hour or half hour at first if the child is teary saying good-bye. If your child can't be calmed or feels sick, almost every ski area will post signs at the bottom of all lifts alerting you to contact the children's center. A growing number of ski areas hand out pagers to parents.

Three- to Five-Year-Olds

Most ski-school programs start children on skis around age three, combining a day-care program with a learn-to-ski experience that should include time just playing in the snow. The newest and easiest lift for beginners to ride is the Magic Carpet, a slow-moving conveyor belt that sits on the snow. Kids simply stand on it as it carries them a short distance up the slopes. Four-and five-year-olds learn skiing much faster than three-year-olds. If your preschooler doesn't like skiing, don't force it. He probably will next year.

School-Age Kids

Starting at age five or six, children have gained the coordination and muscle control to pick up skiing quickly. They learn best in a group setting where they will practice what they learn over and over under the supervision of an expert who can correct them until skiing becomes part of their muscle memory. Many ski instructors feel private lessons are not as helpful as group lessons at this age.

Snowboard lessons begin around age seven or eight in most resorts; a few start kids as young as five. Children need to be a certain minimum weight in order for the board's edges to make solid contact with the snow, which is what allows them to turn.

Make sure your kids have enough time to simply play in the snow before their lessons begin. They'll be better able to pay attention and be less distracted by the novelty of the snow.

Teens

Resorts with night skiing can be an advantage for teens, since that age seems to have an endless supply of energy. Many ski areas offer a wide variety of supervised nighttime activities just for teens along with activities the entire family can enjoy. Select a compact village or small ski town for your vacation and your teens can explore the shops, cafes, and recreational offerings safely on their own. If your teens are accomplished boarders, look for a resort with a variety of snowboard parks, including those with special terrain features. Private lessons and group lessons work well for this age group. Girls might enjoy a women's-only clinic.

Many ski areas provide special teen programming over holiday periods. These programs, usually set up through the ski school, provide a supervised ski experience for teens, who are grouped according to their ability. Ski instructors offer ski tips, but the programs are designed to be fun and less structured than formal lessons.

CLOTHING

Dress children as you would dress yourself—in plenty of warm and comfortable layers. You wouldn't want to be stuffed into a snowsuit that makes you feel like the Pillsbury Doughboy; choose clothing you would feel comfortable moving in. Note that children get cold faster than adults.

Ski clothing must be waterproof and insulated. Don't dress kids in jeans or corduroy pants. Parkas should zip easily and have plenty of pockets. Ski bibs, similar to overalls, eliminate the need to keep things tucked in; there's nothing worse than taking a spill and standing up with a pile of snow melting in your pants. Choose thin layers of high-quality clothing: long underwear can be Thinsulate, a cotton/polyester blend, or silk. Turtlenecks provide a layer of warmth and neck protection.

> ❄
>
> "Proper gloves are a key—cotton mittens are a disaster. Also, kids want to have fun and sometimes the parents lose sight of that. If kids aren't having fun, they're not going to want to learn."
>
> —*Sarah Reed,*
> *Director of Children's Ski School,*
> *Jackson Hole Mountain Resort, Wyoming*
>
> ❄

Never wear long muffler-type scarves, as they can get caught on a chairlift or underneath skis. Tubelike fleece "turtles," also called neck gaiters, keep heat in and can double as a faceguard or hat when needed. Most resorts have hot tubs and heated swimming pools; don't forget to pack your swimsuits!

Headgear

Kids lose considerable heat from their heads and should wear hats except in spring skiing conditions. Many children wear helmets to prevent head injuries, and more and more adults are beginning to wear them as well. Ski-school directors and ski patrollers on the whole approve of them, asserting that more children wear them in the East than the West because eastern snow conditions are hard and icy. Others note that helmets are helpful protection against small children's collisions with chairlifts and each other.

A few experts warn that helmets can limit peripheral vision and that the weight of them may cause neck injuries, but overall, helmets get a thumbs-up from industry experts. Many kids like to wear helmets to give them the sporty look of a ski racer. Goggles can be snapped onto the back of the helmet, making them harder to lose.

If you buy your child a helmet, make sure it fits at the time of purchase: Children should not grow into helmets. You should be able to get a minimum of two years' of use out of a helmet, since a child's head does not grow at anywhere near the rate of her feet.

Mittens and Gloves

Gloves have individual fingers; mittens have only a thumb. Mittens are warmer than gloves and are better for younger children. On a really cold day, add a very thin liner under a mitten for extra warmth. Gloves are better for older kids as they allow greater dexterity. Never allow kids to ski in knit or woven mittens or gloves, as these can actually stick to the lifts and are not particularly cold resistant or waterproof. Instead, select a waterproof material such as Gore-Tex.

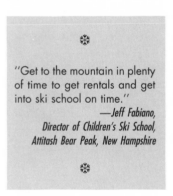

❄

"Get to the mountain in plenty of time to get rentals and get into ski school on time."
—Jeff Fabiano,
Director of Children's Ski School,
Attitash Bear Peak, New Hampshire

❄

When you outfit your child with gloves, buy a set of mitten guards, little cords with clips on each end. One attaches to the glove, the other to the sleeve of the jacket. Then, while you're at it, get a set for yourself. If you have young children, you will be ripping off your gloves every few minutes to help with any number of minor and major adjustments to their gear.

Goggles and Glasses

Make sure you have proper eye covering for your kids. Goggles are essential in snowy conditions and help protect children's eyes and surrounding skin from the cold. They can double as dark glasses on a sunny day, although some children will not wear goggles in warm weather because they're too hot.

Your children must wear dark glasses or goggles on a sunny day or risk damaging their eyes. Children's ski instructors mention the lack of eye covering as the biggest mistake made by parents; many instructors will not allow a child to attend ski school unless he has some sort of eye covering.

Sunblock

Sunblock is as important an item in your child's wardrobe as a jacket. Lip protection also is essential. At high altitudes the exposure to ultraviolet rays is great, and the reflective effect of the snow increases the need to be diligent about applying sunscreen. See page 17 for more about preventing sunburn.

DOWNHILL SKIING

Gear and Equipment

If your kids are ready for lessons, they're also ready for well-made ski equipment. Select the right gear for your kids and your vacation will start out on the right foot. If your children are uncomfortable, they may refuse to ski.

Families who take a ski vacation for a few days once or twice a year should plan to rent equipment until their children are old enough to make it worthwhile investing in equipment. If you're heading to a destination resort for more than a few days, rent equipment once you get there so that any problems can be corrected on-site. If you're driving in for a weekend ski break, rent equipment before you leave home to avoid standing in the rental lines when you should be on the slopes.

> ❄
>
> "Dress kids appropriately, in layers. And label everything!"
> —Kathy Copeland,
> Woollywood Ski School,
> Mammoth Mountain, California
>
> ❄

Families who ski for more than ten days each season should consider buying equipment for their kids. If you're lucky, you can get through two seasons with skis, boots, and clothing. If you buy bindings whose lower limits start with your child's current weight, you can usually use the bindings on several sets of skis. Often, boots will fit for only one season.

Many reputable ski shops sell used kids' equipment that their customers have traded in for new at the beginning of the season. A growing number of shops have season-long equipment-leasing programs for kids. Ski shops won't sell or lease anything that's unsafe or out of date. Ski swaps offer used equipment at rock-bottom prices, but educate yourself about what to look for before you go; talk to your local ski shop and find out what's important in a child's binding, ski or snowboard, and boot.

Skis and Bindings

The most frequent mistake parents make is buying (or renting) kids' skis too long. Beginners of any age should have skis that reach to between their chin and nose when the child stands next to the skis standing on end. Shaped skis are sized differently and are shorter in length. As children progress in ability, the length of the skis can increase. If you buy skis too long, your child will have difficulty trying to maneuver that much ski across the snow. Select newer model skis with bindings that meet industry safety standards, called DIN standards, which determine a binding's release based on the size and ability of the skier. Reputable ski shops can set bindings to suit your child.

Boots

Boots have two functions: to keep the feet warm and to provide control over the skis. If you buy boots too big, your child's foot will slide around, the heel will blister, and she won't have enough control of the ski. Kids should wear just one pair of socks. Ski boots are so well insulated that two pairs of socks are unnecessary and often uncomfortable as they bunch more easily. If it's really cold, the sock can be part wool and a bit thicker.

Most ski boots have insulated padded liners that can be pulled out of the boots' hard plastic shell. Boots with removable liners allow you to take the liners out and dry them. Removable boot liners also provide a more reliable fit since you can feel through the soft padding to where the toes press when you're shopping for boots. Make sure the child walks around with the boot liner in the boot and is wearing his or her ski socks. Test kids' boots in their bindings. Used boots show wear at the tips and heels from walking on pavement. Any boot that is too curved in these areas will not fit properly in a binding.

SNOWBOARDING

Snowboards are here to stay, and even the old holdouts against boarders like Park City Mountain Resort, Utah, and Alpine Meadows Ski Resort, California, now allow them. You can't ignore the statistics: Snowboarding is increasing by an average of 20 percent each year, and the numbers keep growing.

Lessons for kids start at age seven or eight, and most ski areas now have pint-size rental boards and boots and special classes for young beginners. Ski resorts have added snowboard parks with special terrain features such as half pipes (just what it sounds like, half a tube or pipe sculpted out of snow), quarter pipes (half a half pipe—just one side), spines (long spines of snow to board over and catch some air), tabletops (a mound of snow with the top leveled off), whales (a huge mound of rounded snow), chutes, ridges, and bumps. There's even a special snow-grooming tool called a pipe dragon that cuts half pipes perfectly.

Equipment

There are three major styles of snowboards: freestyle boards, freecarve boards, and alpine boards. Freestyle boards are designed for doing tricks; they maneuver a bit like a skateboard. Freecurve boards are designed for all-mountain riding in a wide variety of conditions. They are used with a soft boot and typically have wide tips so you can ride powder as well as execute freestyle tricks. Most children start out on freecarve boards. Alpine boards are designed more for speed and for carving turns on harder snow; they're not as well suited for tricks. They are more popular in Europe than in the U.S. and Canada.

Clothing for snowboarders tends to be different from clothing for skiers, and it's not just fashion dictating the look. Pants are reinforced (and often padded for beginners) where they will make contact with the snow most—at the knees and on the bottom. Jackets are longer and reinforced across the bottom. Gloves are longer too, so a boarder can trail his or her hand through the snow for balance while carving turns.

> ❄
>
> "Kids are a good example to parents of how to take on a new sport. They're playful and not afraid to try new things."
> —*Kim Bender,*
> *Instructor, Nordic Center,*
> *Beaver Creek Resort, Colorado*
>
> ❄

CROSS-COUNTRY (NORDIC) SKIING

There are three types of cross-country skiing: track, telemark, and backcountry. Both backcountry and track skiers cross rather flat terrain using a kick-and-glide motion. Backcountry skiers simply take off across open meadows and woods, creating their own trail. Track skiers ski on tracks produced by special grooming machines. The telemark ski allows skiers to also ski on a downhill course, lifting the heel to make long sweeping turns. It's very tricky. Most families track ski at Nordic centers until everyone is experienced enough to try backcountry skiing.

Nordic centers are found next to nearly every ski resort mentioned in this book. They range from small places with a few dozen kilometers (distances in cross-country skiing are referred to in kilometers rather than miles) of groomed trails, to hundreds of kilometers of terrain for all different abilities.

Most centers have rentals and lessons available at their base lodge. Many have pulkes, little trailers on skis, which parents can use to pull younger kids. Some centers have restaurants, cafés, lodging, and hut-to-hut possibilities.

Because you expend so much more energy cross-country skiing, clothing needs are different. Wear light layers of clothing and avoid 100 percent cotton, as it holds moisture when you sweat. Instead, choose polyester, silk, wool, or any special blend that wicks moisture away from your body.

STAYING HEALTHY

Preventing Ski Injuries

Have your equipment checked out before you ski and make sure your bindings are adjusted to your weight and ability. If you borrow equipment for your kids, you'll need to make sure the bindings are adjusted for your child's weight and ability and reset when returned.

> ❄
>
> "Putting your children in lessons for more than one day gives instructors the chance to help kids remove any mental barriers that get in the way of learning. Whether your child is 3 or 17, the confidence gained from learning something new translates to all other things in life."
>
> —Pèter Ingvoldstad,
> Snow Sport University Director,
> Smuggler's Notch, Vermont
>
> ❄

More than 60 percent of all ski injuries occur on the first and last runs, so don't push yourself at the beginning or end of the day. Do a few stretches before you head out—runners' warm-up exercises will help you loosen up. Ski in keeping with your physical shape. Take it easy at first if you're not in great condition. If you feel tired, quit instead of taking that one last run.

Make sure your kids know the rules of the slopes. All kids should be familiar with signs and fences that indicate off-limit terrain. Beginners should be taught how to approach the chairlift to avoid injuries. Ski poles should be carried so that the tips stay down. Be aware of snow conditions; icy patches and mush make it more difficult to control your skis or snowboards and can tire kids quickly. Take the time to learn your way around the mountain; most areas offer short, free mountain tours in which a ski instructor or mountain host gives skiers an on-skis overview of the mountain.

The most common snowboard injury is to the wrist; beginners are advised to wear wristguards, and a few areas rent them along with snowboards.

Good skills are the best way to help prevent injuries, so lessons should be a regular part of any ski trip—no matter how good your kids think they are. The better skiers and snowboarders your kids are, the less likely they are to get hurt. Ski patrols report that many injuries occur when teenage boys of varying abilities ski together. The more experienced boys take their buddies down an advanced run; the beginners try to keep up, ski out of control, and get hurt.

Effects of High Altitude

If you're skiing in the Rocky Mountains or the Sierra Nevada you're likely to be at elevations of 7,000 and 8,000 feet. Ski resorts in the Midwest and East are at much lower elevations. There is less oxygen and less humidity available to you at a high altitude than at sea level, and a variety of slightly unpleasant symptoms can result. You might find yourself with a headache (the most common side effect of high altitude) or with nausea, insomnia, diarrhea, constipation, restlessness, shortness of breath, nasal congestion, a cough, a fast heartbeat, or fatigue. The minor symptoms will disappear over a few days as your body adjusts.

Here are some things you can do to help adjust to high-altitude conditions:

- Don't overdo: Exercise in moderation the first few days.
- Drink plenty of liquids.
- Reduce alcohol intake (alcohol has a greater effect at high altitudes).
- Get plenty of sleep.
- Avoid salty foods.
- Eat foods high in carbohydrates.

Sunburn

At high altitudes the atmosphere is thinner and the sun can burn you very quickly: For each thousand feet gained in altitude, your UV radiation increases by 2 percent. Add the snow factor and its ability to reflect back 80 to 95 percent of the sun's rays and sunblock is a necessity.

Apply sunscreen of at least SPF 15 to your own and your child's face, ears, and neck, and reapply every two hours, even on cloudy days. Give your child his or her own sunscreen—most ski shops sell sunscreen in small tubes attached to a string that can hang around your child's neck. Sunblock sticks can be used without taking off your gloves. Make sure all family members wear goggles or sunglasses at all times.

TAKE LESSONS!

With the ubiquitousness of well-thought-out learn-to-ski and learn-to-snowboard programs that often feature exciting terrain gardens, many children prefer spending the day in classes with other kids. Even so, allow plenty of time to ski together as a family so your kids can show you what they've learned and won't feel that you are dumping them in ski school so you can have fun skiing without them.

Let the trained, skilled instructors teach your kids to ski. Your children inevitably will listen to them more attentively, resent them less, and learn the proper way to ski instead of picking up all of your bad habits. When a parent teaches his own child, the child has someone handy and safe to blame for problems and mistakes.

Private lessons that last only an hour or two are less valuable for younger kids, who find it difficult to put what they are taught into practice intellectually. Kids need to experience the right way to ski with their body. That's why it's important for children to be in all-day ski lessons, where an instructor can repeatedly correct bad posture and, in an encouraging way, tell kids how to do things right. Once kids reach an age when they can remember and apply ideas, private lessons are beneficial.

The best programs have:

- Instructors who specialize in teaching children and know how to make such instruction fun.
- Beginner facilities that are separated from the rest of the mountain. Special terrain gardens are fun but not necessary.
- Instructors who can communicate their goals clearly to any parent who asks, both at the beginning of the lesson and at the end when they summarize what the child needs to work on.
- Classes that group kids by both age and ability, so that a ten-year-old beginner isn't in with four- and five-year-olds, and kids of different ages and abilities aren't grouped together on slow days.
- Follow-up meetings in which your child's ski instructor lets you know what your child can and cannot do, and identifies which runs are most appropriate for your child to ski.

Keep in mind that your child's experience will be colored by the other kids in the lesson. If a nine-year-old girl has an important bonding experience with another girl her age, she's definitely going to want to return the next day if her new friend will be there. If the class is filled with twelve-year-old toughies, she may refuse to go back.

Pay attention to the quality of your children's skiing to get a sense of what they are really learning, and listen carefully to their comments and impressions. When my son described one of his instructors as "the kind of adult who pretends to like children but you know he really doesn't," I knew it was time to request another instructor.

Every ski resort listed in this book offers adult lessons for skiers and snowboarders of all abilities. Most have special women-only classes or clinics, and some also offer classes in extreme skiing, skiing the bumps, and racing. This book goes into detail only on children's ski schools at each resort. If you want more information on other ski-school programs, simply call the number listed at the front of each chapter.

OUT OF THE CONDO AND ONTO THE SLOPES

Skiing gives kids more to whine about than any other sport. Count the stiff boots, constricting clothes, damp socks, endless opportunities for getting cold, and the number of times kids will fall on a hard, cold, sometimes wet surface, and you have a potential nightmare vacation for parents.

To avoid the morning rush, do as much as possible the night before: Put ski clothes out, set boots by the door (make sure they're dry), stuff your backpack with dry mittens, goggles, and other dry snacks, and make lunches if you can. Write your child's name on all clothing including jackets, sweaters, hats, goggles, and mittens.

If your kids will be in ski school, identify their skis and poles by writing their names in indelible ink on masking tape (even on rental skis) and sticking the tape to their equipment. Most ski schools require some type of identification on equipment, and many parents waste time scrambling to create ID labels on the morning they arrive. Make sure kids' wrist watches are waterproof.

Make sure your children eat a healthy breakfast to give them energy for a busy day, and tuck some high-energy snacks such as nuts, raisins, or energy bars into their pockets. Meet at a prearranged place at a certain time with the lure of a hot chocolate or special treat.

Decide in advance what your children will be expected to carry and what you will carry for them. Kids seven and older can carry their own skis and boards. Inexpensive ski carriers that lock poles and skis together in

> ❄
>
> "Many parents think siblings will be more comfortable if they are placed together in the same ski or snowboard class. But it often happens that the older child is hampered and the younger child never learns to adapt to a new situation. Go with the decision of the pros when it comes to placing siblings in ski school."
>
> —*Maggie Loring,*
> *American Skiing Company,*
> *Director of Perfect Turn, Inc.*
> *and Technical Director of SKIwee USA.*
>
> ❄

a device with a handle can be quite handy; most ski shops carry several types.

Attach as much gear to younger kids as you can so you're not spending your fun money replacing sets of glasses, mittens, and hats. Invest in mitten guards, hat guards, and glasses lassoes.

Tips for a Successful Ski Day

- Make sure children are well rested and well fed and have plenty of healthy, high-energy snacks in their pockets.
- Make sure they eat a healthy lunch and have a restful lunchtime.
- Make sure they quit when they're tired; children slow down and tire with amazing suddenness. It's time to quit when they droop.
- Remember that heavy spring snow tires children faster than the lighter powder.
- Make sure kids know where the bathrooms are.

SKICABULARLY

Ski Terms

alpine skiing – another name for downhill skiing

carving – wide, beautifully executed turns

cross-country skiing – (also called Nordic skiing) a type of skiing on trails or in the backcountry across meadows and fields where you step and glide on a narrow ski that allows your heel to lift

DIN (Deutsche Industrial Norm) – safety standard for a binding's release, calibrated on the size and ability of the skier

hourglass skis – skis that are narrower in the middle than on the ends, allowing for easier turning; also called shaped skis, parabolic skis, sidecuts, and supersidecut skis

Nordic skis – narrower skis used for cross-country skiing

parallel – when the two skis travel down the mountain side by side in parallel

Perfect Turn – system of ski instruction developed at Sunday River, Maine

powder hound – someone who loves to ski deep powder snow

SKIwee – system of children's ski and snowboard instruction developed by *Ski* magazine and used in many ski resorts

sled dogs – extremely short skis, just a couple of feet long; also called hot feet

telemark skis – downhill cross-country skis that leave the heel free to move

traverse – skiing across the mountain, rather than down the fall line
wedge – the name for the shape a beginner's skis must make in order to
   turn and stop; formerly known as a snowplow
wedge christie – a parallel traverse with a wedge turn

Snowboard terms

berms – mounds of snow
carving – creating wide sweeping turns down the mountain
half pipe – imagine a pipe cut in half, now make it big and out of snow;
   snowboarders execute tricks off its edges
hits – jumps
pipe dragon – the grooming machine that cuts half pipes
quarter pipe – half a half pipe
rails – metal or pvc pipes on the snow for sliding and jumping
scorpion – a grooming machine that cuts half pipes
shred – to snowboard brilliantly ("That guy can really shred!")
spine or *razorback* – a long narrow pile of snow with a pointed top and
   wider base, like a triangle
tabletop – a huge pile of snow with a flat top
whales – enormous mounds of snow

Mountain Characteristics

black-diamond trail – an expert or advanced run
blue square trail – an intermediate run
bump – slang for mogul
chute – a steep and narrow run, often edged by rocks or trees
cruiser – a long, wide, smoothed-out run without any bumps
extreme skiing/boarding – a daring form of downhill skiing and snowboarding off steep drop-offs and nearly vertical faces; skiers often
   hike into the backcountry to reach this challenging natural terrain
fall line – the line your skis would take by themselves as they traveled
   down the mountain
glade – a narrow trail through the trees
green circle trail – a beginner's run
moguls – bumps of snow usually caused by the turning action of skiers
   on steep, ungroomed slopes
steep – sharply angled face of the mountain
terrain park – special area of the mountain with man-made jumps and
   other fun features

Types of Lifts

gondola – an enclosed lift, usually holding four to ten people

high-speed chairlift – looks like a typical chairlift, but it moves passengers much faster than a standard chairlift. It has a detachable grip that separates the chair from the cable. The chair slows for loading, then reattaches to the cable and to speed to the top

Magic Carpet – a conveyor belt–like lift that moves beginning skiers up the snow

surface lift – a lift where skiers ride on the surface of the snow, rather than elevated; there are a variety of types—poma, ropetow, handle tow, and J-bar

tram – a much larger enclosed lift, the size of a cable car

PACKING LIST

long underwear

insulated socks

sweaters or fleece layers

turtlenecks

waterproof pants or ski bib, insulated

waterproof jacket, insulated

neck gaiter

mittens or gloves

mitten guards

hat

headbands

goggles

dark glasses

fanny pack

daypack

after-ski lounging attire

waterproof insulated boots

sunblock

lip protector

swimsuit (the most frequently forgotten item in a skier's suitcase)

UNIVERSAL SKIER'S AND SNOWBOARDER'S RESPONSIBILITY CODE

1. Always stay in control and be able to stop or avoid other people or objects.
2. People ahead of you have the right of way. It is your responsibility to avoid them.
3. You must not stop where you obstruct a trail or are not visible.
4. Whenever starting downhill or merging into a trail, look uphill and yield to others.
5. Always use devices to help prevent runaway equipment. (Bindings should have "ski brakes" that are automatically employed when a boot is released from the binding.)
6. Observe all posted signs and warnings. Keep off closed trails and out of closed areas.

7. Prior to using any lift, you must have the knowledge and ability to load, ride, and unload safely.

A few extra rules for the kids—obvious to the rest of us but not necessarily to them:

- Don't wiggle around on the chairlift.
- Wait your turn in line and don't push.
- Don't ski over other people's skis.
- Keep your poles down—"you could poke someone's eyes out."
- Don't throw snowballs at strangers.

Now, let's hit the slopes!

THE WEST

California

Alpine Meadows Ski Resort

Address: P.O. Box 5279, Tahoe City, California 96145
Telephone: 800-441-4423 or 530-583-4232 (ski resort information); 800-949-3296 (lodging)
Web site: http://www.skialpine.com

Although Alpine Meadows consists of more than 2,000 acres of skiable terrain, the place has a small-town atmosphere. Both locals and out-of-towners are loyal to the mountain, preferring Alpine Meadows's down-home personality and quiet laid-back ambience to some of the flashier ski resorts such as Squaw Valley p. 48 or Heavenly Ski Resort p. 31 down the road. Since it recently opened its gates to snowboarders, increasing numbers of families who want a simple ski vacation without all the bells and whistles flock to Alpine Meadows. All trails lead down to the one base lodge, so it's easy to meet the family for lunch or a hot-chocolate break, even when you don't ski together.

Powder hounds have a field day here with vast expanses of untracked snow, and Alpine Meadows's steep and extreme slopes will please the fast and the fearless for days on end. Intermediates can find trails down from every lift and beginners have one section of the mountain just for themselves. You can always find a sunny slope; 360 degrees of sun exposure means that on a clear day the California sun shines down on you all day long and breathtaking views of sparkling Lake Tahoe are commonplace. Since Alpine Meadows is one of the last resorts in this area to close in the spring, skiing in April and May yields bargain rates and spectacularly sunny weather.

Alpine Meadows is about skiing, not nightlife. There are a few inns near

MOUNTAIN STATISTICS
Base elevation: 6,835 feet
Summit: 8,637 feet
Vertical drop: 1,802 feet
Skiable acres: 2,000
Annual average snowfall: 420 inches
Snowmaking: 185 acres, 10 of 12 lifts
Night skiing: none
Season: mid-November to May
Lifts: 12 (1 6-passenger high-speed chair, 1 high-speed quad, 2 triples, 7 doubles, 1 surface lift)
Terrain: 25% beginner, 40% intermediate, 35% advanced
Lift tickets: adults $47, children 7 to 12 $10, senior 65 to 69 $28, age 70 and over free.

FAMILY STATISTICS
Day care: Not available
Children's lessons: 530-583-4232
Baby-sitting: 800-838-ARTS; Wonder Years, 530-581-5623 are two privately run babysitting concerns
Baby gear: Baby's Away in North Lake Tahoe rents cribs, strollers, car seats, high chairs, and other items; 530-581-3930
Medical: Tahoe Forest Hospital, 530-587-6011

the entrance to the ski resort, but most guests stay in the vicinity of nearby Tahoe City, where they can find more aprés-ski activities. There is no day care available at the base of the mountain, and the children's ski-school program starts at age 4.

How to Get There
Alpine Meadows is 45 miles west of Reno-Tahoe International Airport, 13 miles south of Truckee, and 6 miles northwest of Tahoe City. Driving time from San Francisco is 3.5 hours (200 miles); from Sacramento, 2 hours (120 miles).

Where to Stay
Moderate
Stanford Alpine Chalet is about a quarter mile from Alpine Meadows: Guests can walk or take the free shuttle to the slopes. A small sledding hill is just across the road, and the chalet has saucers and sleds for guests to use. Most rooms have one queen-size and one twin bed, but several rooms have a queen-size and two twins or bunk beds. A full hot breakfast is included in the rates. Families congregate in the large common room, which has a big fireplace and windows that look out onto the ski area, along with games and family movies on Saturday night. A complimentary social hour nightly from 5 to 6 P.M. features wine and appetizers. A fixed-menu dinner is served in the restaurant. $104–180 per night. 1980 Chalet Road, Alpine Meadows, P.O. Box 6436, Tahoe City, CA 96145; 530-583-4625.

River Ranch Lodge is a wood-shingled historic inn two miles down the road from the ski resort. It's situated along the Truckee River, so the lodge's restaurant and many of the guest rooms look out on the icy water rushing by. The lodge is best suited for small families who are comfortable in one room with two double beds or for families with older children who don't mind taking two rooms. There are no connecting rooms. $105–140. Highway 89 at Alpine Meadows Road, Tahoe City, CA 91645; 530-583-4264.

Sunnyside Lodge has 23 guest rooms, all with views of Lake Tahoe. Rates include a continental-breakfast buffet with home-baked specialties; tea and cookies are served each afternoon. Most rooms have one king-size bed or two queen-size beds; two two-room suites are available with a queen-size bed in one room, a sleeper sofa in the living area, and an honor bar and wet bar. The front desk sells discounted lift tickets to Alpine Meadows, which is six miles away. Kids 3 and under stay free in their parents' room; extra people are $15 for two. $100–165. 1850 West Lake Boulevard, Tahoe City, CA 96145; 800-822-2SKI, 530-583-7200.

Granlibakkan is its own small ski resort where the number and variety of accommodation possibilities definitely dwarf the tiny ski area with two sur-face lifts. This resort offers attractive ski packages with both Alpine Mead-ows (p. 27) and Squaw Valley (p. 48) and has a small sledding hill that is handy for letting the kids play in the snow before they try to ski. A small cross-country center offers lessons and rental equipment; downhill lessons and rentals also are available. Units range in size from standard hotel rooms to studios and one- to six-bedroom condos and townhouses. A complimen-tary hot buffet breakfast is included in the rates no matter where you stay. Hotel rooms tend to be too small for most families, but studios have two twin beds and a Hide-A-Bed, plus a kitchen and a living-room area with a fireplace. The six-bedroom townhouse has six bathrooms, an enormous living room, and a state-of-the-art kitchen. A sledding area rents saucers. $69–970. 725 Granlibakken Road, P.O. Box 6329, Tahoe City, CA, 96145; 800-543-3221.

Budget

Tahoe City Inn has a variety of room types, including some with heart-shaped tubs in the bedroom, but families will prefer the two-bedroom "de-luxe" units that have a microwave oven, small refrigerator, coffeemaker, TV, and VCR. The Inn has a collection of 500 movies, including Disney features, that guests can borrow at no charge. Standard rooms have two beds, and a rollaway can be added. $42–88. 790 North Lake Boulevard, Tahoe City, CA 96145; 800-800-8246, 530-581-3333.

Lake of the Sky Motor Inn, six miles from Alpine Meadows, has rooms with two full-size beds. This basic motel has a heated swimming pool, tele-phones, and TVs. $69–105. 955 North Lake Boulevard, P.O. Box 227, Tahoe City, CA 96145; 530-583-3305.

Children's Ski School

Children's ski and snowboard lessons are available for ages 4 through 12. Snow School, for children ages 4 to 6, includes a two- or four-hour group ski lesson, snacks, lunch, lift ticket, and equipment rentals. The school has its own playrooms and lunchroom area. Kids Ski Camp, for ages 6 through 12, offers half- and full-day ski and snowboard sessions. Children are grouped by ability, not age, which means classes can contain a wide range of ages.

Day Care
There is no day care at Alpine Meadows but private babysitters can be hired.

Snowboarding
Hot Wheels Gully is particularly popular with boarders; its natural half pipe in between the trees creates ample opportunities for jumping. A terrainpark, Roo's Ride is on the Kangaroo Trail. The Gravity Cavity half pipe is located on Red-Green Trail.

Cross-Country Skiing
Royal Gorge Cross Country Ski Resort (see page 46) is a 40-minute drive from Granlibakken (see page 29).

Other Activities
Ice Skating: Squaw Valley USA, just a few miles down the road, has a recreational area at the top of the tram station called High Camp. There's an Olympic-size ice rink overlooking Lake Tahoe (rental skates are available), bungee jumping from the highest elevation tower in the world, and the 1960 Olympic Winter Museum; 530-583-6985.

Deals and Discounts
Lift and lodging packages are discounted in the early and late season. Two-for-one tickets and lodging start mid-April and run through the end of the season.

Kids ages 6 to 12 ski free with the purchase of a two-hour intermediate or expert ski or "snowboard" lesson.

The Bed and Boards package combines lodging and lift tickets and starts at $59 per person. Ticket may be used for a beginner lesson package or a full-day lift ticket.

❄ Heavenly Ski Resort

Address: P.O. Box 2180, Stateline, Nevada 89449
Telephone: 800-2-HEAVEN (central reservations), 702-586-7050
Web site: http://www.skiheavenly.com

A giant of a resort spanning two states, Nevada and California, Heavenly Ski Resort is one of the largest ski areas in the United States. From its peak on a clear day (and bright, sunny days are plentiful) you can see Lake Tahoe, the world's third largest alpine lake, shimmering at your feet along with the roofs of the gaming casinos of Nevada below. It's a resort that has something for everyone.

Heavenly attracts people who like to ski during the day and relax in their condo by the fire at night, as well as those who prefer to spend their time feeding quarters into the slot machines and watching big-name entertainers. Many people who come to Heavenly stay on the California side of the resort and never see the bright lights and all-night action on the Nevada side. Other skiers come to Heavenly to take advantage of the cut-rate casino lodging packages and to wander past the roulette wheels and blackjack tables in the evening while their kids explore mammoth video-game parlors.

You can easily ski Heavenly for a week. Its two mountains offer countless runs geared to all abilities. On the California side, long cruising trails on top make it an intermediate skiers' paradise, while experts can thrash their thighs on the steep bump runs such as legendary Gunbarrel farther down. Plentiful opportunities for glade and tree skiing abound. Gentle, wide, well-groomed turf is found on both sides of the mountain, giving beginners and intermediate skiers plenty of

MOUNTAIN STATISTICS
Base elevation: 6,540 feet (California);
    7,200 feet (Nevada)
Summit: 10,040 feet
Vertical drop: 3,500 feet
Skiable acres: 4,800
Annual average snowfall: 340 inches
Snowmaking: 67% of all trails
Season: mid-November through April
Night skiing: none
Lifts: 26 (1 aerial tram, 6-passenger
    high-speed chair, 3 high-speed
    quads, 8 triples, 7 doubles,
    6 surface lifts.)
Terrain: 20% beginner, 47%
    intermediate, 33% advanced
Lift tickets: adults $47, youth 13 to 15
    $34, children 6 to 12/seniors 65+
    $22, under 5 free.

FAMILY STATISTICS
Day care: not available
Children's lessons: Snow Explorers, ages
    4 to 12, 702-586-7000
Baby-sitting: Choices for children, 916-
    541-5848
Baby gear: Baby's Away in South Lake
    Tahoe rents cribs, high chairs,
    strollers, toys, and other items; 916-
    544-2229
Medical: Barton Memorial Hospital,
    916-541-3420

variety. Boarders rank it as one of the best in the West for its natural terrain and its snowboard park.

Heavenly has a well-run children's ski school that operates from two sites: the Nevada- and California-side base areas. On-mountain child care is limited to private babysitting; at press time there is no daycare center, but Heavenly's long range plan includes a children's center.

If you want a novel ski experience, take a breakfast ride on the *Tahoe Queen*, an authentic Mississippi-style paddle wheeler, across the lake to North Lake Tahoe. From there you can shuttle to Squaw Valley before heading back across the lake. Each way takes two hours, but it's a relaxing, one-of-a-kind experience. Nature-loving adults and kids should be sure to take advantage of the "Ski with a Ranger" mountain tour program lead by U.S. Forest Rangers who describe Heavenly's mountain, the geology of Lake Tahoe, and the mountain wildlife that inhabits the area.

How to Get There

Reno-Tahoe International Airport is 58 miles from the resort, about an hour by car or shuttle. Driving times: San Francisco, 3.5 hours (198 miles); Sacramento, 2 hours (100 miles). Once you're on Lake Tahoe's South Shore, Heavenly operates free shuttles to the ski resort from many lodging properties.

Where to Stay

Expensive

Ridge Tahoe Resort has its own private 10-passenger gondolas to whisk its guests to the slopes on Heavenly's Nevada side. As you might guess, it's deluxe, exclusive, and very convenient. Accommodations range from regular hotel rooms to spacious one- and two-bedroom condos with full kitchens, fireplaces, and wet bars. Also on the premises are a gourmet restaurant, deli/cafe, small grocery store, ski shop and lockers, and casino shuttle service. Families wanting to avoid the bright lights and hustle of downtown find this secluded resort just perfect. $160–425. 400 Ridge Club Drive, P.O. Box 5790, Stateline, NV 89449; 702-588-3553.

Moderate

Harrahs has an enormous game room called the Family Fun Center bursting at the seams with video games, pinball, air hockey, and little rides for toddlers. The resort's standard hotel rooms are spacious and feature two bathrooms, each with their own miniature color TV, a real kid-pleaser. Guests can choose from a variety of restaurants, plus an indoor heated swimming pool, Jacuzzi, health club with gym and sauna, and massages by appointment. The casino takes up the entire main floor and the game room is one level down. Ski packages are available midweek. Children 15 and under stay free in their parents' room, and rollaway beds and cribs are available free of charge, upon request. $119–150. Highway 50 at Stateline, PO Box 8, Stateline, NV 89449; 800-648-3773, 702-588-6611.

Harvey's Resort Hotel and Casino has a children's day camp that runs from 8:30 A.M. to 3:30 P.M. and 6 to 10 P.M. year-round for kids ages 6 to 13 and offers games, outdoor activities, and self-defense classes. Lunch and snacks are provided, and after-hours baby-sitting can be arranged. The resort is like a small city, with eight restaurants, a health club and spa, outdoor heated pool, beauty parlor, huge game arcade, gift shops, and a ski shop that rents children's and adult's ski clothing and equipment. Rooms are priced according to view, but most have in-room coffeemakers and honor bars and two queen-size or one king-size bed. A free continental breakfast is served to all guests. Ski packages are an excellent value and are available for two and three nights. Children under 18 stay free in their parents' room, and there is no charge for rollaways. $99–190. Highway 50 and Stateline Street, P.O. Box 128, Stateline, NV 89449; 800-427-8397, 702-588-2422.

Lakeland Village Beach and Ski Resort has accommodations ranging from deluxe hotel rooms to four-bedroom townhouses. All have full kitchens, fireplaces, and decks. Surrounded by pine forest, the resort is set on a quarter mile of private beach and features hot tubs, an outdoor heated pool, restaurants and shops, ski rentals, and shuttles to Heavenly. $75–255. 3535 Lake Tahoe Boulevard (Highway 50), South Lake Tahoe, CA 96150; 800-822-5969, 530-544-1685.

Forest Inn Suites has apartment-like suites with full kitchens in either one-bedroom-and-one-bath or two-bedroom-and-two-bath configurations. A complimentary breakfast comes with the room. There are two pools, spas, a sauna, and a game room with video games, a pool table, and Ping-Pong. $90–$215. 1 Lake Park Way, South Lake Tahoe, CA 96150; 800-822-5950, 530-541-6655

Embassy Suites is an attractive full-service hotel in South Lake Tahoe that doesn't have the gaming glitz of other properties—as no gambling is allowed—but that does have an indoor swimming pool and a game room for the kids. Two-room suites have minikitchens with a refrigerator, microwave oven, and coffeemaker. The sofa bed in the living area creates extra sleeping quarters. A continental-breakfast buffet that includes cooked-to-order dishes is served each morning in the six-story atrium lobby. $129–600. 4130 Lake Tahoe Boulevard, South Lake Tahoe, CA 96150; 800-362-2779, 530-544-5400.

Budget

Camp Richardson Resort, about eight miles from Heavenly, is a find for families, especially those who want to combine cross-country skiing or snowshoeing with their downhill fun. Basic hotel rooms are available in the Lodge and the Beach Inn, and families of three or four can stay in one room with two double beds. Larger families or those wanting a kitchen should opt for cabins, which range in size from studios to two bedrooms, all with lake views and full kitchens. One-bedroom cabins can fit up to seven people and two-bedroom cabins can sleep up to eight people. Groomed trails for cross-country skiing or snowshoeing along the lake start here, and sleigh rides are available as long as there's snow on the ground. The resort has a small general store, beachfront restaurant, and deli. None of Richardson's accommodations have telephones or TVs. Rooms $59; cabins $85–129. 2100 Jamison Beach Road, P.O. Box 9028, South Lake Tahoe, CA 96158; 530-541-1801.

Best Western Timber Cove Lodge is right on the beach, so kids can play in the snow that covers the gently sloping sand. Children under 12 stay free in their parents' room. Rollaway beds cost $20 extra per night. Rooms have a king-size bed or two double beds; lakeside rooms have doors leading out to the lake. Winter specials are an excellent value and include breakfast. $49–84. 3411 Lake Tahoe Boulevard, South Lake Tahoe, CA 96150; 800-528-1234 (for reservations), 800-972-8558 (winter packages), 530-541-6722.

Children's Ski School

The Nevada and California side of Heavenly both have Snow Explorers ski schools for kids ages 4 to 12 and snowboarding schools for ages 7 to 12. Kids are divided into classes depending on their age and ability. Pagers are available to parents for $4 a day. Each ski school has its own children's center where kids meet in the morning and return for lunch. The ski school is first come first served and reservations are not accepted, so it's best to arrive a little early on weekends and during holidays.

"Tag-A-Long" private lessons allow parents to accompany their child on a private lesson and monitor the child's skiing progress. The ski instructor provides tips and information for the parents so they can help their own child improve her skiing after the lesson is over. Two children per lesson; 702-586-7000.

Day Care
There is no on-mountain daycare for 1997–98 ski season, but it may be added for the 1998–99 season.

Snowboarding
Expect to see increasing numbers of snowboard competitions as Heavenly reaches out to boarders. The Airport Snowboard Park on the Nevada side of the mountain is on intermediate terrain, and has a huge half pipe, tabletop jumps, quarter pipes, and a rail. Many boarders like the natural steeps and chutes that send them rocketing off rock drops and cliffs or carving around windswept dunes.

Cross-Country Skiing
Sunset Ranch Winter Recreational Area has 200 acres of groomed track, sleigh rides, and snowmobile rentals; 916-541-9001, 916-544-8594.

Camp Richardson Resort has 55 kilometers of groomed trails, ski rentals (including children's), decorated children's trails, a ski patrol, and full-moon tours; 800-544-1801.

Spooner Lake Cross Country has 80 kilometers of groomed trails. Beginners enjoy the flatter trails around Spooner Lake, while more intermediate and advanced skiers can explore the high country trails that have outstanding views of Lake Tahoe. Backcountry cabins can rented by the night. Children's equipment is available. P.O. Box 981, Carson City, NV 89702. (½ from Highway 50 on Highway 28); 702-749-5349.

Other Activities
Ice skating: The South Tahoe Ice Center is located at the South Lake Tahoe Recreation Center, one mile from Heavenly. 1180 Rufus Allen Boulevard, South Lake Tahoe, CA 96150. 530-542-4700.

Horse-drawn sleigh rides: Camp Richardson's corral offers afternoon and dinner sleigh rides; 916-541-3113. Borges Sleigh Rides offers 35-minute horse-drawn sleigh rides along the shoreline of Lake Tahoe. Rides depart across from Caesar's Tahoe at Lake Parkway East, Stateline, NV 89449; 702-541-2953. Sunset Ranch Winter Recreational Area also offers sleigh rides; 916-541-9001, 916-544-8594.

Steamship rides on the *Tahoe Queen* take place throughout the winter on Lake Tahoe, which never really freezes. Morning breakfast rides across the lake to North Lake Tahoe take you to ski Squaw Valley. Each way takes two hours, but it's a relaxing one-of-a-kind ride. There's free pickup at most hotels on a red double-decker bus. End of Ski Run Boulevard along the lake. 530-541-3364.

The MS *Dixie*, an old-fashioned paddle wheeler, makes round trips around Emerald Bay at noon daily, and on weekends they offer an evening ride; 702-588-5678.

Snowmobiling: Lake Tahoe Winter Sports Center, 916-577-2940, 702-588-3833. Sunset Ranch Winter Recreational Area also offers snowmobile rentals; 916-541-9001, 530-544-8594.

Deals and Discounts

Accommodations around Heavenly are plentiful and tend to be priced lower than in other areas thanks to the casino business. All the casinos and lodging properties have great packages, especially midweek. Look into three- or four-day ski-school packages, which offer discounts.

Mammoth Mountain (and June Mountain)

Address: P.O. Box 24, Mammoth Lakes, California 93546; P.O. Box 146, June Lake, CA 93529
Telephone: 888-4MAMMOTH, 888-JUNE-MTN
Web site: http://www.mammoth-mtn.com

Monumental Mammoth Mountain draws a weekend clientele largely from the Los Angeles basin, but hosts visitors from all over the U.S. and beyond throughout the week. Owner Dave McCoy, who welded the parts together for the first chairlift back in 1955, is still actively involved in running the show today, and the current lift count has risen to 31 sophisticated machines. This is one of the last few ski resorts still owned by an individual rather than a corporation.

The closest town to the ski area is Mammoth Lakes, four miles down the road. Many of the accommodations found here—mostly condos—are spread around the town. A car can be useful but is not essential: an efficient shuttle bus takes skiers from town to the mountain and back. An elevated monorail system under construction will eventually link the town of Mammoth Lakes with Mammoth Mountain Ski Area. Phase I has been completed and transports skiers from the vast parking areas to the main lodge.

Mammoth Mountain's sister ski area, June Mountain, thirty minutes away, was opened by the McCoy family in the mid-1980s and is a particularly popular resort with snowboarders thanks to its competition half pipe and snowboard experts–only

**MOUNTAIN STATISTICS—
MAMMOTH MOUNTAIN**
Base elevation: 7,593 feet
Summit: 11,053 feet
Vertical drop: 3,100 feet
Skiable acres: 3,500
Annual average snowfall: 353 inches
Snowmaking: 200 acres, 22 trails
Night skiing: none
Season: November through June
Lifts: 29 (5 high-speed quads, 3 quads, 7 triples, 11 doubles, 2 gondolas, 1 surface lift)
Terrain: 30% beginner, 40% intermediate, 30% advanced
Lift tickets: adults $47, teens 13 to 18 $34, children 7 to 12, $23, 6 and under free.

FAMILY STATISTICS
Day care: Small World Child Care at the Mammoth Mountain Inn, main base area, 760-934-0646; June Mountain Day Care, 619-648-7609
Children's lessons: Woollywood Children's Center, 760-934-0658; June Children's Ski School, 619-468-7609
Baby-sitting: A list of sitters is available through the day-care center, 760-934-0646
Medical: Mammoth Hospital, 760-934-3311

terrain park. Lift tickets are cheaper for June Mountain alone, but if you buy a ticket for Mammoth it is good for June Mountain as well. Family facilities at June Mountain include a small children's day-care center and ski school.

Mammoth is known for its long season accompanied by gloriously sunny springlike weather. At its summit, it offers some of the highest lift-served skiing in the continent and in recent years has been the official training center for the U.S. Ski Team. That should tell you that this former volcano has long, steep, challenging faces along its sides. Intermediate skiers won't be disappointed either, since there are plenty of endless wide-open cruising runs. Beginners have always enjoyed the lower part of the mountain with its gently sloped broad boulevards, perfect for learning to turn and stop. Newcomers may be confused by the helter-skelter arrangement of lifts, which are numbered in the order they were built rather than by their order on the mountain. Study the trail map carefully or take a mountain tour your first day out.

Children's programs are concentrated at Woollywood Children's Center and the Mammoth Mountain Inn, both at the main base area. Mammoth Mountain's lovable mascot, "Woolly," an enormous furry mammoth, skis around the slopes and waves to kids. Special areas are set up just for kids, with little adventure zones, tiny slalom courses, and roller bumps.

How to Get There

Mammoth has a small airport that receives flights on Mountain Air Express (800-788-4247, 310-595-1011) from Long Beach and Elrod and Associates Aviation, Inc. (202-252-8055) from Fresno. A free shuttle bus connects the Main Lodge, Warming Hut II, and downtown. Parking shuttles are available. Driving times: Los Angeles, 5 hours (320 miles); San Francisco, 6 hours (360 miles).

Where to Stay

Expensive

Mammoth Mountain Inn has brightly colored, attractive rooms, suites, and apartment-style units, the latter with fully equipped kitchens and one or two bedrooms. It houses Mammoth Mountain's child-care facility for nonskiing children and is right across the street from the Woollywood Children's Center. This is the only full-service hotel at Mammoth Mountain, with a 24-hour desk, several restaurants, ski valets, ski storage, laundry facilities, a game room, and room service in the package. Standard rooms have one or two double or queen-size beds; studios have one bedroom with a queen-size bed and a fold-out couch. Two-bedroom units come with a loft and can sleep up to 12 people. Rollaway beds are not available. $112–445. P.O. Box 353, Mammoth Lakes, CA 93546; 800-228-4947, 760-934-2581.

Moderate

Hidden Valley Condominiums is extremely popular with families because of its proximity to town and the shuttle stop. Units range from a studio or studio/loft combination to a one-bedroom-and-loft unit that can accommodate six. Prices depend on furnishings. Guests can use two separate spa complexes. $100–180. Lake Mary Road, Mammoth Lakes, CA 93546; 800-462-5571, 760-934-7303.

Mammoth Ski and Racquet Club, one-quarter mile from the lifts, offers a great location with beautiful views of the mountains. Its units range from studio units with a loft that can sleep up to four people, to two-bedroom condos with lofts can handle up to eight people. All units have fully outfitted kitchens. All guests can use the two Jacuzzis and thirteen saunas on the property. There are discounts for stays of three days or more. $135–230. 248 Mammoth Slope Drive, P.O. Box 3846, Mammoth Lakes, CA 93546; 760-934-7368.

Budget

The Shiloh Inn has simple rooms, with kitchenettes, that can accommodate up to four people. All rooms have either a king-size bed and a single sofa sleeper, or two queen-size beds and a minirefrigerator, microwave oven, wet bar, and complimentary continental breakfast. Other features include covered parking, ski lockers, laundry facilities, an indoor pool, a sauna, a steam room, and a free airport shuttle. Children 12 and under stay free in their parents' room, but rollaways cost $15 per night. $119–145. 2963 Main Street, Mammoth Lakes, CA 93546; 800-222-2244, 760-934-4500.

La Vista Blanc is a standard condo complex with utilitarian decor, but it's clean and a good choice if you're pinching pennies. Ranging in size from studios to three bedrooms with a loft, units have full kitchens and sleeper sofas. The complex is a half block from a shuttle stop that takes guests to the Main Lodge. $90–240. Meadow Lane, P.O. Box 1565, Mammoth Lakes, CA 93546; 800-462-5571, 760-934-8328.

Children's Ski School

Woollywood Ski School programs start at the Woollywood Children's Center, a one-stop shopping spot with kid-size ski and snowboard rentals, a kids' ski shop, lunch room, and meeting area. Junior Explorers are 4- to 6-year-olds who take small group lessons with an emphasis on having fun and achieving success. Beginners start indoors, practicing balance and learning how to move their skis before they head out. Explorers, ages 7 to 12, progress more rapidly; beginners end up on a chairlift in the afternoon of their first day on skis. Snowboarders, called Big Kahunas, start group lessons at age 7. All classes are full or half day, and private lessons are available. Woollywood stays open through the end of spring breaks. If you're visiting late in the season, call first to make sure lessons are available.

An optional ski-school/day-care combo is available for ages four to nine. The staff takes them to Woollywood, gets their equipment, and places them into ski school. Lessons are two hours in the morning followed by lunch and a short break, and two hours in the afternoon; 760-934-0646.

Day Care

Small World Child Care, at the Mammoth Mountain Inn across from Woollywood and the Main Lodge, takes newborns through preschoolers and older kids who do not wish to ski. Each age division has its own room: Infants to 18-month-olds have indoor activities such as movement, music, toys, and quiet/nap time in cribs; toddlers 18 to 24 months have art, music, movement, and rest time. Snow is brought indoors for this age group to play with. The advanced toddler room, for 2- to 3-year-olds who are not toilet trained, has all the above activities but also features outdoor snow play and sometimes a gondola ride. A preschool room for 2-year-olds and up who are toilet trained has a small sledding area outside, and offers snow play, art, music, movement, and quiet time. Videos are not shown at this facility, and beepers are available on request.

June Mountain is much smaller but offers similar services; 760-648-7609. Advance reservations are required for both facilities.

Snowboarding

Mammoth's snowboard features continually change. Its official snowboard area, The Unbound, usually has a terrible T, a diamond, tabletops, whoop-dee-dos (several bumps close together), jump boosters, and a quarter pipe. Skiers are welcome, too.

June Mountain has a world-class half pipe, and Boardertown Snowboard Park with a variety of hits and jumps.

Cross-Country Skiing

Nestled between Ansel Adams and John Muir Wilderness, with the Crystal Crag and Mammoth Crest rock formations towering above, *Tamarack*

Lodge's 45 kilometers of track go around six alpine lakes. The track is groomed daily for both skating and classical technique, and a complete base lodge has ski rentals (including kids' sizes and little trailers parents can put young children in) and lessons for all ages and abilities. A log-cabin lodge built in the 1920s houses a four-star restaurant serving breakfast and dinner and standard hotel-rooms. Fifteen wilderness cabins with full kitchens and one, two, or three bedrooms are connected by ski trails in close proximity to the lodge and are quite popular with families. There's a sledding hill (bring your own sled) and easy, moderate, and difficult ski trails. Twin Lakes Road, Mammoth Lakes, CA 93546; 619-934-2442.

Sierra Meadows Ranch offers cross-country skiing on 25 kilometers of groomed and tracked trails. Rental equipment is available for all ages, as are snowshoes, saucers, and sleds. Moonlight tours require that skiers have some experience. Other guided tours and lessons for all ages are available. 1 Sherwin Creek Road, Mammoth Lakes, CA 93546; 760-934-6161.

Other Activities

Dog Sled Adventures takes families on fun-filled *dogsled rides*: (sleds hold two adults and two kids) through the woods to a scenic overlook. Dinner packages are available, as are kennel tours and puppy petting. P.O. Box 7791, Mammoth Lakes, CA 93546; 619-934-6270.

Snowshoe rentals are available at Tamarack Lodge (619-934-2442).

Sledding: A little rope tow with handles pulls riders to the top of two 600-foot-long tube runs. Sledzs; Highway 203, Mammoth Lakes, CA 93546; 760-934-7533.

Sleigh rides: Sierra Meadows Ranch (760-934-6161) offers lunch rides, meadow rides, dinner rides, and moonlight rides. Advance reservations are required.

Snowmobiling: rides and equipment are available from DJ Snowmobile Adventures (760-935-4480) and Mammoth Snowmobile Rentals (760-934-5946).

Deals and Discounts

Midweek lift and lodging packages are available at a great savings, and late-season packages start in April (skiing goes into June), when ticket prices drop and lodging is discounted. Kids 6 and under ski free.

❄ Northstar-at-Tahoe

Address: P.O. Box 129, Truckee, California 96160
Telephone: 800-GO-NORTH (central reservations), 530-562-1010
Web site: http://www.skinorthstar.com

Just the right size" is how my daughter describes Northstar. When a resort is too big, it can be frustrating to figure out your way around—but when it's too small, you're quickly bored. Northstar has enough terrain to keep a family of intermediate skiers busy for a ski week. It also offers an unusual base "floor plan" that is well suited for families.

Many of the resort's facilities, including the lift-ticket office, ski-rental office, a large ski shop, licensed day-care center (parents get pagers), and restaurants are found at the lower village, next to the parking lots and shuttle bus stop. A high-speed gondola takes skiers up to the more secluded mountain base of the ski lifts where you'll find the main lodge, cafeteria, restaurant, ski school, and cross-country base. This separation allows more freedom of movement for families away from the hustle and bustle and traffic of a typical ski-resort base. The Nordic Center trails are just steps from the main lodge, making it convenient for families with both types of skiers to meet for lunch.

The ski area is the winter centerpiece for a self-contained community of condos and private homes that extend for more than a mile from the slopes. Free shuttles run all day and into the night, and many older children who want to sleep in or quit early can take the bus by themselves, as buses never leave the Northstar community. Nightlife tends to be quiet, spent by the fire, in the rec center, or in the few restaurants.

MOUNTAIN STATISTICS
Base elevation: 6,330 feet
Summit: 8,610 feet
Vertical drop: 2,280 feet
Skiable acres: 2,400
Annual average snowfall: 350 inches
Snowmaking: 50% of runs
Night skiing: none
Season: Thanksgiving to mid-April
Lifts: 12 (1 gondola, 4 high-speed
    quads, 2 triples, 2 doubles,
    3 surface lifts)
Terrain: 25% beginner, 50%
    intermediate, 25% advanced
Lift tickets: adults 23–59 $46, young
    adults 13 to 22 $38 children 5 to
    12 $10, 4 and under free.

FAMILY STATISTICS
Day care: Minors' Camp Child Care
    Center, ages 2 to 6, 530-562-2278
Children's lessons: 530-562-2471
Baby-sitting: Minors' Camp keeps a list
    of local baby-sitters; 530-562-2278
Baby gear: Baby's Away in North Lake
    Tahoe rents car seats, cribs, strollers,
    high chairs, toys, and other gear;
    530-581-3930
Medical: Tahoe Forest Hospital,
    530-587-6011

Northstar doesn't have the dramatic terrain and sheer faces of Alpine Meadows (see page 27) and Squaw Valley (see page 48) just down the road. It has built its reputation as a place that is safe, easy, and convenient for families. Its ski school and bunny slopes are highly regarded, and it was one of the first resorts to add an unusual terrain park, featuring spines, rolls, little jumps, and special trails for both skiers and boarders. Guests praise its meticulously groomed, manicured corduroy slopes.

Although expert skiers won't find any death-defying steeps, Northstar's black diamond trails on the back side, while a little tamer than many others, will keep any advanced skier happy. Because this is a midsize resort, Northstar emphasizes service, and their staff is very helpful indeed.

Children can ski for $10 per day.

How to Get There

Reno-Tahoe International Airport is 40 miles from the resort. Once you're inside the Northstar community, shuttles take you anywhere you need to go, but if you plan to visit farther, you'll need a car. Driving times: San Francisco, 3 hours (196 miles); Sacramento 1.5 hours (96 miles).

Where to Stay

Most people who ski Northstar stay on the 6,000-acre property in private homes, condos, or hotel rooms. Shuttle buses run regularly throughout all the areas and drop skiers in front of the Village.

Hotel rooms are right at the base village, which also houses the restaurants and the lift-ticket office. These rooms offer ski-in-and-out convenience but have few concierge services. There are two types of rooms: One has two queen-size beds, and the other has a queen-size bed in a loft and a lounge area with a small kitchen. $169–224 per night.

Condominiums are scattered in clusters among the trees and granite outcroppings. The most expensive units are along the ski trail so you can ski home. They range in size from studios to four-bedroom suites. Two-bedroom and larger units have a washer and dryer. All units have fireplaces and fully equipped kitchens. Prices depend on location and amenities. $159–454.

Private homes vary in design and amenities. All are custom built and are beautifully maintained and elegantly decorated. Three-, four-, and five-bedroom homes feature fireplaces, fully equipped kitchens, and washers and dryers. $374–619.

Children's Ski School

The "Starkids" program for children ages 5 to 12 features programs for different ages and abilities. A Magic Carpet lift, in which kids stand on a moving band, makes it easy for first-timers to get up a slight slope without having to worry about what their hands are doing. The full-day program includes lunch in the children's lunch/playroom on the main mountain (which also has a clothes dryer that is in constant use!).

The "Ski Cubs" program for 3 and 4 year olds is taught by day-care instructors in the safe, fenced slope behind the day-care facility. Parents should sign up through the day-care center. The 5- and 6-year-olds who are in the day-care program and have signed up for a ski lesson are brought from the day care to the ski school by a teacher.

The snowboard program, "Shredkids," is open to children as young as 5, but the ski-school staff recommends that participants be 7 or 8 years old. Free lessons are available for intermediate and advanced skiers and snowboarders age 13 and over.

Day Care

Minors' Camp Child Care Center is a state-licensed day-care center that can accommodate up to 60 kids between the ages of 2 and 6 in a colorful and cheerful playroom decorated with murals of forest scenes. Parents are all given a pager. Lessons are available for 3- to 6-year-olds. The younger group, ages 3 and 4, step out the back door to their own tiny ski area to practice and get used to moving around on skis. The 5- and 6-year-olds start out in this area, but as they progress they are taken up the gondola for lessons.

Snowboarding

Snowboarding is allowed everywhere at Northstar, but snowboarders congregate below the lookout chairlift on the half pipe and various terrain features sculpted for their enjoyment. Terrain features on other parts of the mountain vary throughout the year but usually include two half pipes. The resort groomer that creates perfect half pipes.

Cross-Country Skiing

Northstar's Cross-Country Ski Center offers 65 kilometers of groomed and tracked trails. Warming huts, picnic tables, and spectacular views of Lake Tahoe are found throughout the system. Trails extend from both sides of the downhill ski mountain, leading back to the day lodge, ideal for a family that includes both downhill and cross-country skiers. Equipment rental, a ski shop, and lessons (including children's) are available at the cross-country lodge; 530-562-2475.

Royal Gorge Cross Country Ski Resort, (see page 46) has 328 kilometers of groomed track.

Other Activities

Sleigh rides travel around the area and are offered depending on the weather. Central reservations, 800-GO-NORTH.

Snowshoeing: Special groomed snowshoe trails and snowshoe rentals can be found at Northstars' Cross-Country Ski Center. Rentals, 530-562-2475.

Snowmobiling: One- and-two-hour tours are offered through the surrounding forests. Rental clothes are available if you need extra protection; 530-562-2267.

Northstar Swim and Racquet Club: Formerly known as the rec center, the facility has an outdoor heated lap pool (adults only), outdoor spas, a sauna, a workout room, and a youth center with pool tables, video games, and Ping-Pong.

Deals and Discounts

Free one-hour clinics for high intermediate to advanced skiers and boarders are available for ages 13 and up.

Stay and Ski Free packages offer free lift tickets with lodging over certain dates, especially mid- to late March and selected times throughout the season.

Membership in Vertical Plus ($49) offers discounts on lift tickets for adults and children. A special wristband records the number of vertical feet skied, accumulating points for rewards.

Mommy, Daddy, and Me is a free 1-hour clinic of how to enjoy skiing with your 3 to 5 year old child. The program takes place Sunday through Friday at 2:15 p.m.

Royal Gorge Cross Country Ski Resort

Address: P.O. Box 1100, Soda Springs, California 95728

Telephone: 800-500-3871, (outside Northern California), 800-666-3871 (in Northern California), 530-426-3871

Web site: http://www.royalgorge.com

The biggest cross-country ski resort in North America, Royal Gorge has two overnight lodges, one in the heart of the trail system reached by a short sleigh ride, and the other an old mountain inn at the end of a lodge-to-lodge trail. This unusual cross-country center has 328 kilometers of groomed track and 88 different trails. Beginner, intermediate, and advanced trails follow loops, lead to downhill ski areas (with good restaurants), and travel past ten warming huts spread throughout the track system where steaming cups of tea await skiers. Experts who want real challenges can try one of the lift-serviced trails. A ski patrol roams the tracks in case you need help. At the end of the day they sweep the entire trail network to make sure no one is left stranded.

Four surface lifts take the work out of accessing certain trails and interconnect points. Skiers can travel to a beautiful wilderness lodge for a meal, a warming hut, or the lodge at several different ski areas for lunch on the vast number of interconnect trails.

The downhill ski resorts Alpine Meadows (see page 27), Squaw Valley (see page 48) and Northstar-at-Tahoe are a short drive away.

MOUNTAIN STATISTICS

Base elevation: 7,000 feet
Summit: 7,532 feet
Vertical drop: N/A
Skiable acres: 9,172
Annual average snowfall: 450 inches
Snowmaking: 15 kilometers
Night skiing: none
Season: mid-November to mid-May
Lifts: 4 surface lifts
Terrain: 28% beginner, 44% intermediate, 16% advanced
Lift tickets: adults $19.50, children 10 to 14 $8.50, under 10 free.

FAMILY STATISTICS

Day care: Not available
Children's lessons: Pee Wee Snow School Ages 4 to 12
Baby-sitting: None
Baby gear: Baby's Away in North Lake Tahoe rents cribs, strollers, car seats, high chairs, and other items; 530-581-3930.
Medical: Tahoe Forest Hospital, 530-587-6011

How to Get There

Royal Gorge is in the Lake Tahoe area, 45 minutes from Reno-Tahoe International Airport. Van and limo services are available at the airport.

Where to Stay

The Wilderness Lodge is four kilometers into the trail system. Rates include ski instruction, breakfast and lunch buffets, gourmet candlelit French cuisine, tea time and hors d'oeuvres, moonlight ski tours and video clinics. Children 5 to 16 receive children's rates; those under 5 are not permitted (they're better off at the Rainbow Lodge, listed below). Amenities include a sauna and hot tub. Adults $150 per weekend night, $135 per midweek night. Kids $115 per weekend night, $105 per midweek night.

Rainbow Lodge is a bed-and-breakfast built in the 1920s of granite and timber. Its popular dining room features French and California cuisine. Three styles of rooms are available. The best for families include those with a queen-size and twin bed with space to add a rollaway, or a family suite with a queen-size bed in one area and a bunk set in the other. Rates include breakfast. Children over six, $15 per child per night. $79–135.

Children's Ski School

Kids' classes are divided into two age groups. Peewee Snow School, for ages 4 to 12, offers equipment, lunch, the lesson, and other on-snow activities. The programs operate from the family center in the main base area. Full- or half-day programs are available.

Day Care

There is no day care at Royal Gorge.

Other Activities

See the listing on Squaw Valley, page 48 for activities in the North Lake Tahoe area.

Deals and Discounts

Midweek packages offer excellent savings. On Tuesday, two-for-one learn to ski packages are available, and on Wednesdays, trail passes are discounted to $10, and on Thursday, there's a discount for a combination equipment rental and trail pass.

Squaw Valley USA

Address: Olympic Valley, California 96146
Telephone: 800-545-4350 (central reservations), 530-583-6985
Web site: http://www.squaw.com

MOUNTAIN STATISTICS

Base elevation: 6,200 feet
Summit: 9,050 feet
Vertical drop: 2,850 feet
Skiable acres: 4,000
Annual average snowfall: 450 inches
Snowmaking: 340 acres
Night skiing: 3.5 miles of trails open until 9 P.M.
Season: mid-November to Memorial Day, June or July
Lifts: 30 (150-passenger cable car, 30-passenger automated gondola, 6-passenger gondola, 4 high-speed quads, 1 quad, 9 triples, 10 double, 3 surface lifts)
Terrain: 25% beginner, 45% intermediate, 30% advanced
Lift tickets: adults $48, youth 13 to 15 half price, children 12 and under $5, seniors 65 to 75 $24, 75+ free

FAMILY STATISTICS

Day care: Toddler Care, ages 2 to 3, 530-581-7280
Children's lessons: Children's World, ages 4 to 12 530-581-7225
Baby-sitting: A list is available from Children's World; 530-581-7225
Baby gear: Baby's Away in North Lake Tahoe rents cribs, car seats, high chairs, strollers, toys, and other gear; 530-581-3930
Medical: Truckee Tahoe Hospital, 530-583-3439

One of the crown jewels in the group of ski resorts that ring Lake Tahoe, Squaw Valley will soon have a base village that will rival those of the Colorado giants like Vail, Breckenridge, and Aspen. The resort opened with a few lifts in 1949 but grew dramatically when it hosted the 1960 Olympic Winter Games. Lodging was largely scattered around the towns of Truckee and Tahoe City until a first-class hotel and several other ski-in-and-out lodgings were built in the charming valley. Intrawest, the company that developed Whistler Resort and Mont Tremblant in Canada, recently acquired 15 acres of day-skier parking lot and plans to build an extensive base pedestrian resort village.

Skiing is spectacular for people of all abilities on this titan of a mountain, the second largest in the United States. Devotees of steep descents will be challenged by some of the most extreme black-diamond skiing west of the Rockies, while intermediates will find avenue after avenue of wide undulating cruisers groomed to velvety perfection. There's plenty for beginners, too, with a protected learn-to-ski area near the children's center and numerous gentle slopes. Its base elevation of 6,200 feet offers skiing right off the parking lot, but the majority of the lifts are at an 8,200-foot-high upper base accessible by gondola or cable car. Squaw's reputation as a resort frequented by arrogant speedsters on skis and boards has been tempered by a vigilant ski patrol. Signs scattered throughout the resort read SKI TOO FAST, LOSE YOUR PASS.

Nonskiing and nighttime action are concentrated at High Camp, an upper mountain "village" with an ice-skating rink, lift-served snowtubing, bungee jumptower, restaurants, and shops. Skiers who start their day late can ski until 9 P.M. (using the same lift ticket), on 3.6 miles of uninterrupted night-lit vertical from High Camp to the valley floor below. The night-lit slope includes a terrain park, half pipe, and ear-splitting sound system. The terrain park and pipe are regroomed every afternoon to keep them in jumping shape for the evening. The rest of the après-ski action takes place in the restaurants and bars of the base village and at the Resort at Squaw Creek.

A well-designed 12,000-square-foot children's center offers one-stop shopping for rentals, meals, lift tickets, and lessons. Parents can use a special reserved parking area while they drop off the kids before they head off for their own day of skiing. Squaw was one of the first ski areas to offer deeply discounted children's lift tickets, and today you still pay just $5 per child 12 and under.

How to Get There
Reno-Tahoe International Airport is 45 miles from Squaw Valley. Drive times: San Francisco, 3.5 hours (196 miles); Sacramento, 1.5 (100 miles); Reno, 50 minutes (42 miles).

Where to Stay
Squaw Valley has a number of private homes for rent, plus several condominium hotels, a youth hostel, and a high-end resort hotel with ski-in-and-out capabilities. Squaw Valley Central Reservations (800-545-4350) can help book your stay within the valley and surrounding area. The North Tahoe Resort Association can help book reservations for homes, cabins, and condos located within a ten-mile radius of the ski area. 800-824-6348.

Expensive
Resort at Squaw Creek has its own private chairlift that carries guests to the main Squaw Valley ski area. This first-class hotel is the most luxurious in the area and features five restaurants, from delis to fine dining, its own ice-skating rink, cross-country ski center, an outdoor heated pool, three outdoor Jacuzzis, a complete fitness center and spa with treatments and massages, and a shopping promenade. Half of its 403 rooms are one- and two-bedroom suites, and a few have kitchens. Its "Mountain Buddy" program offers activities throughout the day for kids 4 to 13. The program is

organized like a day camp, running all day or for half days and also from 6:30 to 9:30 P.M. Activities include arts and crafts, games, sledding, ice skating, swimming, and a hot tub. Kids 18 and under stay free in their parents' room and family ski packages are available. $259–850. 400 Squaw Creek Road, Olympic Valley, CA 96146; 800-327-3353, 530-583-6300.

Squaw Valley Lodge, closer than any other property to the main base area, has individually owned studios and one- and two-bedroom suites that can sleep up to six people. Furnishings are contemporary and attractive; personal touches like artwork and accessories vary. Studios have small but complete kitchenettes, while larger units have full-size kitchens. A family of four can manage comfortably in a spacious studio if the kids don't mind sharing a bed—a bedroom area is separated off from the main living area by a bookcase. Some studios have lofts with a sofa bed and extra bath. A sauna, steam room, massage room, three indoor and two outdoor hot tubs, concierge and bell staff, covered parking, ski locker and valet, and movies and VCR rentals on-site complete the package. $160–550. 201 Squaw Peak Road, Olympic Valley, CA 96146. Mailing address: P.O. Box 2364, Olympic Valley, CA 96146; 800-922-9970, 530-583-5500.

Olympic Village Inn, about one and a half blocks from the lifts, looks just like a Swiss A-frame chalet. Its one-bedroom suites have kitchenettes, a queen-size bed in the bedroom, and a queen-size sofa bed in the living room. Some units come with a fireplace, and all can accommodate four people. Amenities on site include eiderdown comforters, a swimming pool, five hot tubs with a mountain view, a ski-check area, a small gift shop, and laundry facilities. $165–215. 1900 Chamonix Place, Olympic Valley, CA 96146; 800-845-5243, 530-581-6000.

Plumpjack Squaw Valley Inn at the base of the tram building is stylishly modern. You'll find feather comforters on beds, plush terry robes, an honor bar, VCR, cable, room service, and a five-star restaurant on the premises. Most rooms have one king-size or two queen-size beds, and some have connecting doors. Other extras include a swimming pool and cozy bar. $170–270. 1920 Squaw Valley Road, P.O. Box 2407, Olympic Valley, CA 96146; 800-323-7666, 530-583-1576.

Moderate
Granlibakken is its own small ski resort where the number and variety of accommodation possibilities definitely dwarf the tiny ski area with two sur-

face lifts. This resort offers attractive ski packages with both Squaw Valley and Alpine Meadows and has a small sledding hill that is handy for letting the kids play in the snow before they try to ski. A small cross-country center offers lessons and rental equipment, downhill lessons and rentals also are available. Units range in size from standard hotel rooms to studios and one-to six-bedroom condos and townhouses. A complimentary hot buffet breakfast is included in the rates no matter where you stay. Hotel rooms tend to be too small for most families, but studios have two twin beds and a Hide-A-Bed, plus a kitchen and a living room area with a fireplace. The six-bedroom townhouse has six bathrooms, an enormous living room, and a state-of-the-art kitchen. A sledding area rents saucers. $69–970. 725 Granlibakken Road, P.O. Box 6329, Tahoe City, CA 96145; 800-543-3221.

River Run Condominiums, three miles from Squaw Valley, have one, two, or three bedrooms, some with lofts that contain two twin beds. The largest units can accommodate 8 to 12 people. All have their own washers and dryers, fireplaces, and decks that look out over the river. Other amenities include a hot tub, Jacuzzi, and small sauna. $170–260. 135 Alpine Meadows Road, P.O. Box 6747, Tahoe City, CA 96145; 530-583-0137.

Budget
Tahoe City Travelodge is well maintained, attractively appointed, and has rooms large enough for a family of four. Rooms have one king-size or two double beds and all are big enough to accommodate one rollaway ($10 extra charge). Some rooms have a microwave oven and small refrigerator, and all rooms have a coffeemaker. After skiing, soak in the hot tub on a deck overlooking the lake. Rooms are priced according to their view, and kids under 17 stay free in their parents' room. The motel is a ten-minute drive from Squaw Valley. $79–119. 455 North Lake Boulevard, P.O. Box 84, Tahoe City, CA 96145; 800-578-7878, 530-583-3766.

Lake of the Sky Motor Inn, six miles from Squaw Valley, has rooms with two full-size beds. This basic motel has a heated swimming pool, telephones, and TVs. $69–105. 955 North Lake Boulevard, P.O. Box 227, Tahoe City, CA 96145; 530-583-3305.

Children's Ski School
Squaw Valley's learn-to-ski area for kids is fenced off and lies right out the back door of the children's center. Intermediates and advanced classes are

taken up the tram or gondola to ski. A preferred parking area in front of Squaw Valley's Children's World makes it easy to drop off kids for day care or ski school. Parents can buy their own lift tickets when they sign up their kids and head up the Red Dog lift, which allows them access to the rest of the mountain. The huge children's facility was designed after the staff had visited children's ski facilities around the country; they took the best ideas and put them into practice at this state-of-art center.

Snow School, for ages 4 to 6, accommodates all skill levels with full- and half-day programs. Junior Mountain, for ages 7 to 12, focuses on fun, skiing development, and skiing etiquette. Snowboard lessons are available for this group, too; 530-581-7225.

Day Care
Toddler Care for 2- and 3-year-olds is in Children's World at the base of the mountain. Daily activities include arts and crafts, music, snow play, and story time. The 3-year-olds can take an optional one-and-a-half-hour ski lesson. Full- and half-day programs are available; 800-545-4350.

Snowboarding
Central Park has a series of tabletops, rails, spines, a half pipe, and other ridable snow sculptures. The park is open from all day, closes from 4 to 4:15 for grooming and reopens until 9 P.M. for night skiing.

Cross-Country Skiing
Resort at Squaw Creek has 25 kilometers of groomed trails, plus ski rentals, including children's sizes, and group and private lessons for all ages and abilities; 800-327-3353, 530-583-6300.

Other Activities
High Camp, at the top of the tram station, is the center for nonskiing action in the Valley. You'll find an Olympic-size ice rink overlooking Lake Tahoe (rental skates available), bungee jumping from the highest-elevation permanent tower in the world, and the 1960 Olympic Winter Museum; 530-583-6985.

Full-moon hikes start from this area. Three different snowshoe hikes— easy, intermediate, and difficult—are led by guides who talk about the history and natural features of the area. Adult-size snowshoes are available for rent but children's sizes are not. In March, the swimming lagoon, pool, and spa open for spring skiers and are free with every lift ticket.

The base of High Camp, el. 6,200, in the valley, features a movie theater with five o'clock showings, a climbing wall in the bottom of the cable-car building, and a small ice-skating rink at the Resort at Squaw Creek.

Deals and Discounts

Kids 12 and under pay $5 per ticket. Call central reservations and ask about packages when you start planning your trip. Lift ticket prices include night skiing.

Colorado

Aspen Mountain

Address: Aspen Skiing Company, P.O. Box 1248, Aspen, Colorado 81612

Telephone: 800-525-6200, 970-925-1220

Web site: http://www.skiaspen.com

Aspen, with its 300 shops and boutiques, 30 art galleries, and nearly 100 bistros, restaurants, and bars, makes the society pages and movie magazines as the premiere winter hangout of the rich and famous. You will see skiers in Aspen whose ski-vacation price-tag total would send a kid to an Ivy League college for a year or two, but don't let Aspen's image of wealth and exclusivity intimidate you. It's not reserved for the rich and famous alone.

Aspen's charming compact village with its beautifully preserved historic buildings is small enough to explore on foot, yet diverse enough to satisfy the most jaded shopaholic. An excellent bus system ferries visitors around town. If you're on a budget you can stay for less just outside of town and still enjoy all that Aspen has to offer.

Four different ski areas are situated within a few miles of one another: Aspen Mountain, Buttermilk Mountain, Snowmass Ski Area (see page 94), and Aspen Highlands. Aspen Mountain's rugged peaks shoot skyward just behind the town. Called Ajax by the locals, its steep faces and knee-shattering mogul runs make it equally appropriate for strong intermediate and expert skiers. This mountain has virtually no beginner terrain.

MOUNTAIN STATISTICS
Base elevation: 7,945 feet
Summit: 11,212 feet
Vertical drop: 3,267 feet
Skiable acres: 631
Annual average snowfall: 300 inches
Snowmaking: 218 acres
Night skiing: none
Season: late November to mid-April
Lifts: 8 (1 gondola, 1 high-speed quad, 2 regular quads, 1 high-speed double, 3 doubles)
Terrain: 35% intermediate; 35% advanced, 30% expert only
Lift tickets: adults $59; youth 13 to 27 $39, children 7 to 12 $35, under 7 and over 70 free.

FAMILY STATISTICS
Day care: at nearby Snowmass (970) 923-0570 or Buttermilk Mountain (970) 920-0935
Children's lessons: at Snowmass, Ski Area Buttermilk Mountain, or Aspen Highlands; 800-525-6200 or 970-925-1220 (ask for ski school)
Baby-sitting: Super Sitters (970-923-6080), Kidstime Referral Service (970-925-KIDS)
Baby gear: Baby's Away rents cribs, strollers, car seats, toys, etc. 970-920-1699.
Medical: Aspen Valley Hospital, 970-544-1216

Snowboarders are not allowed on Aspen Mountain, but the same excellent bus system takes boarders to three other nearby ski areas that welcome them.

Buttermilk Mountain, a small but good beginner and intermediate mountain, has a snowboard park and day-care center. The children staying in any of Aspen's lodgings are transported here for all-day ski or snowboarding lessons in a special purple bus called Max the Moose Express.

Snowmass Ski Area, 13 miles away (see pages 94–95), is a behemoth of a mountain known for its well-groomed intermediate cruising runs and a compact base village with many ski-in-and-out hotels and condominiums.

Aspen Highlands, considered the most extreme mountain and a favorite of boarders and mogul hounds, is 2 miles from Aspen. One lift ticket allows you to ski all four mountains, and discounted lift tickets are available for snowboarders and skiers ages 13 to 27. The trail-rider pass for kids 7 to 12 costs even less.

Aspen visitors with very young children often hire baby-sitters to take care of infants and toddlers back at the hotel or condo, and there is a drop-in day-care center in town for toddlers. If you want one-stop shopping for day care, ski school, and lodging, you're better off staying at Snowmass and exploring Aspen in the evening or on a nonski day.

How to Get There

Aspen is 220 miles from Denver, about a four-hour drive by car or shuttle bus. Many guests fly into Eagle County Airport, located 70 miles east of Aspen, or into the small airport in Aspen that is served by four airlines— United Airlines, Aspen Mountain Air, Western Pacific, and Mountain Air Express—and has direct flights from Minneapolis, Chicago, Los Angeles, and Dallas. Direct flights into Eagle County Airport are available from many other parts of the country.

Don't bother with a rental car if you fly in (even into Denver). The bus system is so good you won't need a car and there are taxis available in the city of Aspen.

Where to Stay

Expensive

The Gant has attractive one- to four-bedroom condos, combining the convenience of extra space and a kitchen with the concierge services of a first-class hotel. It's in downtown Aspen about two-and-a-half blocks from the lift and offers a complimentary skier shuttle. As a bonus, there is a swimming pool and tennis courts. $310–635. 610 West End Street, Aspen, CO 81611; 800-345-1471, 970-925-5000.

Aspen Alps, conveniently located alongside the gondola, has condos with two to four bedrooms. Free cribs are available, and there's an outdoor pool, hot tub, spa, and massage services. $400–1100. 700 Ute Avenue, Aspen CO 81611; 800-228-7820, 970-925-7820.

Historic **Hotel Jerome** opened in 1889, and its Victorian grandeur, luxuriously appointed rooms, and top-flight service make it a favorite with parents who want to be pampered. The public rooms are stunning with crystal chandeliers, vintage furnishings, and sumptuous woodwork. The spacious hotel rooms have high ceilings and are decorated with period antiques. There are two excellent restaurants, an outdoor pool with a Jacuzzi, and a fitness center that kids can use with supervision. $395–1300. Aspen Mountain is four blocks away. 330 East Main Street, Aspen, CO 81611; 800-331-7213, 970-920-1000.

Moderate

Aspen Square has 105 condos, consisting of studios, and one- and two-bedroom units, all with full kitchens. There's a pool and a hot tub, and the hotel is located in the center of town across the street from the ski area. Rollaways are free of charge. $215–445. 617 East Cooper, Aspen, CO 81611. 800-862-7736, 970-925-1000.

Hotel Aspen is a small contemporary hotel with 45 standard rooms and suites. It's about three blocks from downtown Aspen and one block from a shuttle stop. Its ski packages for five nights and four days of skiing can be a good deal. Rollaways cost $10 per night, but cribs are free. $129–594. 110 West Main Street, Aspen, CO 81611; 800-527-7369, 970-925-3441.

T-Lazy-7 Ranch sits five miles outside of town and offers apartments and cabins of all sizes with kitchens and fireplaces but no telephones or TVs. A shuttle takes skiers to the slopes. Activities available on-site include snowmobile tours, private sleigh rides, cross-country trails, and western party nights. $75–300. P.O. Box TT, Aspen, CO 81612; 888-875-6343, 970-925-7254.

Budget

Mountain Chalet is just a little more than a block from Aspen Mountain and has a variety of room configurations comfortable for families, such as a king-and-two-twins combination, a queen-and-sofa-bed combination, and bunk rooms. Several four-bedroom apartments are available, as are a few rooms with a wet bar and fireplace. A full breakfast, included in the rates, is served to all guests in the dining room. Other features include a game room, fitness room, sauna, steam room, Jacuzzi, and pool. $130–240. 333 East Duerant Avenue, Aspen, CO 81611; 970-925-7797.

Molly Gibson Lodge is eight blocks from the lifts and has a low-key, easy-going ambience. A free shuttle takes you to the slopes, and there's an indoor and an outdoor pool and two outdoor Jacuzzis. Standard rooms run $200 per night. 101 West Main Street, Aspen, CO 81611; 800-356-6559, 970-925-3434.

Children's Ski School
Parents can register children ages 3 and up for ski school at Aspen Mountain and will be escorted by ski instructors to their lessons at Buttermilk Mountain via the Max the Moose Express bus; 800-525-6200 or 970-925-1220 (ask for ski school).

Day Care
Aspen Mountain has no programs for kids, but you can take your tiny ones—18 months to 3 years old—to the Snow Cubs program at Snowmass Ski Area (970-923-0563). Night Hawks—also at Snowmass—is an evening child-care program for children 3 to 12, and is staffed by ski-school personnel (970-923-0570).

The Kids Club Daycare Center in Aspen offers drop-in care for toddlers 12 months to 2 years (970-925-3136). Super Sitters has screened and bonded baby-sitters who will come to your hotel or condo (970-923-6080).

Teens
The Aspen Youth Center (970-925-4939) has pool tables, basketball, Ping-Pong, and video games.

Snowboarding
Aspen Mountain does not allow snowboarding on the front side. Snowboarding is allowed on powder tours on the backside of Aspen Mountain.

Cross-Country Skiing
Nearly 48 miles of Snow-Cat groomed trails connect Aspen and Snowmass Village with terrain for beginners, intermediates, and experts.

Aspen Cross Country Center, on the tracks at the Aspen Golf Course (308 South Mill Street, Aspen, CO 81611), can set you up with skis, accessories, rentals, lessons, and tours; 970-925-2145.

Snowmass Lodge & Club Touring Center offers more than 30 kilometers of tracks that connect with the Aspen Snowmass Nordic System. It offers professional and guided tours, a rental shop, and a small restaurant. If you've purchased a multiple-day downhill ticket and want to try cross-country skiing, you can trade in one ticket for a free group lesson, ski rental, and the use of the trail system; 970-923-3148.

Other Activities

Fly-fishing: Cast a line into the Roaring Fork River. Oxbow Outfitting (800-421-1505, 970-925-1505) and Blazing Adventures (800-282-7238, 970-925-5651) will supply gear, transportation, and instruction.

Hot-air balloon rides: Float over the Rocky Mountains in a hot-air balloon with Adventures Aloft (970-925-9497) or Unicorn Balloon Company of Colorado (970-925-5752).

Ice skating: Aspen Ice Garden 233 West Hymen Avenue, Aspen, CO 81611; 970-920-5154. Silver Circle Ice Rink offer skating at the base of Aspen Mountain in front of the Grand Aspen Hotel; 970-925-6360.

Sleigh rides: Burlingame Dinner Rides (970-925-1220) offers a 20-minute sleigh or heated Sno-Cat ride to Burlingame Cabin, where you'll find a roaring fire, reindeer, entertainment, and a Southwestern meal.

Aspen Adventures Sleigh Rides and Snow-Cat Tours (970-920-4FUN) or T-Lazy-7 Ranch (970-925-4614, 970-925-7040) offer sleigh rides around the valley.

Snowmobiling: T-Lazy-7 Ranch (970-925-4614, 970-925-7040).

Spa: The Aspen Club is a tony first-class health-and-racquet club with a day spa, indoor tennis courts, and a sports-medicine institute; 970-925-8900.

Paragliding is becoming more and more popular in ski areas, with riders taking the chairlift up and then launching off the side of the mountain, floating above the spectacular alpine scenery. Aspen Paragliding, 426 South Spring Street, Aspen, CO 81611; 970-925-7625.

Snowshoeing: Take a break from skiing and try a snowshoe trek. Rent snowshoes for $11 a day at Ute Mountaineer (970-925-2849) and take a free guided tour of the wildlife and ecology of the area (970-925-5756).

Other guided trips are available with Blazing Adventures (800-282-7238, 970-925-5651) or the Aspen Cross Country Center (970-925-2145).

Swimming: There's a year-round swimming pool at the James E. More City of Aspen Pool that offers family swims, a kid's splash time, water games, and kayak lessons. Maroon Creek Road, Aspen, 81611 CO; 970-920-5145.

Deals and Discounts

Aspen is short on freebies and deals, but here are a few: guided snowshoe treks (see above) are free; Use It Again Sports (970-925-2483) may have clothes and equipment to fit your kids; many restaurants have early-bird specials, and there's a McDonald's in Aspen that is particularly low on atmosphere and prices.

Discounted early- and late-season packages are available.

❄ Beaver Creek Resort

Address: P.O. Box 7, Vail, Colorado 81658

Telephone: 800-243-8053 (reservations), 970-375-6688; 800-859-8242 (lodging)

Web site: http://www.snow.com

 This luxurious self-contained mountain resort, ten miles down the road from its sister, Vail (see page 112), has one of the best children's ski schools around. Beaver Creek is a meticulously planned ski village rated among the best in the country for its lodging and overall service.

Like any well-designed ski village worth its snow, Beaver Creek has everything in one spot: shops, ski rentals, lift tickets, accommodations, day care, and restaurants. If you don't want to ski, there are plenty of options at the resort or just down the road at Vail. Many accommodations offer views of the slopes, and ski-in-and-out lodging is abundant, making Beaver Creek especially convenient for families. The resort's lift ticket is interchangeable with Vail, Keystone, and Breckenridge.

The layout of lifts and trails has been as carefully thought out as the design of the pedestrian village. Beginning skiers tend to head to the top of the mountain where easy, smooth trails head off in a number of directions. Intermediates can ski the entire mountain; even the toughest runs have intermediate trails down. A new high-speed quad links Beaver Creek with Arrowhead Mountain next door, which creates even more intermediate skiing. There are plenty of black-diamond runs, double-black-diamond trails, and some bone-rattling bumps for the experts. Kids

MOUNTAIN STATISTICS
Base elevation: 7,400 feet
Summit: 11,440 feet
Vertical drop: 4,040 feet
Skiable acres: 1,625
Annual average snowfall: 331 inches
Snowmaking: 550 acres
Night skiing: none
Season: late November to mid-April
Lifts: 14 (6 high-speed quads, 3 triples, 4 doubles, 1 surface lift).
Terrain: 34% beginner, 39% intermediate, 27% advanced
Lift tickets: adults $55, children 6 to 14, $37, under 6 free.

FAMILY STATISTICS
Day care: Small World Play School Nursery, ages 2 months to 6 years, 970-845-5325 (reservations required)
Children's lessons: Children's Skiing Center; 800-475-4543, 970-479-3239
Baby-sitting: Vail Babysitting, 970-827-5279; Baroni Baby Sitting, 970-476-9126; Rocky Mountain Baby Sitters, 303-949-2069
Baby gear: Baby's Away rents cribs, strollers, car seat, high chairs, and other gear; 970-926-5256
Medical: Vail Valley Medical Center, 970-476-2451

adore the fanciful terrain gardens such as the Indian Burial Ground; Tomb-stone Territory, the colorful ski-through ghost town; and Nears Cave, a fanciful gold mine where kids can take home a piece of fool's gold.

Every aspect of Beaver Creek's children's ski school is well thought out. The minute your child leaves the ticket office/kids' ski accessories shop, "tatch-it" guns (devices retailers use to attach price tags to clothes) attach his goggles to his hat and the hat and mittens to his jacket. Kids get big, fat buttons as they enter ski school, to which they affix the flashy gold-and-black stickers they receive every time they learn a new ski skill.

Most Thursday evenings intermediate and expert skiers can participate in a torch-lit ski-down. All skiers, including the kids, receive a glow stick to carry down the darkened slopes of Haymarket, a beginner's run. The evening culminates in a fireworks grand finale.

How to Get There

Eagle County Airport is about 25 miles west of Beaver Creek and is serviced with direct flights by many major airlines. Shuttle buses run regularly be-tween the airport and the resort. Denver International Airport is about 2½ hours away by car and shuttle services operate between the airport and Beaver Creek. Regular shuttles are available to Vail, a 20-minute, $2 bus ride away.

Where to Stay

Expensive

Hyatt Regency Beaver Creek, in the center of Beaver Creek's pedestrian village and just steps from the slopes, is one of the resort's best-located hotels. The Camp Hyatt children's program entertains youngsters 3 to 12 (must be toilet trained) who don't want to ski during the day and offers activities until 10 P.M. in the evening. The hotel's full-service spa refreshes parents' aching muscles. Kids under 18 stay free in their parents' room. $240–450. 136 East Thomas Place, P.O. Box 1595, Avon, CO 81620-1595, 800-233-1234, 970-949-1234.

The Inn at Beaver Creek is at the base of Strawberry Park Express chair-lift and has the closest lift access in Beaver Creek. It's a cozy, upscale es-tablishment with hotel rooms, two condos, and two-room suites. There's an outdoor heated pool and tub, an indoor sauna, a steam room, free un-derground parking, and a free shuttle. Children 12 and under stay free in parents' room. Rooms and suites $300–600, condos $675–1250. 10 Elk Track Lane, Beaver Creek, CO 81620; 800-859-8242, 970-845-7800.

Moderate

Embassy Suites has two-room suites that can sleep up to four and include kitchenettes, VCRs, fireplaces, and separate living rooms. A complimentary continental breakfast is included in the rates. There's an indoor and outdoor pool, sauna, and Jacuzzi. The hotel provides a shuttle to the lifts, and ski storage. $135–500. 26 Avondale Lane, Beaver Creek; P.O. Box 2578, Avon, CO 81620; 800-362-2779; 970-845-9800.

Budget

The Christie Lodge in Avon, about 5 minutes and 2.5 miles from Beaver Creek Resort, is an affordable option in a pricey neighborhood. It's undistinguished, but its clean and comfortable one-bedroom suites have kitchenettes and fireplaces and can accommodate two adults and two children. $109–199 47 East Beaver Creek Boulevard, P.O. Box 1196, Avon, CO 81620; 800-551-4326, 970-949-7700.

Comfort Inn in Avon offers a free continental breakfast to guests. If it's not too cold your kids can play at the playground next door or splash in the outdoor heated pool and hot tub. Most rooms have two queen-size beds. Kids under 18 stay free in their parents' room and rollaways cost $10 per day. $167–187. 161 West Beaver Creek Boulevard, Avon, CO 81620; 800-221-2222, 970-949-5511.

Children's Ski School

The layout of the children's ski-school headquarters couldn't be better designed. Sign your kids up for lessons next to the ski-accessories shop where you can pick up a set of goggles or a tube of sunblock if you need it. Kids are fitted for skis and boots at the rental area, then head off in several different directions depending on their age. Classes are separated by age and ability: 3-year-olds, Mini Mice, have their own introductory ski class (must be toilet trained), 4- and 5-year-olds, Mogul Mice, have their own lessons, while kids in first grade through the age of 12 ski together in ability-based groups. Teens have special programs over peak holiday periods. Because so many kids come for a week, there are themes for each day, such as Ski-cology Day, Friendship Day, Race Day, Treasure Hunt Day, Circus Day, and Ski Patrol Day. Snowboard lessons start at age 6.

Day Care

Children from age 2 months to 6 years are placed in three groups, each in its own room at the Small World Play School Nursery (970-845-5325).

Babies from 2 to 15 months share one room. Caregivers interview parents about their child's schedule so they can try to duplicate it. Parents are given a complimentary pager.

Toddlers are so busy going from one activity and toy to the next that their day is relatively unstructured, but they do have an art project, circle time, and nap time after lunch.

Preschoolers have a more structured day with art, music, movement, circle time, and snow play. After lunch they watch a short video and take naps.

Reservations are required, especially over peak holiday periods. Because so many guests stay a week, many children are enrolled for the full week but take off a day or two when plans shift; cancellations can provide a space that day.

Kid's Night Out Goes Western is a supervised kids-only evening that includes music, games, storytelling, a pizza dinner, and a Western show. It takes place on Tuesday evenings at Beaver Creek Village at 5:30 P.M.; 970-476-9090.

Teens
Special teen programs are offered through the ski school during holiday periods.

Snowboarding
Free snowboarding trail maps are available at any activities desk and at on-mountain information kiosks. Beaver Creek's Stickline Snowboard Park is set among the trees and has banks, hits, tabletops, log slides, and a huge gully. The resort also has a half price. For information on snowboarding, call 970-476-3239.

Cross-Country Skiing
McCoy Park offers lift-served mountaintop Nordic skiing. The park is accessible via the Strawberry Park Express chairlift and offers 32 kilometers of double tracks with a skating lane. As you might expect, views are spectacular and you don't have to work very hard to get them. Lessons, rentals, and guided tours are available. Kids in a group lesson need to be accompanied by an adult; 970-845-5313.

Other Activities
Avon Recreation Center: This state-of-the-art fitness center has a 15,000-square-foot Aquatics Area that contains a lap pool, diving well, leisure pool, and a 150-foot slide encircled by a lazy river. In addition, there's a

steam room, sauna, and Jacuzzi. 0325 Benchmark Road, Avon, CO 81620; 970-949-9191.

Dogsledding rides start from Cordillera about nine miles out of Beaver Creek. Outfitters can pick you up at your hotel. 970-476-9090.

Hot-air balloon rides with Mountain Balloon Adventures (970-476-2353) take riders five years and older over the Vail Valley and beyond, offering views that stretch from the Continental Divide to Rocky Mountain National Park.

Ice skating: Beaver Creek's outdoor skating rink (970-949-9090), atop the new art-center complex, has a cooled floor so if the weather warms you can still skate in the open air. Rental skates of all size are available.

Snowshoeing: McCoy Park (970-845-5313), the cross-country area at the top of the Strawberry Park Express chairlift, offers rental snowshoes and ten different trails for snowshoers to explore.

Snowmobiling: Take a backcountry tour into the White River National Forest. Outfitters Piney River Ranch (970-476-3941) or Nova Guides (888-949-6682, 970-949-4232) will pick you up and take you to the forest, which is south of Mintern, about seven miles away.

Sleigh rides: Bundle up in a horse-drawn sleigh for a brisk ride through the forests and meadows. Beaver Creek Stables, 970-845-7770; 4 Eagle Ranch, 970-926-3372.

Deals and Discounts

Early season discounts on lift tickets can be purchased until the week before Christmas.

❄ Breckenridge Ski Resort

Address: P.O. Box 1058, Breckenridge, Colorado 80424
Telephone: 800-221-1091, 970-453-2918 (lodging); 970-453-5000
Web site: http://www.snow.com

Breckenridge's popularity with skiers from all over the world is due to a first-class ski experience, combined with an authentic western town that offers all of the services and amenities you'd find in any community where people live year-round. In the old-town section of Breckenridge, quaint streets are fronted by gracious Victorian buildings, many of which were built more than 130 years ago. The area was first settled about 10,000 years ago by Anasazi Indians. The town enjoyed a boom in the Victorian era thanks to prospectors who discovered a rich vein of gold in the nearby Blue River. The old mining town eventually went from boom to bust but then boomed again with prosperity as a popular ski resort.

Breckenridge Ski Resort has four linked mountains; the untamed summit of one of them can only be reached on foot. As you might imagine, its steep pitches and chutes are for experts only. The lower mountains and their easygoing cruisers and smooth, wide bowls keep families of intermediate boarders and skiers happy for days at a time. There are 6 high-speed quads servicing the 4 peaks. Study the trail map before you hit the slopes as the combination of high-speed quads that have been added to make up for some of the shortcomings of the older, slower chairs can seem confusing at first.

There are three main base areas; two have their own children's day care and three have a ski-school facility. The age

MOUNTAIN STATISTICS

Base elevation: 9,600 feet
Summit: 12,998 feet
Vertical drop: 3,398 feet
Skiable acres: 2,031
Annual average snowfall: 300 inches
Snowmaking: 504 acres
Night skiing: none
Season: early November to May
Lifts: 19 (6 high-speed quads, 1 triple, 7 doubles, 5 surface lifts)
Terrain: 14% beginner, 18% intermediate, 8% advanced intermediate, 22% advanced, 38% extreme
Lift tickets: adults $55, children 6 to 14 $37, under 6 free

FAMILY STATISTICS

Day care: Peak 8 Children's Center (ages 2 months to 5 years) or Peak 9 Children's Center (ages 3 to 5 years), 800-789-SNOW
Children's lessons: Peak 8 and 9 Children's Centers, 800-789-SNOW, ext. 3258
Baby-sitting: The Children's Center provides a list: 800-789-SNOW
Baby gear: Baby's Away rents car seats, cribs, strollers, backpacks, high chairs, and other items; 970-668-1571
Medical: Breckenridge Medical Center 970-453-9000

and needs of your family will determine which facility you select. Only one of the three base areas has facilities for babies and toddlers and a different facility houses the ski-school program for three and four year olds. Inform yourself before you select a lodging to make sure you find the most convenient base area for your family.

Long recognized by snowboarders as friendly, welcoming, and challenging, Breckenridge's snowboard parks are some of the best in the country. Snowboarding lessons for kids operate from every base area, and adults can take special day clinics on boards. The ski area is also known for its excellent women's clinics.

Breckenridge is partnered with Vail, Keystone, and Beaver Creek and offers an interchangeable multi-lift ticket at all 4 resorts.

How to Get There

Breckenridge is 104 miles west of the Denver International Airport. A number of airport-shuttle companies provide door-to-door service. With in the resort, there is a free shuttle-bus system to transport skiers between lodging and the ski area. The Summit Stage is a free county-wide bus service that will take you to Keystone, Arapanoe Basin, and anywhere else you want to go in Summit County.

Where to Stay

Expensive

Beaver Run Resort and Conference Center (http://www.colorado.net/thebeave) couldn't be better set up for families. It has an indoor minigolf course; its own children's ski school, Kinderhit, for 2½- to 6-year-olds; an infant-and-toddler nursery; two swimming pools; eight hot tubs; a game arcade; and deluxe accommodations. Hotel rooms and deluxe studios accommodate families. A quad chair on the property allows for ski-in-and-out accessibility. There's ski storage and a free shuttle to town. $120–880. 620 Village Road, P.O. Box 2115, Breckenridge, CO 80424; 800-525-2253, 970-453-6000.

Breckenridge Hilton is located slopeside right across the street from the day-care center. Lift-ticket purchases, recreational activities, dinner reservations, and all sorts of other things can be arranged through the guest-services desk. Both hotel rooms and suites are available, and a number of them have connecting doors. Amenities include an indoor swimming pool and hot tubs, an outdoor swimming pool, fitness center, massage services, ski storage, and shops. Children stay free in their parents' room. $89–

265. 550 Village Road, P.O. Box 8059, Breckenridge, CO 80424; 800-321-8444, 970-453-4500.

Moderate

Village at Breckenridge has ski-in-and-out units about 50 yards from the lifts and a short walk from historic downtown Breckenridge. Possibilities include hotel rooms, studio apartments, and one-, two-, and three-bedroom condos. The most luxurious units have Jacuzzi tubs in the master bathroom, fireplaces, balconies, and Lodgenet, an in-room movie-and-video-game service. The nine on-site restaurants have children's menus, plus there's an indoor and outdoor pool, nine hot tubs, a billiard hall, and a game arcade. $60–800. 535 South Park, Breckenridge, CO 80424; 800-800-7829, 970-453-2000.

Twilight Inn is a cozy bed-and-breakfast right next door to the Daily Planet Bookstore. Rates include a lavish continental breakfast and use of the steam room and hot tub. Several of its rooms are perfect for families: two connect with a shared bath, and one has a double bed and two twins. Other rooms have two queen-size beds, two double beds, or a single queen-size bed. The inn is about ten minutes from the lifts and about two blocks from the shuttle stop. $90–125. 308 Main Street, P.O. Box 397, Frisco, CO 80443; 970-668-5009, 800-262-1002.

Budget

Breckenridge Park Meadow Lodge, one mile from the lifts, is rustic with mountain-lodge decor. Studios and one-bedroom units feature kitchenettes. There is a hot tub, a game room, and a lounge. $145–230. 213 North Main, Breckenridge, CO 00924; 800-344-7669.

Holiday Inn Resort Summit County offers a free skier shuttle to all four ski areas in the Summit county area. Its "Holidome" is an undercover sports center with an indoor heated pool, hot tubs, saunas, exercise machines, Ping Pong, pool table, and tanning beds. Children under 19 stay free in their parents' room, and kids age 12 and under eat free in the Holiday Inn restaurant. Rooms have either one king-size bed and a sofa sleeper, two queens, or one king. Be sure to ask about promotional packages and the "best breaks" rate when you book your stay: The price can drop considerably. $159–220. I-70 exit 203, P.O. Box 4310, Frisco, CO 80443; 800-465-4329, 970-668-5000.

Children's Ski School

Ski instruction is offered at both the Peak 8 and 9 Children's Centers (800-789-SNOW, ext. 3258). Ski school for toilet-trained 3-year-olds takes place in the morning, but your kids can stay and play away the afternoon. Children 4 and 5 years old get two hours of ski instruction in the morning and two hours in the afternoon. Children 6 to 12 have full-day and half-day classes. Teens are grouped in separate classes whenever possible, usually over holiday periods. Group snowboarding classes are available for kids 8 and older; private instruction can be arranged for kids age 7 and younger.

Day Care

Breckenridge has two child-care facilities, both called Kid's Castle. Peak 8's children's center takes children two months to five years old and is the only facility to take infants and toddlers. Infants have their own playroom, separate from the room for toddlers and the additional large playroom for 3 to 5 year olds. Reservations are essential, especially for the younger ages as space is limited. The facility also has a rental shop downstairs, ticket counter, ski school, and cafeteria. Peak 9 has a Kid's Castle that takes children ages 3 to 5. Both facilities have colorful and engaging rooms and toys for indoor play that includes music and art, and preschoolers enjoy regular daily outdoor snow play, such as sledding, building snowmen, and walks, weather permitting. Reservations required; 800-789-7669, 970-496-7201.

Teens

There's an indoor skateboard park in town called Big Fish; 970-547-0216.

Snowboarding

A six-acre snowboard-park terrain garden provides challenges for boarders of all levels with a half pipe, rails, spines, fun boxes, rolls, waves, bridges, and additional snow structures. Skiers are welcome.

Cross-Country Skiing

Breckenridge Nordic Center has 18 kilometers of groomed trails. Its day lodge has equipment rentals, including children's sleds, plus lessons and a ski shop; 970-453-6855.

Frisco Nordic Center has 35 kilometers of trails that go around Lake Dillon. Rentals and lessons are available; 970-688-0866.

Other Activities

Breckenridge Recreation Center has climbing walls, a fitness center, swimming pools with a slide and rope swing, hot tubs, basketball, tennis, racquetball, volleyball courts, and steam rooms. Day care is available on the premises; 970-453-1734.

Dogsledding: Tiger Run (970-453-2231).

Historic town tours are offered by the Summit Historical Society (970-453-9902).

Horseback riding: Guided tours with Western Safari Ranch (800-530-8883) last one hour in bad weather and two hours on a sunny day.

Ice skating: An outdoor ice rink at Maggie Pond (970-453-9601) is in Breckenridge between the town and the ski area.

Sleigh rides: Nordic Center dinner sleigh rides (970-453-2005) include a delightful dance-hall show.

Snowmobiling rides of all lengths, from one hour to half-day and dinner rides are available from White Mountain Tours (800-668-5323), Good Times Snowmobiling (800-477-1448), or Swan River Adventure Center (800-477-0144).

Deals and Discounts

Ski Free Stay Free packages are available at certain properties from approximately early November to Christmas (excluding Thanksgiving) and early January to mid-February. If guests purchase 4, 5, or 6 nights of lodging and 3, 4, or 5 days of lift tickets they receive a one-night stay and one lift ticket free of charge.

Copper Mountain Resort

Address: 209 Ten Mile Circle, P.O. Box 3001, Copper
Mountain, Colorado 80443
Telephone: 800-458-8386 (central reservations)
Web site: http://www.ski-copper.com

Copper is known for affordable prices, a convenient layout, and good, solid skiing. The look of this planned village is slightly utilitarian, lacking the Bavarian charm of Vail, the elegance of Aspen Mountain, or the Western mystique of Jackson Hole Mountain Resort. Its accommodations, however, are all a short walk from the ski mountain, making this a particularly convenient resort for families. Even during the peak season its lodging-and-lift-ticket packages are some of the lowest around when you consider what you get—accommodations a few steps from the lifts and dry, champagne-powder snow.

The skiing is naturally separated into three ability-based areas, with most of the advanced terrain on one side, the intermediate terrain in the middle, and beginner hills on the other side. A free shuttle system throughout the resort connects the different base areas. To make skiing Copper attractive to beginners, families who are just learning to ski can use the beginner lifts (K and L) for free during selected weeks throughout the season. When they progress to intermediate terrain, they must buy regular lift tickets, but Copper's children's lift-ticket prices (to age 14) are a low $20. The late-season packages are some of the most affordable anywhere in Colorado, and kids 14 and under stay free most of the time.

Most of the children's programs are in

MOUNTAIN STATISTICS
Base elevation: 9,712 feet
Summit: 12,313 feet
Vertical drop: 2,601 feet
Skiable acres: 2,433
Annual average snowfall: 280 inches
Snowmaking: 270 acres
Night skiing: none
Season: mid-November through late
   April
Lifts: 21 (3 high-speed quads, 6 triples,
   8 doubles, 4 surface lifts)
Terrain: 21% beginner, 25%
   intermediate, 36% advanced, 18%
   extreme
Lift tickets: adults $49, children 6 to 14
   $20, under 6 free.

FAMILY STATISTICS
Day care: Belly Button Bakery/Babies
   in the Mountain Plaza building, ages
   2 months to 4 years; 800-458-8386
   (or 970-968-2318), ext. 6345
Children's lessons: Ski School ages 4 to
   12; 800-458-8386 ext. 6331
Baby-sitting: Day care will help arrange
   evening baby-sitting; 800-458-8386
   (or 970-968-2318), ext. 6345
Baby gear: Baby's Away rents high
   chairs, cribs, strollers, car seats, toys,
   and other items; 970-668-1571
Medical: Copper Medical Center, 970-
   968-2330

one building—Kids Headquarters and Family Skiing Center—that also houses a rental shop, a cafeteria, and a play area. One call to central reservations can reserve lodging, lessons at the ski school, day care, and such extras as evening sleigh rides.

On weekends, the parking lot can be packed with suburbanites hailing from Denver, Colorado Springs, or Fort Collins. The resort stops selling tickets once the parking lot is filled to limit the number of skiers on the mountain.

Copper will see major changes in the next few years, as it recently was purchased by Intrawest, the company that transformed Whistler Resort and Mont Tremblant into pedestrian villages with much charm and personality. Intrawest plans to spend $340 million in the village and another $30 million on the mountain over the next ten years.

How to Get There

Copper is 73 miles west of Denver, and shuttles are available for the short trip from the Denver International Airport. Once you're at the resort, a shuttle system operates within its boundaries. Older kids can travel to and from their lodging to the slopes or the sports center safely, as the buses never leave the Copper community. The free Summit Stage takes visitors to and from the other ski resorts and towns in the area.

Where to Stay

Moderate to expensive

Copper Mountain hotels and condos. An enormous variety of accommodations are available at Copper and nearly all can be booked through Copper Mountain central reservations. Describe your budget and your family's needs and you'll be directed to a number of places from which to select. Properties within a short walk of the ski mountain range from hotel rooms and studios to four-bedroom condos with kitchens and fireplaces. These tend to be moderately priced, but some are expensive and others are available at budget rates; hotel rooms $145–255, condos $155–610. P.O. Box 3001, 209 Ten Mile Circle, Copper Mountain, CO 80443; 800-458-8386.

Club Med offers an all-inclusive family ski package with options galore. If you tire of downhill or cross-country skiing, try bungee jumping, Snow-Cat skiing, heliskiing, ice skating, and sleigh rides. Rooms are quite small, and it's nearly impossible to squeeze in an extra bed or crib, so parents should ask for rooms with connecting doors. Their own ski-school program starts out from the club's front door. Prices include lift tickets, meals, lodging, ski instruction, and entertainment. Ages 12 and up $110-140; under twelve $70–100. 50 Bueller Place, Copper Mountain CO 80443. 800-CLUB-MED.

Budget
Super 8 Motel has simple rooms with a queen-size or two double beds. Its complimentary continental breakfast features a toast bar with toast, bagels, and pastries that can further keep your costs down. Children under 12 stay free in their parents' room. $49–100. 808 Little Beaver Trail, Dillon, CO 80435; 800-800-8000, 970-468-8888.

Children's Ski School

The Kids Headquarters and Family Skiing Center, located in the Clock-tower building at the base of the resort, has the children's ski school and rental shop, plus a kids' cafeteria. The ski school provides learn-to-ski programs for kids age 4 to 12 and snowboard lessons for kids 8 to 12. The youngest groups start indoors where they practice skilike movement patterns on a marked carpet before heading outside. Beginners use the Kids' Arena just out the door. Children are grouped first by age, then by ability. A Ski School Satisfaction Guarantee means that if you're not happy with a lesson, you receive a refund. 800-458-8386 ext. 6331.

Day Care

Day care is available for children from 2 months to 4 years of age. The Belly Button Bakery, for 2- to 4-year-olds, was so named because the kids bake cookies in the morning and serve them when their parents pick them up. Belly Button Babies are ages 2 months to 2 years. Two different rooms accommodate the two age groups in cheerful, toy-filled play spaces. Belly Button Bakery babies get to head outside to the Belly Button Bump where they play in the snow and build snowmen. If they're 3 or 4, they can strap on some skis, walk around, and slide down the gentle slope. Reservations are required; 800-458-8386 (or 970-968-2318), ext. 6345.

Snowboarding

The Snowboard Park has 15 different hits and jumps and other snowboard features including a half-pipe are found throughout the mountain. Visitors can participate in a series of snowboard races held on select weekends throughout the season: giant slalom, slalom, and freestyle. Four boys' divisions and two girls' age divisions allow younger boarders to have a chance at the prizes, which can range from snowboard equipment to clothes.

Cross-Country Skiing

Twenty-five kilometers of groomed tracks and skating lanes start from the Union Creek base area and meander through the wooded valleys of the Arapahoe National Forest. Rentals, including children's sizes and lessons, are available. One day of a multi-day downhill lift ticket can be exchanged at the beginning of the day for a cross-country ticket. 970-968-2318 ext. 6342.

Other Activities

Guests who book through central reservations have free access to **Copper Mountain Racquet and Athletic Club** (303-968-2826), which includes indoor tennis courts, an indoor pool, saunas, steam rooms, exercise classes, massage services, and a nursery.

Horse-drawn dinner *sleigh rides* take guests, bundled in blankets, up to a cozy heated cabin for a Western dinner and singalong; 970-968-2232.

Ice skating: An outdoor rink is on Westlake in the center of the village. On Saturday night there's a roaring bonfire and hot chocolate is served. Skates can be rented.

Snowshoeing is available at the cross-country center. 970-968-2318 ext. 6342.

The neighboring town of Silverthorne has more than 125 **outlet stores** at exit 205 off I-70; 970-468-9440.

The Silverthorne Recreational Center, 11 miles away, is a great stop on a snowy day. Four pools—a lap pool, deep pool with a slide, shallow play pool for toddlers with a whale slide, and a pool with a 130-foot corkscrew slide offer something for all ages. There are all of the traditional spa facilities—steam, sauna, hot tub, exercise equipment, and weights—plus volleyball and basketball courts and an indoor running track. A childcare center on site cares for children six months to six years while their parents work out. 430 Rainbow Drive, Silverthorne, CO 80498; 970-262-7370.

The Breckenridge Recreation Center, 14 miles from Copper, has a fitness center, swimming pools, hot tubs, basketball and volleyball courts, and steam rooms; 0880 Airport Road, Breckenridge, CO 80424; 970-453-1734.

Deals and Discounts

Shop the packages and go late in the season, after the first week of April, when it's less crowded. Another good value time is between Christmas and President's Day weekend. Buy discounted lift tickets at Wal-Mart or Safeway stores in the nearby town of Frisco, or at any sporting-good store in the area.

❄ Crested Butte Mountain Resort

Address: 12 Snowmass Road, Mount Crested Butte, Colorado 81225
Telephone: 800-544-8448, 970-349-2333
Web site: http://www.cbinteractive.com/skiing/

A stroll down Elk Avenue, the main downtown street of the quaint western hamlet of Crested Butte, is a trip back to the turn of the century when silver and gold mining were king. Crested Butte started life as a supply stopover for miners who settled in the area to make their fortune from the rich fingers of silver or gold veining the mountains.

MOUNTAIN STATISTICS
Base elevation: 9,375 feet
Summit: 12,162 feet
Vertical drop: 2,775 feet
Skiable acres: 1,160
Annual average snowfall: 300 inches
Snowmaking: 11 of 13 lifts
Night skiing: none
Season: mid-November to mid-April
Lifts: 13 (2 high-speed quads, 3 triples, 4 doubles, 4 surface lifts)
Terrain: 13% beginner, 29% intermediate, 11% advanced, 47% expert
Lift tickets: adults $47, children 12 and under pay their age.

FAMILY STATISTICS
Day care: Whetstone Building, ages 6 months to 7 years; 800-444-9236, 970-349-2259
Children's lessons: Children's Ski Center, ages 3 to 12 years, 800-444-9236, 970-349-2259
Baby-sitting: Chamber of Commerce (800-545-4505) and the Crested Butte Marriott Resort (970-349-2390) keep a list of sitters.
Baby gear: Once Upon a Time (970-641-0823) in Gunnison (28 miles away) rents high chairs, car seats, and all kinds of other things.
Medical: Crested Butte Medical Clinic 970-349-6651

The old-time main street hasn't changed that much, and now its beautifully preserved shops, restaurants, and homes have been designated a National Historic District. Even the residents call it "The Last Great Colorado Ski Town."

Three miles up the valley, the butte from which the town and ski area take their name soars skyward. Backed by the dramatic 12,162-foot-high peak, the ski village—a comfortable modern, condo- and hotel-filled resort community—nestles into its side.

Crested Butte is the home of the U.S. Extreme Free Skiing Championship and the U.S. Extreme Snowboarding Championship. Most families won't be trying to free-fall into steep chutes and couloirs or ski Extreme Limits, North America's largest and steepest lift-served terrain. But just knowing it's there raises Crested Butte a few notches in any jaded teen's rankings. If you have the courage and the conditioning, take a free, ski patrol–guided tour of the extreme terrain.

Don't panic—the plentiful novice terrain is excellent and is placed on the lower portion of the mountain, well out of the way of any extreme skiers or speedsters. Intermediates have a long list of choices, too, with ballroom-smooth cruisers and tranquil through-the-trees runs. Children's learn-to-ski programs are nurturing for the little ones and exciting and encouraging for older kids. There's even a fuzzy seven-foot skiing teddy bear, Bubba, Crested Butte's official mascot.

Kids 12 and under pay their age for lift tickets with the purchase of an adult lift ticket. Skiers who visit from opening day to the start of the Christmas holidays or during the last two weeks of the season receive free lift tickets.

How to Get There
American Airlines, Delta, Western Pacific, and United Express fly into Gunnison/Crested Butte Airport. Alpine Express meets every flight and provides door-to-door shuttle services between Gunnison Airport and Crested Butte, 30 miles away. Driving times: Denver, 5 hours (230 miles).

Where to Stay
Most accommodations are clustered around the ski area, although there are some choices for families who want to be in town.

Expensive
Crested Butte Marriott Resort, 35 yards from the slopes, is the only ski-in-and-out hotel. It features children's menus in its restaurants, nightly movies for the kids, and a game room. Standard rooms have two queen-size beds, an in-room coffeemaker and a minirefrigerator. King suites, presidential suites, and concierge-level rooms offer more space and amenities. For evenings or nonski days there's an indoor heated pool and sauna, indoor and outdoor hot tubs, and a video game room. $99–600. 500 Gothic Road, Mt. Crested Butte, CO 81225; 800-544-8448, 970-349-2390.

All units in **The Plaza** have kitchens, fireplaces, and washers and dryers in their deluxe two-and three-bedroom condo suites. The property is about 125 yards from the lifts, and guests get the use of the sauna, steam room, hot tubs, and private ski and boot lockers. $131–579. 11 Snowmass Road, Mt. Crested Butte, CO 81255; 800-544-8448, 970-349-2900.

Village Center Condominiums are ski-in-and-out, just steps from the slopes. Units include one, two, and three bedrooms, with fully equipped kitchens and fireplaces. $135–485. 600 Gothic Road, Crested Butte, CO 81225; 800-521-6593, 970-349-2111.

Moderate

Sheraton Hotel at Crested Butte is 200 yards from the lift. Standard rooms have two king-size or queen-size beds, a minirefrigerator, and coffeemaker. Kids under 12 stay free in their parents' room, but if you need more beds it's $8 per night for a rollaway. The hotel has indoor and outdoor swimming pools, two outdoor hot tubs, a coin-operated laundry, and ski storage for guests. $70–175. 6 Emmons Road, Mt. Crested Butte, CO 81225; 800-544-8448, 970-349-8000.

Three Seasons Condominiums have one-, two-, and three-bedroom units with fully equipped kitchens. Facilities include a hot tub, indoor pool, game room, laundry facilities, plus a small grocery, liquor store, and post office. $115–425. 701 Gothic Road, Mt. Crested Butte, CO 81225; 970-349-5342.

License Plate House is one of the most unusual lodgings we've ever seen. The exterior of an old barnlike building in the heart of town has been covered entirely in license plates from the 1920s, '30s, and '40s. Its two bedrooms can sleep up to six people on a queen-size bed, a full bed, and a queen-size sleeper sofa. The kitchen has all appliances including a washer and dryer. The minimum stay during ski season is five to seven nights. $225. 400 Elk Avenue, Crested Butte, CO; 970-349-9999.

Budget

Scandinavian-style **Nordic Inn** has standard hotel-type rooms and chalets with kitchens, all about 300 yards from the lifts. It's an excellent value given its location. Its amenities include a fireside lounge with a small library and game room complimentary continental breakfast, and an outdoor hot tub and Jacuzzi. Chalets accommodate between six and eight people, and hotel rooms have two doubles or one queen-size bed. Rooms $95–175, chalets $222–325. P.O. Box 939, Crested Butte, CO 81224; 970-349-5542.

Manor Lodge is centrally located about 250 yards from the lifts and features ski movies during daily happy hour. Suites are best for families, with one queen-size bed, a sofa sleeper, and a wood-burning fireplace. The restaurant has a kids' menu and there's a guest laundry and complimentary sweet rolls and coffee each morning. $65–135. 650 Gothic Road, Crested Butte, CO 81225; 970-349-5365.

Children's Ski School

The Kids' Ski and Snowboard World (800-444-9236, 970-349-2259), located in the Whetstone building, offers a variety of kids' learn-to-ski programs. The ski and snowboard school divides kids from age 3 to 7 into two groups: Cubs, who are 3 years old, and Polar Bears, ages 4 to 7. The Cubs' program is geared to first-time skiers, offering a one hour one-on-one session combined with day care. The Polar Bears program of group lessons and indoor and outdoor ski exercises is for skiers of all ability levels. The Grizzly Bears program is for skiers of all abilities, ages 8 to 12. Shred bears are 8 to 12 year olds of all abilities who want to snowboard. Kids 8 to 17 who are experienced skiers can participate in a Rip session for a challenging adventure.

Tag-a-long lessons are private lessons in which parents are allowed to tag along and observe. This allows parents to help their child progress and ski safely after the lessons, and allows parental involvement in the instruction as well.

Day Care

A nursery for babies from 6 months old to toilet trained toddlers still in diapers is located in the Whetstone building (800-444-9236, 970-349-2259), and allows parents to enroll their kids for as little as an hour or as long as a full day. Once kids (up to age 7) are toilet trained, they can participate in a preschool program in a different room. Each day includes organized activities, arts and crafts, games, quiet time, and snow play if the weather is good. Half-day and all-day sessions are available.

Teens

Teens 13 to 17 can join a program that lets them have fun with their peers and improve their skiing at the same time. It's available for every type of skier, from never-evers to extreme skiers. Sessions are full and half day. The town of Crested Butte operates a Teen Center with billiards, Foosball, Ping-Pong, and sponsored activities; 970-349-5039. Adventurous teens should check out the No Limits Center high-adventure recreation courses (page 82).

Snowboarding

The snowboard park features log slides, quarter pipes, gaps, and other various jumps and hits.

Cross-Country Skiing

Crested Butte Nordic Center is in the heart of downtown. Groomed trails take you around the outskirts of town on 30 kilometers of groomed track.

The center offers rental packages and lessons for both skating and classical skiing, and children's sizes are available. The facility operates from the corner of Second Street and Whiterock Avenue, P.O. Box 1269, Crested Butte, CO 81224; 970-349-1707.

Other Activities

Dogsled tours explore backcountry on a sled pulled by 12 Alaskan huskies, 970-641-1636.

Horse-drawn **sleigh rides** with Just Horsen Around (970-349-9822) tour downtown Crested Butte and the scenic countryside nearby.

Hot-air balloon rides offer spectacular views of the mountains; 970-349-6712.

Winter **horseback riding** at Fantasy Ranch (970-349-5425) starts at the Skyland Lodge and meanders around Crested Butte Mountain.

No Limits Center: This international business (800-954-6487) specializes in adventure and pushing personal limits in sports. Courses are offered in extreme skiing as well as winter mountaineering, ice climbing, dogsledding, rescue training, and avalanches. It provides a central booking system for adventure activities.

Deals and Discounts

Kids under 12 pay their age. Visit Crested Butte between late November and December 20 or April 7 to 20, when both kids and adults ski for free, with the exception of Thanksgiving weekend.

Keystone Resort

Address: P.O. Box 38, Keystone, Colorado 80435
Telephone: 800-468-5004, 970-496-4242 (central reservations)
Web site: http://www.snow.com

Families who just can't seem to get out of the condo until noon find Keystone an excellent buy: The same lift ticket you purchase for the day is good for skiing at night. You can actually ski from 8:30 A.M. to 9:00 P.M. During peak season, structure your day to avoid the crowds by skiing in the morning, taking a siesta or a break in the middle of the day, and heading out again midafternoon.

Keystone's elevation starts at 9,300 feet, making it one of highest ski areas in the U.S. It's partnered with Breckenridge Ski Resort, about 14 miles away (see page 68), and Vail and Breckenridge and offers an interchangeable multi-day lift ticket between all four resorts. Shuttles transport skiers among the three areas so you can easily sample each of the ski resorts.

Keystone is a planned ski community with two centers of activity: the ski-resort base area and a complex of shops, restaurants, and hotels that border a picturesque lake which freezes in the winter for ice skating. The two are a short shuttle ride apart. The dozens of condominium clusters around the resort are connected to the central areas by the same excellent shuttle-bus system. The resort lacks the western charm of Crested Butte Mountain Resort or even Breckenridge Ski Resort next door, but its compact layout, convenience, and solid skiing more than make up for it. Over the next ten years, expect the look to change. The ski-resort base is being developed by Intrawest (the

MOUNTAIN STATISTICS
Base elevation: 9,300 feet
Summit: 12,200 feet
Vertical drop: 2,900 feet
Skiable acres: 1,755
Annual average snowfall: 230 inches
Snowmaking: 859 acres (48% of terrain, but 100% of Keystone Mountain)
Night skiing: 205 acres until 10 P.M.
Season: mid-October to mid-May
Lifts: 20 (2 high-speed gondolas, 4 high-speed quads, 1 regular quad, 3 triples, 5 doubles, 5 surface lifts)
Terrain: 13% beginner, 36% intermediate, 51% advanced
Lift tickets: adults $55, children 6 to 14 $37, under 6 free.

FAMILY STATISTICS
Day care: Keystone Children's Center, ages 2 months and up, 800-239-1622 (reservations required)
Children's lessons: Children's Ski School, ages 3 to 14, 800-239-1622
Baby-sitting: The Children's Center has a list of names, 970-496-4181.
Baby gear: Baby's Away rents car seats, cribs, strollers, backpacks, high chairs, and other gear; 970-668-1571
Medical: Summit Medical Center, 970-668-3300

company that created Whistler Resort's charming pedestrian village) and transformed into an expansive pedestrian village called River Run.

Most families rent a condo and pick up groceries in Dillon on their way in. Nightlife is rather quiet in Keystone, and unless you're enjoying Colorado's largest night-skiing operation, you'll be cozying up around the fire anyway. One-stop shopping is a trademark of Keystone, and you can (and should) make all reservations—lift ticket, ski school, child care—when you book your lodging.

The skiing season can start early at Keystone, even when nature doesn't cooperate, since the resort has the biggest snowmaking system in the Rockies. The ski area extends over three mountain peaks. Most of the beginner runs are on Keystone Mountain, and intermediates are indulged with corn silk–smooth highways and amusing through-the-trees glade runs throughout all three mountains. An area called The Outback is left ungroomed and offers challenging terrain for the advanced skier.

How to Get There

It's easy to fly into the Denver International Airport and shuttle to Keystone, about 118 miles or a two-hour drive away. Eagle County Airport is 60 miles west of Keystone and is served by American, United, and Delta Airlines. Once you're there, a county-wide bus system, The Summit Stage, will take you to Breckenridge, and anywhere else in Summit County. In addition, Keystone has its own clearly marked shuttles that ferry guests from lodging to skiing and restaurants.

Where to Stay

Accommodations are clustered around the village area and its skating lake and the ski mountain. Many condos fan out from both of those central areas. Most condo clusters have their own pool.

Expensive

Chateaux d'Mont is an elegant condominium complex just steps from the lifts. Two-and three-bedroom suites vary in their furnishings but all are exquisitely appointed with no detail spared. Two-and three-bedroom units all have one private bath per bedroom, their own hot tub, and a full gourmet kitchen that guests will find stocked with snacks and drinks on arrival. Premium service is the trademark of this posh resort that coddles its guests with nightly turn-down service, fresh flowers, and plush terry robes. $400–840. Near Mountain House. 800-468-5004, 970-468-4242.

River Run Condominiums are in the new River Run base area about 75 yards from the gondola. One-to four-bedroom condos have fireplaces and full kitchens and are decorated with a southwestern flair. $254–839. 800-468-5004.

Moderate
Keystone Condominiums come in all shapes and sizes and are all on the shuttle-bus route to the ski area. Most have a fully equipped kitchen, housekeeping service, and complimentary access to the Keystone Fitness Center. Rates are determined by a unit's proximity to the mountain, but all units are a quick and easy ride away from the slopes. Options include studios, condo units up to four bedrooms, and private homes with three to five bedrooms. Condos $110–900; homes $300–1,000. 800-468-5004.

Keystone Lodge looks over picturesque Keystone Lake, which offers ice skating in the winter. The lodge is a large, modern complex with attractive hotel rooms decorated with a western flair. There are standard rooms with two queen-size beds or loft rooms with a loft upstairs and pull-out couch downstairs. The shops, restaurants, and bars in the complex are a few steps away, and a bus station with shuttles to the slopes is adjacent to the property. $150–320. 800-468-5004, 970-468-4242.

Budget
Dillon Super 8 Motel, a short drive from the resort, is a typical no-frills motel whose rooms have either one queen-size bed or two double beds. Kids under 17 stay free in their parents' room, and a simple continental breakfast is included in the rates. Rollaways are available. $59–119. 808 Little Beaver Trail, Dillon, CO 80435; 800-800-8000, 970-468-8888.

Some of the rooms in the *Snowshoe Motel* have kitchenettes, and there is one two-room suite with a kitchen and its own whirlpool tub. $75–140. 521 Main Street, Frisco, CO 80443; 800-445-8658, 970-668-3444.

Children's Ski School
Children are divided into five different age groups: children age 3 usually participate in ski school through the day care; age 4; ages 5 and 6; ages 7 and 8; and ages 9 and 10. The school will not put children of different ages and abilities together, no matter how few children are enrolled; if just one child is age 7 or 8, that child receives individual instruction. The beginner area is separated from the rest of the mountain and intermediates and advanced-level kids ski just about anywhere on the mountain. Super-

vised activities are available before and after ski school, running until 5 P.M. During holiday periods, teens get a full-day program and ski together as a group, more for fun than instruction.

Day Care
Keystone's Children's Center is at the base of Keystone Mountain and accommodates children ages two months and up. Infants ages two to eleven months have their own room and a caregiver-to-child ratio of one to three. Parents are provided with complimentary beepers to stay in touch with the center. Toddlers ages one and two have their own room and a schedule of activities including arts and crafts, lunch, group games with parachutes and balls, and free play. Ages three and up can participate in the Snowplay program or the Learn to Ski program. The Snowplay program includes lots of time out of doors—riding the gondola, feeding the ducks in the pond and the horses in the stable, sledding, and taking walks. The Learn to Ski program, for three-year-olds, consists of a two-hour lesson where the kids become accustomed to wearing boots and skis and spend time on the slopes learning the basics of skiing in a fun way. The rest of the day they spend in the day-care facility.

Teens
A teen snowboarding program for 15- to 18-year-olds is offered from March 8 to April 7 and includes a day-long lesson and lift ticket. It gives older teens the chance to learn some new skills in a fun social setting.

Snowboarding
Keystone was a snowboard holdout until the 1996–1997 season when the mountain welcomed boarders for the first time. Area 51, the Snowboard Park, features two half pipes, rails, and various hits. A snack bar, the Sprite Hut, in the snowboard park, sells drinks and snacks.

Cross-Country Skiing
The Keystone Cross Country Center has 25 kilometers of trails at the base of the mountain. Another groomed five kilometers is accessed by the gondola. Skiers can explore above the timberline to an elevation of about 12,100 feet. Moonlight tours are offered once a month. Lessons and rental equipment is available for adults and children age six or over; 970-496-4275.

Other Activities

Keystone Activities Center can book all of the following activities at 800-354-4FUN.

Dogsled rides: Siberian huskies from Good Times Snowmobiling (800-477-1448) pull your sled on mountain trails that are between Keystone and Breckenridge.

Ice skating: Keystone Lake (970-496-7103) freezes in winter to make the largest outdoor skating rink in North America. Regular skating takes place on one end, and a hockey rink is set up on the other. Rentals of all sizes are available.

Keystone Fitness Center is near the lodge and lake. All guests staying at Keystone have access to its swimming pool, aerobic center, weight machines, hot tub, and sauna; 970-496-4118.

Sleigh rides: Choose from a 30-minute scenic afternoon ride or a dinner sleigh ride. The dinner ride is a 20-minute sleigh ride through open meadow past original Keystone homesteads to a rustic restaurant warmed by a wood-burning stove. A cowboy singer entertains throughout the four-course meal; 800-354-4FUN.

Snowmobiling tours are available up to the Continental Divide and to an abandoned mining town. Good Times Snowmobiling (800-477-1448) and Tiger Run (970-453-2231).

Snowshoes can be rented through the Nordic Center at the Yurt. Snowshoers can start their trek at either the base of the mountain or at the top of the gondola.

Deals and Discounts

Keystone's ski season is one of the longest of any destination resort in Colorado. April tends to be a very snowy month in Colorado, with far fewer crowds, rock-bottom prices, powder snow, and sunshine.

The central-reservations staff can tell you about other discounts and packages offered throughout the season.

❄ Purgatory Resort

Address: #1 Skier Place, Durango, Colorado 81301

Telephone: 800-525-0892 (central reservations) 970-247-9000

Web site: http://www.ski-purg.com

Purgatory's trademark rolling terrain was formed about 45,000 years ago during the last ice age when a glacial shift created vast headwalls and moraines. The resort chose to capitalize on the striking natural rollercoaster-like steps, rather than bull-doze the runs smooth.

Snowboarders and skiers of all abilities will find terrain to suit them. Beginners will find easy terrain on the front side of the mountain where there's also a kid's terrain park and a NASTAR race course. More than half the trails are designated as intermediate and the grooming is some of the best in the West. The back side of the mountain offers more challenging runs for adrenaline junkies and thrill seekers who have the legs to withstand them. The weather at this resort is consistently rated some of the best in the country, with big nighttime dumps of powder and warm sunny days in which to enjoy these ski-perfect conditions.

Some lodging is available at the base of the mountain, but most of it is 25 miles away in Durango, a western-style town tucked into the Four Corners region of Colorado that has served as a gateway into the San Juan Mountains for fur traders, miners, prospectors, and ranchers for more than a hundred years. Now it's populated by vacationers who travel here, especially during the summer when they come to visit Mesa Verde National Park. Named a World Heritage Site by the United Nations along with such natural wonders as the Great Wall of China and the Egyptian pyramids,

MOUNTAIN STATISTICS
Base elevation: 8,973 feet
Summit: 10,822 feet
Vertical drop: 2,029 feet
Skiable acres: 1,200
Annual average snowfall: 289 inches
Snowmaking: 255 acres (9 of 11 lifts)
Night skiing: none
Season: late November to mid-April
Lifts: 11 (1 high-speed quad, 4 triples, 4 doubles, 2 surface)
Terrain: 23% beginner, 51% intermediate, 26% advanced
Lift tickets: adults $40, kids 6 to 12 $18, seniors 65 to 69 $22, under 6 and over 70 free.

FAMILY STATISTICS
Day care: Cub Care, ages 2 months to 5 years, 970-385-2144 or 800-525-0892 (reservations required)
Children's lessons: Ski School, ages 3 to 12 years, 970-385-2144 (reservations required)
Baby-sitting: Day care has a list of available sitters, 970-385-2144
Medical: Mercy Medical Center, 970-247-4311.

Mesa Verde is famous for its ancient Anasazi cliff dwellings and is a must-see stop less than an hour's drive from Durango.

Believe it or not, winter is the off-season here, a phenomenally good deal for skiers. Lodging prices in Durango drop after the busy summer-vacation season quiets down, and you can find accommodations for as low as $50 per night, many with skier shuttles. Fort Lewis College sits above the town, and like any college town, the place is packed with cheap eateries, pizza parlors, and hamburger joints. For those who want to make the first tracks of the day, there are a variety of choices for ski-in-and-out lodging and a selection of condominiums several miles away serviced by skier shuttles.

Purgatory's Total Ticket program allows visitors to purchase a four-day (or more) lift ticket and exchange a day of skiing for any one of seven major vacation activities in southwest Colorado, such as a ride on the historic Durango & Silverton Narrow Gauge Railroad, a tour of Mesa Verde National Park, a sleigh ride, or a snowmobile tour.

How to Get There
Durango–La Plata County Airport is the closest full-service airport to Purgatory. American Airlines, United Express, and Mesa Airlines, America West Express fly in daily during the winter season. Albuquerque Airport in Albuquerque, New Mexico, is an easy four-hour drive away, with no major mountain passes to cross. Airport and skier shuttles are readily available, and a shuttle and trolley service in town carries visitors into town or up to mountain. The resort is 6 hours (368 miles) from Denver.

Where to Stay
Expensive
Purgatory Village Hotel has ski-in-and-out accommodations ranging in size from standard hotel rooms to three-bedroom condominium suites. Most of the units have wood-burning fireplaces and their own washers and dryers. Restaurants, bars, a deli-grocery store, and a ski shop with ski rentals are steps away, and there's a heated swimming pool, rooftop hot tubs, and a sauna. $120–295. Skier Place, Durango, CO 81301; 800-693-0175, 970-385-2100.

Leland House and the *Rochester Hotel* are sister inns across the street from each other in the historic downtown area of Durango. Leland House has rooms and suites decorated with antiques, all with kitchen facilities and private baths. The Rochester Hotel, originally built in 1892, has rooms decorated in an Old West motif. A complimentary gourmet buffet breakfast is offered to guests of both hotels at the Rochester Hotel dining room. No skier shuttle. $88–140. Cribs $15 per night, extra person charge $15 per night. 721 East Second Avenue, Durango, CO 81301; 970-385-1920.

Moderate

Best Western Lodge at Purgatory is a 150-yard walk from the lifts and offers a more affordable option if you want to stay at the base area. If you've skied your legs to jelly, you can take the lodge's free shuttle back to your room. Some rooms have kitchenettes and there's an indoor pool, hot tub, and laundry facility. Children under 12 stay free in their parents' room. $95–275. 49617 Highway 550, Durango, CO 81301; 800-637-7727, 970-247-9669.

East Rim Condominiums have full-size kitchens, fireplaces, a variety of bedroom configurations, and are within walking distance of the base area. $120–345. 44 Sheol Street, Durango, CO 81301; 970-247-5528.

Historic Jarvis Suite in downtown Durango is just off the main street. Guests travel back and forth between the ski-resort base area on a complimentary skier shuttle. The hotel-type rooms can accommodate one to four people; other options include studios and one- and two-bedroom units with full kitchens. $89–159. 125 West 10th Street, Durango, CO 81301; 800-824-1024, 970-259-6190.

Silver Pick is a mile from the ski base and has a variety of accommodations including one- and two-bedroom condos and deluxe hotel rooms. You can rent your skis and other winter gear right there. Kids keep busy in the game room with Nintendo, cards, and board games. Units have kitchens and fireplaces and there's a laundry, restaurant, and hot tub. Children under 12 stay free in their parents' room. $69–300. 48475 Highway 550 North, Durango, CO 81301; 800-221-7425, 970-259-6600.

Budget

Iron Horse Inn offers one of the best deals in the region. Its two-level suites with fireplaces offer families excellent privacy for the price. Ask for one of the renovated rooms. There is a small general store and a guest laundry on the premises, plus a ski shop, gift shop, restaurant, bar, indoor pool, and sauna. No shuttle is available, so you'll need a car. $59–129.

5800 North Main Avenue, Durango, CO 81301; 800-748-2990, 970-259-1010.

Days Inn looks like just about any other standard motel in the U.S., but this one has a free skier shuttle and free continental breakfast, making it a good buy for budget-conscious families who plan to eat out. The indoor Junior Olympic pool, two giant Jacuzzis, and a fitness room are handy when the weather turns foul. Standard rooms have one king-size or two queen-size beds, and a few rooms have connecting doors. $59–95. 1700 County Road 203, Durango, CO 81301; 800-329-7466, 970-259-1430.

Children's Ski School

The Polar Bears program offers an introduction to skiing for kids age 3 and 4. Kids start out on cross-country-style skis strapped to their own boots as the staff feels Nordic skis are easier to use and more comfortable. Snow playtimes are available, too, along with story time and indoor games. Full- and half-day programs are available and prices include equipment.

The Grizzly Bears program for 4- and 5-year-olds uses alpine skis and boots. Skiing is the main emphasis, but outdoor and indoor playtime, story time, and indoor games are offered as well. Full- and half-day programs are available, and rental equipment costs extra.

Kids ages 6 to 12 are in the Kodiak Clan and meet adjacent to the Twilight lift, where they get serious ski lessons. The kids are divided by ability, age, level of interest, and previous experience. Snowboarders participate in the Shred Bears program, which requires that they weigh 35 pounds or more. If they are too light, the edge of their board won't contact the snow and they can't turn. Half- and full-day lessons are available, and rental equipment is extra.

Day Care

Kids 2 months to 5 years are cared for in one facility. Cub Care, a nonskiing program for kids ages 2 months to 3 years, operates from 8:30 A.M. to 4:30 P.M. daily. There is a special infants' room and nap area and playrooms for toddlers. Full and half days are available.

Children ages 3 to 5 can enroll in a learn-to-ski program (see Children's Ski School, above) combined with day care. While they're inside, they're amused with toys, projects, games, and small play equipment; 970-247-9000.

Snowboarding

The resort's terrain park is on Pitchfork, a snowboard arena with nine half pipe, ramps, tabletops, and jumps. The natural steplike quality of Purgatory's terrain creates sensational natural jumps.

Cross-Country Skiing

The Purgatory Nordic Center (970-247-9000) offers 16 kilometers of groomed trails. The Total Ticket exchange, which includes an all-day trail pass, a lesson, and rental equipment, enables you to exchange a day of downhill for a day of cross-country skiing.

Other Activities

Dinner sleigh rides: Buck's Livery (970-297-9000) offers horse-drawn sleigh rides through the woods at the base of the ski mountain to a cozy mountain cabin where a western rib-eye steak dinner is served. There are two departures nightly.

Durango & Silverton Narrow Gauge Railroad (970-247-2733) operates during the winter months from Durango to Cascade Canyon. This is a beautiful ride in winter through the mountains with a stop for a picnic lunch. Reserve seats when you reserve your lodging, as this narrow gauge train driven by an antique coal-fired locomotive has become quite popular. It heads into a wilderness area that can't be reached by car.

Guided naturalist tours take place every Sunday. Volunteer naturalists and interested guests head out into the forest and learn about wildlife and forest ecology. 970-247-9000.

Mesa Verde National Park tour: Guided and self-guided tours of this ancient ruin (970-529-4461) operate during the winter months, although a few portions are closed. If it's a cold day, visitors can understand why the early inhabitants built their homes to catch the sun in winter and shade in summer. Locals call it the Machu Picchu of North America.

Snowmobiling: Tours leave from the base and take you to an area on a mountain crest in the high country just north of the resort head. Snowmobile Adventures at Purgatory; 970-247-9000, ext. 141. 970-247-9000.

Snowshoeing: Rent snowshoes at the cross-country center and explore its trails or rent them at the base of the mountain and head out into the woods. 970-247-9000.

Tubing: The Alpine Snowcaster is a 600-foot groomed tubing run in the beginners area. There's a surface lift to pull riders (and their tubes) up the hill; it's lit for night tubing. 970-247-9000.

Trimble Hot Springs: Soak in three different natural mineral-water pools, with temperatures that range from 70 to 110°F. It's particularly beautiful when the snow is falling. 6475 County Road 203, Durango, CO 81301; 970-247-0111.

Deals and Discounts

Purgatory's range of budget accommodations are some of the best in the industry. The central-reservations staff can tell you about packages and airline partners.

❄ Snowmass Ski Area

Address: P.O. Box 1248, Aspen, Colorado 81612
Telephone: 800-215-7669; 970-923-2000
Web site: http://www.skiaspen.com

Families like the convenience of Snowmass—no schlepping the kids and their gear more than a few steps before you get to the lifts—as much as they like the skiing. The resort was ingeniously designed to allow most guests to ski in and out of their hotel or condominium accommodations and walk to several shopping areas that have family-style restaurants. If your condo is not within walking distance of the supermarket, simply hop on one of the frequent shuttle buses and you'll be there in a few minutes. Snowboarders are welcome everywhere, and there are excellent childcare and ski-school programs for children ages 18 months to 12 years.

Families who wish to indulge in a fine-dining experience can ski Snowmass and shuttle a few miles down the road to Aspen for a gourmet meal. But most families tend to stay and eat in the Snowmass Village Mall where all restaurants feature a children's menu. There are pizza parlors, hamburger joints, soup bistros, as well as restaurants offering more sophisticated cuisine. Parents who want to enjoy a fine-dining experience while their kids are in ski school or day care can have a served, sit-down gourmet meal on the mountain while the kids are having their own fun. On a sunny day, ski to Krabloonik, a deluxe on-mountain restaurant where you can sit on the patio and sample dishes containing elk, buffalo, and exotic mushrooms.

MOUNTAIN STATISTICS
Base elevation: 8,104 feet
Summit: 12,310 feet
Vertical drop: 4,206 feet
Skiable acres: 2,580
Annual average snowfall: 300 inches
Snowmaking: 130 acres
Night skiing: none
Season: late November to mid-April
Lifts: 18 (7 high-speed quads, 2 triples, 6 doubles, 3 surface lifts)
Terrain: 10 % beginner, 52% intermediate, 18% advanced, 20% expert
Lift tickets: adults $59, youth 13 to 27 $39, children 7 to 12 $35, under 7 free.

FAMILY STATISTICS
Day care: 18 months to 3 years, 970-923-0563; 4 years to kindergarten, 970-923-0570
Children's lessons: 800-525-6200, 970-925-1220
Baby-sitting: Super Sitters, 970-923-6080; Kidstime Referral Service, 970-925-KIDS
Baby gear: Baby's Away rents cribs, strollers, backpacks, car seats, toys, and more; 970-920-1699
Medical: Aspen Valley Hospital, 970-544-1261

Snowmass was initially developed in 1967 to complement Aspen Mountain (see page 57), and it became known as an intermediate skiers' paradise, with a vast and immaculately groomed selection of middle-of-the-road turf, but with little to offer the advanced skier. Not anymore—now the fast and the fearless can ski Hanging Valley and hang on to their hats as they drop through the glades on this and other precipitous steeps. Raw beginners tend to congregate on the two beginner runs on the lower part of the mountain. Intermediates and experts don't bother with these lifts, letting novices have the place to themselves.

The layout of the lifts and trails on this giant of a mountain is cleverly planned so that it's easy to move around from area to area. All parts of the mountain are easily reached from the base village. The skiing is so immense that lift lines are generally sparse. A new speed course has opened where skiers and boarders receive race instruction, a helmet, and an opportunity to ski up to 65 miles per hour!

One lift ticket allows you to ski four mountains—Aspen Mountain, Aspen Highlands, Buttermilk Mountain, or Snowmass Ski Area—and discounted lift tickets are available for snowboarders and skiers ages 13 to 27. Trail-rider passes for kids from 7 to 12 are further discounted. Free skier shuttles connect the four mountains.

How to Get There

Snowmass is 220 miles from the Denver International Airport, and it takes about four hours to drive in your own car or take a shuttle. Many guests fly into Eagle County Airport, about 70 miles east of Snowmass, or into the small airport in Aspen; there are now four airlines—United Airlines, Aspen Mountain Air, Western Pacific, and Mountain Air Express—that service Aspen's Pitkin County Airport and offer direct flights from Minneapolis, Chicago, Los Angeles, and Dallas. Direct flights into Eagle County Airport are available from many parts of the country.

Don't bother with a rental car if you fly in (even into Denver) because the bus system is so good you won't need a car, and taxis are available in the city of Aspen.

Where to Stay

Almost all of the accommodations, with a couple of exceptions, at Snowmass Village are condos and many are ski-in-and-out. Village Property Management can help with condo rentals, 970-923-4350.

Expensive

Chamonix is a luxury condo property that offers the services of a first-class hotel. Its one-, two- and three-bedroom units are contemporary and have full kitchens, washer/dryers, and the use of a pool and hot tub. 476 Wood Road (on the mountain at the Wood Run Lift), $239–1,302. Snowmass, CO 81615; 800-365-0410, 970-923-3232.

The Snowmass Lodge & Club is an excellent choice for families who enjoy a mix of downhill and cross-country skiing, as the area's Nordic ski trails start just outside the door. It's a five-minute ride to the Snowmass base lodge via shuttle bus. One-, two- and three-bedroom villas, and standard, premium, and deluxe hotel rooms can accommodate groups of just about any size. Its facilities are some of the most extensive in the area, featuring tennis courts, heated pools, a complete athletic club, restaurants, snack bars, ski storage, laundry facilities, and a 24-hour desk. $63–809. 0239 Snowmass Club Circle, Box G-2, Snowmass, CO 81615; 800-525-0710, 970-923-5600.

The Silvertree Hotel is the only full-service ski-in-and-out hotel in Snowmass and it offers all the amenities one would expect from any good first-class hotel. The biggest bonus, though, especially for families of toddlers and preschoolers, is its location a few steps away from the day-care center, ski-school office, and the Snowmass Village Mall. Standard hotel rooms can accommodate four in two queen-size beds, but spacious suites will provide families with more room. Within the hotel are three restaurants, a ski shop, several heated pools, a whirlpool, and a sauna. Room service and airport transportation are both available. $140–525. 100 Ebert Lane, Snowmass, CO 81615; 800-525-9402, 970-923-4350.

Top of the Village condominiums are deluxe ski-in-and-out two-, three-, and four-bedroom units with a pool, two hot tubs, an exercise room, and a sauna. Rollaways cost $22 per night, but cribs are free. $420–675. 855 Carriage Way, Snowmass, CO 81615; 800-525-4200, 970-923-3673.

Moderate
Mountain Chalet, just ten steps from the day-care center, is an excellent value because breakfast and lunch are included in the rates. The dining room serves family style, so guests get to know one another over the course of their visit, and children tend to gather in the lounge area or near the complimentary hot-chocolate machine, making friends along the way. Its ski-in-and-out location makes it a perfect spot for families who don't want to do their own cooking. Rooms have a king-size bed (a rollaway can be added), two queen-size beds, or a queen-size bed and queen-size fold-out sofa. Deluxe rooms have fireplaces, and many rooms have balconies. Con-

necting rooms are available. Ski lockers are provided for all guests and the outdoor heated pool, coin laundry, spa, and sauna get plenty of use. $96–245. 115 Daly Lane, Snowmass, CO 81615; 800-843-1579, 970-923-3900.

Wildwood Lodge, just steps from Snowmass Village Plaza and about 400 yards from the lifts, is a pleasant hotel with comfortable rooms and one- and two-bedroom suites. All units come with minifridges and coffeemakers and many of the rooms have balconies overlooking the slopes. Children under 12 stay free in their parents' room. $89–239. 40 Ebert Lane, P.O. Box 5037, Snowmass, CO 81615; 800-525-9402, 970-923-3550.

The Crestwood (http://www.thecrestwood.com) offers units that range from studios to three-bedroom condos with a loft. All are ski-in-and-out, and there's an outdoor pool and two outdoor hot tubs. $206–687. 400 Wood Road, P.O. Box 5460, Snowmass Village, CO 81615; 800-356-5949, 970-923-2450.

Budget
The Laurelwood condos sit two levels above the Village Mall's shops, restaurants, and bistros, and just twenty yards from the slopes. Its large, economical studios have full-size kitchens, fireplaces, a queen-size sleeper sofa and a queen-size bed that can be closed off from the main room. There's daily housekeeping (except Sunday), ski storage, laundry, and the use of two pools and a Jacuzzi. $120–305. P.O. Box 5600, Snowmass Village, CO 81615; 800-356-7893, 970-923-3110.

Aspenwood Condominiums range in size from studios to two-bedroom units with a loft. It's a good option for families watching their budget and it's only 100 yards from ski lifts. Rollaways are free, and extra people over the age of 5 are $12 per night. $184–438. 600 Carriage Way, Snowmass, CO 81615; 800-457-8540, 970-923-2711.

Poklodi Lodge is a simple, clean, hotel-style property that can accommodate up to four people in each room. You can save further by storing your own lunch foods in the minifridge in the room; there's also a coffeemaker, TV, shuttle service, ski storage, laundry, outdoor hot tub, and outdoor heated pool. Best of all, a complimentary breakfast is included in the rates. $85–140. 25 Daly Lane, P.O. Box 5640, Snowmass, CO 81615; 800-666-4556, 970-923-2000.

Children's Ski School

Snowcubs for three-year-olds and Big Burn Bears, for four years through kindergarten age, can receive a ski lesson for a short part of the morning and the afternoon; most kids this age are enrolled at the day-care facility and are picked up for their short lessons by ski instructors. They use the Magic Carpet, a short moving carpeted track that carries them up the hill, to learn to ski. Teaching methods take the child's motor development into account and the emphasis is on fun.

The Bears on Boards program offers a full day of snowboarding instruction for 5- to 7-year-olds. General learn-to-ski programs are available for children from first grade through 12 years of age. The program runs a full day although first-time skiers can get just a half-day lesson in the afternoon. Kids are grouped by age and ability. Since most guests stay from three to five days, the ski school tries to keep the same group of children together with the same instructor for the duration of their visit.

Teen programs for 13- to 19-year-olds are offered on weekends and over holiday periods for the full day or just the afternoon. A speed course for recreational skiers age 13 and up is offered one day a week throughout the year. After attending a clinic in the morning, teens don a helmet and get clocked for speed. During the first hour teens attempt to go 35 to 45 mph; if they pass they can ski 45 to 55 mph, and then go again to try clocking 55 to 65 mph.

Day Care

The resort's day-care and ski-school programs, Snow Cubs and Big Burn Bears are located just steps from the lift-ticket office, the ski-school headquarters, and the Village Mall.

Snow Cubs, for children 18 months to 3 years, is run like a preschool, especially for the 3-year-olds, with art, music, story time, and puppet shows. All children are taken outside to play at least 45 minutes a day, and 3-year-olds are given short ski lessons twice during the day.

There are separate rooms for 18-month-old toddlers and 2-year-olds; one has a water play table containing snow. Three different rooms are available for the 3-year-olds. The 18-month toddlers get a short buggy ride outside unless it's stormy.

Night Hawks is an evening child-care program for children 3 to 12, and is staffed by ski-school personnel; 970-923-0570.

Teens

Every Wednesday evening teens can participate in an organized group activity called Teen Night Out. They can go ice skating, play Ping-Pong in the youth center, watch ski movies, or go swimming. Teens also enjoy the speed course (see page 98).

Snowboarding

A boarders' terrain garden has an extra-wide, extra-long half pipe and a variety of other hits and jumps. The speed course is open to snowboarders.

Cross-Country Skiing

The Snowmass Lodge & Club Touring Center offers more than 30 kilometers of groomed tracks that connect with the Aspen Snowmass Nordic System. Professional tours, guided tours, ski rentals, and a restaurant are in the base lodge. You can trade a downhill ticket for a free group lesson and ski rental; 970-923-3148.

Aspen Cross Country Center (see page 61) also offers Nordic Skiing.

Other Activities

Family Fun Days are held every Thursday afternoon from 2 to 5 P.M. Families enjoy all kinds of activities, complimentary snacks, and goodie bags.

Hot-air balloon rides: Float over the Rocky Mountains in a hot-air balloon with Adventures Aloft (970-925-9497) or Unicorn Balloon Company of Colorado (970-925-5752).

Ice skating: Try the Aspen Ice Garden, 233 West Hymen Avenue, Aspen, CO 81612 (970-920-5154) and Silver Circle (at base of Aspen Mountain, 970-925-6360).

Paragliding is for slightly more adventurous types, and is available through Aspen Paragliding, 426 South Spring Street, Aspen, CO 81611, (970-925-7625).

Sleigh rides: Aspen Adventures Sleigh Rides and Snow-Cat Tours (970-920-4FUN) or T-Lazy-7 Ranch (970-925-4614, 970-925-7040) offer sleigh rides around the valley.

Guided snowshoeing: trips are available through Blazing Adventures (800-282-7238, 970-925-5651).

Snowmobiling: A variety of snowmobile trips are available at T-Lazy-7 Ranch (970-925-4614, 970-925-7040).

Fly-fishing: Cast a line into the Roaring Fork River. Oxbow Outfitting (800-421-1505, 970-925-1505) and Blazing Adventures (800-282-7238, 970-925-5651) will supply gear, transportation, and instruction.

Deals and Discounts

Ski late season into April and get reduced prices, warm weather, and good snow.

Take a free tour of the Krablooniks dog kennels; 970-923-4342.

Steamboat Ski Area

Address: 2305 Mt. Werner Circle, Steamboat Springs, Colorado 80487-9023

Telephone: 800-922-2722, 970-879-0740 (central reservations)

Web site: http://www.steamboat-ski.com

Originally a summer hunting ground for the Ute tribe, Steamboat Springs was later settled by cattle and horse ranchers and Scandinavian immigrants who created the area's first ski trails so that the mail could be delivered more efficiently during the winter. Later, when their work was done, they built ski jumps and hills to amuse themselves. The cow-town atmosphere still pervades downtown Steamboat Springs, but the skiing has changed considerably since the town celebrated its first winter carnival in 1914. Today the downhill action takes place about three miles from town on Mt. Werner and four other peaks, which offer wide-open cruising terrain, tree skiing, and bump runs for skiers or snowboarders of every ability.

Guests can stay at the foot of the mountain in any number of ski-in-and-out hotel and condo properties or can stay a few miles away in town. There is a free skier shuttle that runs between the town and the mountain that takes about ten minutes. All lodging at Steamboat can be booked through central reservations.

Steamboat pioneered the "kids ski free program" in 1982 and they've added plenty of features since to keep families coming back for more time on the hill. The ski-free program allows kids 12 and under to ski free the same number of days

MOUNTAIN STATISTICS

Base elevation: 6,900 feet
Summit: 10,568 feet
Vertical drop: 3,668 feet
Skiable acres: 2,939
Annual average snowfall: 300 inches
Snowmaking: 400 acres
Night skiing: in town at Howelson Hill
Season: Thanksgiving to mid-April
Lifts: 22 (1 gondola, 3 high-speed quads, 1 regular quad, 6 triples, 6 doubles, 4 surface lifts)
Terrain: 13% beginner, 56% intermediate, 31% advanced
Lift tickets: adults $48, children 12 and under $28, seniors 65 to 69 $29.

FAMILY STATISTICS

Day care: Kiddie Corral Child Care, 6 months to 6 years; 970-879-6111, ext. 469 (reservations required)
Children's lessons: Kids' Vacation Center, 2 years to kindergarten; 970-879-6111, ext. 218 (reservations required) 6 to 15 years; 970-879-6111, ext. 531
Baby-sitting: Kid's Adventure Club at Night, ages 2½ to 12 years; 970-879-6111, ext. 469 (reservations required)
Baby gear: Baby's Away rents strollers, cribs, high chairs, car seats, back packs, and other gear; 970-978-2354
Medical: Routt Memorial Hospital, 970-879-1322

as their parents when a parent purchases a ticket for five or more days. It has several limitations but can still save you lots of money. Teen tickets allow 13- to 18-year-olds to ski at reduced prices when their parents purchase a five-day ticket. Other programs for teens make this a resort that does more for this often overlooked age group than most ski areas in the West. Two "kids-only" zones have teepees, a Colorado mine shaft, a log-cabin playhouse, and picnic areas; adults are not allowed unless accompanied by a child.

Some complain that the ski area, about 160 miles from Denver International Airport, is isolated and hard to get to compared to other Colorado ski resorts. It cuts both ways: While it may take you longer to get there, once you're there you won't have the weekend crowds of the resorts that line Interstate 70 out of Denver.

How to Get There

Yampa Valley Regional Airport near Hayden is 22 miles from Steamboat Springs and has service on American, Continental, Northwest, United Airlines, TWA, United Express, Mesa, and Mountain Air Express. The Denver International Airport is about a three-hour drive. The free bus system makes a rental car unnecessary.

Where to Stay

Expensive

Bronze Tree and *Torian Plum* are both condo properties that offer the services of a hotel—swimming pool, hot tub and sauna, ski in and walk or ski out (access near the Christie lift). Most condos are two-to three-bedroom units with a queen-size sofa sleeper in the living room. Units are individually owned and decorated and are quite elegant. There are laundry facilities and ski lockers. $415–465. 1885 Ski Time Square Drive, Steamboat Springs, CO 80487; 800-228-2458, 970-879-8811.

Bear Claw Condominiums are some of the most luxurious in Steamboat, located at the Headwall and Southface lifts. They range in size from studios to four-bedroom units, each one exquisitely decorated with gas fireplaces, full kitchens, and balconies. Facilities include an outdoor heated pool, sauna, health spa, and game room. $215–1205. 2420 Ski Trail Lane, Steamboat Springs, CO 80487; 800-BEAR-CLAW, 970-879-6100.

Moderate

The Ranch at Steamboat (http://www. ranch-steamboat.com) is a couple miles away from the base area, but it feels just right for families and is quieter than some of the base-lodge properties. One-to four-bedroom units are quite spacious with full kitchens, washers and dryers, and private garages. A free shuttle takes you to the lifts. $200–430. 1 Ranch Road, Steamboat Springs, CO 80487; 800-525-2002.

Storm Meadows Townhouses are good for big or combined families. These trilevel three- and four-bedroom townhouses offer ski-in-and-out access from their back doors, and amenities include a spa facility and heated outdoor pool and tub. $400–500. Storm Meadows Drive, 80487; 800-262-5150.

Budget
Ptarmigan Inn, a Best Western property, is well-priced for ski-in-and-out accommodations right on the mountain. Standard rooms have two queen-size beds, but there are three rooms with lofts that are good for families. The Ski School and Kids' Vacation Center are right next door at the gondola building. All units have a small refrigerator plus the Inn offers a restaurant, lounge, heated outdoor pool, hot tub, and sauna. Children 12 and under stay free in their parents' room. $155–185; rollaways $10 per night. 2304 Apres Ski Way, Steamboat Springs, CO 80487; 800-538-7519, 970-879-1730.

Alpiner Lodge is in town about two blocks from a hot-springs pool. Rooms are standard motel fare, with one king-size or two double beds. The property is about three miles from the slopes, but a free city bus picks up and drops off passengers from the edge of the parking lot. Children 16 and under stay free in their parents' room. $60–150; Rollaways are $10 per night. 424 Lincoln Avenue, Steamboat Springs CO 80477; 800-538-7519, 970-879-1430.

Harbor Hotel, one of the oldest hotels in Steamboat, has hotel rooms, suites, and one- and two-bedroom condominiums, some in the original section and some in a newer annex. The hotel is about three miles from the slopes and is on a free city-bus line. $195–230. 703 Lincoln Avenue, Steamboat Springs CO 80447; 800-543-8888, 970-879-1522.

Rabbit Ears Motel, across from Steamboat Hot Springs, has two queen-size beds per room and a day couch that folds into a bed. It's located in the center of town about three miles from the slopes. Some rooms have extras such as a coffeemaker and minirefrigerator, and a complimentary continental breakfast is included in the rates. Kids 12 and under stay free in their parents' room. $89 and up. 201 Lincoln Avenue, Steamboat Springs CO 80477; 800-828-7702, 970-879-1150.

Children's Ski School

The Kids' Vacation Center offers lessons for kids ages 2 to 15. Children 2 to 6 years who want a combination of skiing and day care attend one of three programs: Buckaroos (2 years to kindergarten) have all-day child care and a one-hour private ski lesson. Mavericks (3½ to 4 years) have two one-hour group lessons and fun in the Child Care Center the rest of the day. They must be willing to ski and be toilet trained. Sundance Kids (ages 4 years through kindergarten) enjoy longer lessons. There are three kids-only beginner lifts, two of which are Magic Carpets; 970-879-6111, ext. 218.

Rough Riders are children from 6 to 15 years who want to learn to ski or snowboard. Grouped by age and ability, they can have full-or half-day lessons; 970-879-6111, ext. 531. Special classes for teens are also offered (see Teens section below).

Day Care

The Kiddie Corral Child Care Center accepts children from 6 months to 6 years for half-day or full-day programs. Children are divided by age into three groups, each with a separate room. The infant group (6 to 17 months) enjoys toys, swings, jump-ups, and a small climbing slide and rocking boat. Parents supply food for this age group. Toddlers from 18 months to 2½ years enjoy the water table, painting, riding toys, blocks, and a scheduled quiet/nap time. Preschoolers (ages 2½ to 6) enjoy a day filled with games, crafts, block play, music, and outdoor activities if the weather permits; 970-879-6111, ext. 469.

Kids' Adventure Club at Night programs for ages 2½ to 12 are offered every Tuesday through Saturday evening from 6 to 10:30 P.M. from mid-December to late March. Kids enjoy games, a movie, and rest time. Pizza and snacks are served. Once a week, an activity night is scheduled for kids 8 to 12 that includes visits to a climbing wall or hot-springs pool. For reservations, call 970-879-6111, ext. 469.

Teens

Steamboat ski-school classes are offered for intermediate and advanced teens who want to ski together with an instructor during holiday periods and the month of March. Night Owls, a program designed for 13- to 18-year-olds, features a trip to the Vertical Grip climbing gym or to town for pizza and a movie, allowing teens to mingle. All activities are supervised and run from 6 to 10:30 P.M. Wednesday, Thursday, and Friday nights from mid-December through the end of March. Reservations are required; 970-879-6111, ext. 531.

Teens from all over the world come to Steamboat for a learn-to-ski program that is combined with intensive English language lessons.

Snowboarding
Several terrain parks offer riders plenty of air. A total of three snowboard terrain parks (and one just for kids) consist of tabletops, rollers, a snake run, wu-tang launcher, fun box, and half pipes.

Cross-Country Skiing
Just below the Steamboat Ski Area, the Steamboat Touring Center offers 30 kilometers of groomed trails for skating and track skiing. A free shuttle service runs daily between the Ski Area and the Touring Center offering half-day and all-day trips; 970-879-8180.

Other Activities
Dinner sleigh rides: Horse-drawn sleighs team up with home-style cooking and live entertainment for an evening of fun and food. Windwalker Tours (http://www.cmn.net/~walker), Gondola Square, P.O. Box 775092, Steamboat Springs, CO 80477; 800-748-1642, 970-879-8065.

Dog sledding: The Steamboat Sled Dog Express (970-879-4662) zips you across the countryside in open-air sleds pulled by a pack of racing dogs.

Hot-air ballooning: Three different companies offer balloon rides over the Yampa Valley, giving you a bird's-eye view of Steamboat: Balloons Over Steamboat (970-879-3298), Aerosports Balloonists (970-879-7433), and Pegasus Balloon Tours (970-879-9191).

Hot springs: Steamboat Springs was named for its hot springs. The town has several hot-springs pools, one with a slide (970-879-1828), but a day trip to the Strawberry Hot Springs out of town is great fun. Take a four-wheel-drive trek (or shuttle) about six miles out of town to a hot-springs pool right in the rocks. Change in a teepee. It's a delightful adventure for kids during the day, but at night it turns into a party scene, so plan your visit accordingly; 970-879-0342.

Ice skating is found in town at Howelson Ice Arena; 970-879-0341.

Deals and Discounts

Ski off season, buy the packages, and keep an eye on the Web site for special deals. Because this is a college town, (Colorado Mountain College) there are some very reasonably priced cafés and restaurants.

Lift ticket prices are discounted early and late season.

❄ Telluride

Address: 565 Mountain Village Boulevard, P.O. Box 11155
Telluride, Colorado 81435
Telephone: 800-525-3455, 970-728-6900
Web site: http://www.telski.com

Telluride is often thought of as a mountain exclusively for the experienced family of skiers and snowboarders who wants plenty of adrenaline-pounding steeps and rugged extreme turf. In fact, the resort also has plenty of kind and considerate trails for moseying middle-aged intermediates whose legs aren't exactly what they used to be. "Split grooming" is Telluride's trick to accommodate skiers of different abilities on the same slope: Half the run looks like an upside-down egg carton, offering a workout better than any Thighmaster; the other half is smoothed out to make it easy for less experienced skiers to traverse and turn.

The town of Telluride lies in a narrow valley surrounded by the majestic peaks of the San Juan Mountains. A National Historic District, it was originally settled in the 1870s as a gold and silver mining camp. Now the historic buildings are filled with chic boutiques, fine restaurants, and charming inns. The resort has added an eight-passenger gondola from town to the ski resort that has cut the commute time in half and is a great asset to locals as well as visiting powder hounds who stay in town. The Mountain Village where the ski resort is located is accessible via free 11-minute gondola ride or a short drive or cross-country ski trip. There are increasing numbers of condos, a few hotels, and several restaurants in the Mountain Village, but most of the accommodations are in town.

MOUNTAIN STATISTICS
Base elevation: 8,725 feet
Summit: 11,890 feet
Vertical drop: 3,165 feet
Skiable acres: 1,050
Annual average snowfall: 300 inches
Snowmaking: 155 acres
Night skiing: none
Season: late November to mid-April
Lifts: 13 (2 high-speed quads, 2 triples, 5 doubles, 2 gondolas, 2 surface lifts)
Terrain: 21% beginner, 47% intermediate, 32% advanced
Lift tickets: adults $49, kids 6 to 12 and seniors 65 to 69 $27, 70+ and under 6 free.

FAMILY STATISTICS
Day Care: Mountain Village Nursery, ages 2 months to 3 years, 800-801-4832 or 970-728-4233 (reservations required); The Peaks Hotel & Spa, ages 6 weeks to 5 years, 800-801-4832 or 970-728-6800
Children's lessons: Children's Adventure Center, ages 3 to 12, 970-728-7533
Medical: The Telluride Medical Center, 970-728-3848

The mountain is nicely separated into three ski areas divided largely by abilities. An entire mountain just for beginners is on the western side, serviced by the world's longest quad chair. As you might expect, beginners rank Telluride among their favorite places to ski. Almost 50 percent of the terrain is rated intermediate, but note that some of what is now marked "blue" intermediate terrain used to be black before it was smoothed and straightened by grooming machines. Telluride's bumps are rated the best in the West and its steeps are indeed precipitous.

A day care for infants and toddlers, a highly regarded ski school, and a rental shop are located in a new building at the base of the gondola, offering one-stop convenience for families.

How to Get There

Visitors can fly into Telluride Airport, six miles west of town, or to larger airports in Durango, Montrose, Grand Junction, Gunnison, or Cortez (all one to two hours away) and hop a van into town. Denver International Airport is the closest international facility and is a full day's drive (330 miles) from the resort. A free local shuttle service makes loops through Telluride. The Mountain Village has its own shuttle service.

Where to Stay

Expensive

The Peaks Resort & Spa wants to make sure parents get a vacation, too, so they have a children's program during the day for kids from 6 weeks to 5 years. An evening program for children 2½ to 8 years operates from the Christmas holiday through March and provides dinner, movies, and arts and crafts, from 6 to 10 P.M. daily. Their full-service spa was rated one of the nation's top three resort spas by *Conde Nast Traveler*, and as you might imagine, it offers every possible treatment to relax and rejuvenate its guests. Other guest services include down comforters, ski valets, complimentary shuttles to and from the town and airport, and a full-service beauty salon. Evening baby-sitting in your room is easy to arrange. Rooms, suites and one- to three-bedroom penthouses are available. $355–1500. Telluride Mountain Village, P.O. Box 2702 Telluride, CO 81435; 800-789-2220, 970-728-6800.

Hotel Columbia is located right at the base of the gondola, giving it one of the most convenient locations in town. All rooms have a gas fireplace, fluffy terry robes, a safe, and an honor bar; guests' ski lockers are even outfitted with boot driers. Coffee and tea are served every morning in the library. The hotel has a full-service restaurant, an outdoor hot tub, and exercise equipment. Most rooms are for two, three, or four people, but several larger rooms will accommodate families of up to six people. $150–390. 300 West San Juan Avenue, P.O. Box 800, Telluride, CO 81435; 800-201-9505, 970-728-0660.

Telluride Resort Accomodations handles many of the condominium rentals in the Mountain Village and town. Ranging in size from studios to four bedrooms, all have fully equipped kitchens and fireplaces. Many feature their own washer and dryer, steam showers, and private hot tubs. $110-$2,250. 666 West Colorado Avenue, Telluride, CO 81435; 800-538-7754, 970-728-6621.

Moderate

The Victorian Inn, filled with antiques and unusual period pieces, is located right in the center of town and less than a block from the Cherry lift. The best rooms for families share a hallway bath, and have a queen-size bed and bunk beds in the room. Rooms with private baths have one or two queen-size beds. A complimentary continental breakfast is included in the rates. Children 7 and under stay free. $63–165. 401 West Pacific Avenue, P.O. Box 217, Telluride, CO 81435; 970-728-6601.

Budget

Tomboy Inn is in downtown Telluride, a four-block walk from the lifts. Its rooms are clean and comfortable, although some are a little worn; it's a good value for families on a tight budget. Larger suites have kitchens, and the standard and studio rooms are spacious. Two-bedroom units can accommodate up to six people. $110–300. 619 Columbia Avenue, P.O. Box 100, Telluride, CO 81435; 800-538-7754, 970-728-6621.

The Oak Street Inn has simple rooms that can sleep as many as six people in a variety of bed configurations. Most share a hallway bath with other rooms. Rooms lack TVs and phones, but the downstairs lounge has a TV for guests. The inn is one block from the main downtown street and three blocks from the gondola. Children under 5 stay free. $49–105. 134 North Oak Street, P.O. Box 175, Telluride, CO 81435; 970-728-3383.

Children's Ski School

Children start lessons at age 3: Miners (toilet-trained 3-year-olds) have one-hour one-on-one lessons with an instructor. Utes, 4 to 6 years old, take group lessons. Explorers, 7- to 12-year-olds, receive more time on the snow. Sessions run from 9:30 A.M. to 3:00 P.M. Snowboard lessons are available for 7- to 12-year-olds, and supervision is available before and after ski school (from 8:30 to 9:45 A.M. and 3 to 4 P.M., reservations required). If you're staying for three days or more your child can learn and play with the same group of buddies.

Day Care

The Mountain Village Nursery (800-801-4832, 970-728-7533), in a new brightly lit facility at the base of the gondola, is for children ages 2 months to 3 years. Infants have their own room, and toddlers enjoy two different playrooms. Special sleeping rooms allow napping children a quiet place to rest. Full- and half-day sessions are available and reservations are required.

Teens

The Voodoo Lounge, open every afternoon and evening, is a popular teen hangout featuring video games, dances, and special events; 970-728-0140.

Snowboarding

Take a free "Meet the Mountain" snowboard tour (800-801-4832, 970-728-7533) to learn your way around. An advanced-level 800-foot-long park, Pipe Dreams, is located near the midmountain restaurant and is full of berms, bumps, banks, spines, gap-style jumps, and tabletops. Telluride's half pipe is designed to Olympic specifications and is in Pipe Dreams park.

Cross-Country Skiing

Telluride Nordic Center offers 100 kilometers of Nordic terrain. Rental equipment and lessons are available. Thirty kilometers of trails atop Sunshine Peak are accessible to skiers.

Skyline Ranch is a ski-in-and-out cross-country skiers' heaven. This 110-acre ranch surrounded by U.S. Forest Service land has miles of Nordic trails meandering through the aspens and firs over high alpine meadows, lakes, and ghost towns. Accommodations are available; Nordic skiing is out the back door, and the ranch provides a shuttle to the Telluride Ski Area, 5 miles away; P.O. Box 67, Telluride CO 81435; 970-728-3757.

Other Activities

Horseback riding: Horses walk on trails through the snow on the mesa and beyond. Roudy Roudebush; 970-728-9611.

Hot-air balloon rides with San Juan Balloon Adventures (970-625-5495) leave from the valley floor on days that are perfectly calm to take you soaring high above the town.

Ice skating: An outdoor rink is in the town park at the east end of Telluride; shops in town rent ice skates. There's a small outdoor rink in the Mountain Village behind the Centrum building, but you must rent skates in one of the ski shops in town as no skate rentals are available in the Mountain Village.

Sailplane rides: Glider Bob at Telluride Soaring (970-728-5424) takes you from the airport up into the skies above the ski area for a half- or one-hour ride.

Sleigh rides: Deep Creek Sleigh & Wagon Rides (970-728-3565) and Skyline Ranch (970-728-3757) offer a variety of daytime and dinner rides.

Snowmobile tours with Telluride Outside (970-728-3895) take riders to abandoned mining towns and out on the mesas.

Snowshoeing: The U.S. Forest Service offers guided snowshoe tours of the area. They start from the top of the gondola and head out from there. Rangers talk about the geologic history and wildlife of the area. Rent snowshoes in town, as no rentals are available in the Mountain Village; 970-728-7525.

Historical walking tour: Hour-long tours acquaint visitors with the history of the town and its historic buildings. Dress warmly, as most of the tour takes place outside; 970-728-6639.

Deals and Discounts
Early and late ski packages that offer free lift tickets, lunch, and ski clinics are available if you stay at participating lodging in Telluride. If you stay in a participating lodging in the nearby towns of Ridgway, Cortez, or Ouray, tickets are half-price throughout the season during this time. Ask about January bargain packages.

❄ Vail

Address: P.O. Box 7, Vail, Colorado 81658
Telephone: 800-278-2372, 970-845-5745 (central reservations)
Web site: http://www.snow.com

This glamorous resort lures ski buffs and pleasure seekers the world over with its world-class snow conditions, high-speed lifts, and the awesome variety of its terrain. Picturesque and pedestrian friendly, Vail Village resembles a Tyrolean ski town, and its chic and expensive shops and bistros offer off-slope and après-ski diversions. Much of the lodging is a short walk from the lifts.

With all of its style and panache, you'd think Vail might be too chic to bother indulging guests in some of the less sophisticated winter activities, but this is not the case. The Adventure Ridge area, at the top of the gondola, offers lift-served tubing (six different runs, from gentle to steep), ice skating, broomball, snowshoeing, and laser tag in the snow. After 4 P.M. you can ride the gondola free of charge, and the area stays open until 9:30 P.M. Of course, much more sophisticated adult après-ski fun is abundant; Vail is repeatedly ranked among the top resorts in North America for nightlife and a special supervised "kids' night out" program allows parents the opportunity to go out on the town by themselves.

It's hard to tell at first glance that Vail is the single largest ski mountain in North America because much of the terrain is hidden on the back side of the mountain. The entire front side is evenly divided among beginner, intermediate, and advanced terrain. That means family mem-

MOUNTAIN STATISTICS

Base elevation: 8,120 feet
Summit: 11,450 feet
Vertical drop: 3,330 feet
Skiable acres: 4,644
Annual average snowfall: 341 inches
Snowmaking: 347 acres
Night skiing: one beginner's chair, open until 9:30 nightly
Season: early November to late April
Lifts: 30 [1 12-passenger heated gondola, 10 high-speed quads (including one enclosed), 1 fixed quad, 3 triples, 5 doubles, 10 surface lifts]
Terrain: 28% beginner, 32% intermediate, 40% advanced
Lift tickets: adults $55, children 12 and under $35, under 6 free.

FAMILY STATISTICS

Day care: Small World Play School Nursery, ages 2 months to 6 years, 970-479-2044 (reservations required)
Children's lessons: 970-479-4440 ages 3 to 13 years; (Golden Peak) 970-479-4450 (Lionshead).
Baby gear: Baby's Away rents cribs, high chairs, car seats, strollers, and other gear; 970-926-5256
Medical: Vail Valley Medical Center, 970-476-2451

bers of different abilities can share their ski day: Everyone can ride to the top, ski down the appropriate run, and meet halfway down the mountain for a snack and again at the bottom at the end of the day. The back side of Vail features intermediate and advanced trails that include serious powder and bump runs. One lift ticket buys you skiing possibilities at nearby Beaver Creek Resort (see page 63) and smaller Arrowhead Mountain, and if you buy a multiday ticket and your muscles seize after two days of power skiing the bumps, you can trade your tickets in for a sleigh ride, a snowmobile trip, or an activity that will give those aching, aging muscles a break.

Kids have delightful terrain parks such as Fort Whippersnapper, a 15-acre adventure land that includes Dragon's Breath Mine, the Sluice Slalom Course, and a re-created gold mine called Devil's Fork Mine. At the top of Lionshead gondola, children in ski-school programs can cruise through Indian teepees and acres of obstacles in the Gitchegumme Gulch.

The kids' learn-to-ski program is ranked one of the best in the country along with the program offered at its sister resort a few miles down the road, Beaver Creek. Recent redevelopment has created a new children's center, a base lodge, and ski-in-and-out condos at Golden Peak. A new high-speed quad zips you to the top after you've dropped off the kids. Children's ski-school lessons are also available at the Lionshead base. Older kids and fearless adults should ride the teeth-chattering bobsled course that twists and turns down the side of the mountain.

How to Get There

Eagle County Airport is about 30 minutes from Vail and is serviced with direct flights from many major airlines. Shuttle buses run regularly between the airport and Vail. Denver International Airport is 120 miles away. You really won't need a car in Vail, as the shuttle bus system is excellent.

Where to Stay
Expensive
The Lodge at Vail: Elegant ease is the best way to describe this convenient ski-in-and-out lodge where a family can stay in a condo (called a suite) offering the first-class services of a luxury hotel. Attractive hotel rooms are available, too, but larger families will be most comfortable in a suite with a full kitchen, a living room, and one, two, or three bedrooms. A member of Preferred Hotel & Resorts Worldwide, the Lodge offers a level of luxury and service that is truly world class. Some frequent guests send their skis and luggage ahead of them via overnight mail and fax the lodge their grocery list. The Lodge has a ski valet, two restaurants, a bar, complimen-

tary parking, and is steps away from Vail Village. Baby-sitters can be arranged. There is a children's pool at the far end of the main pool. Children under 12 stay free in their parents' room $330–2,100. 174 East Core Creek Drive, Vail, CO 81657; 800-331-LODG, 970-476-5011.

Manor Vail is near the Children's Center at Golden Peak, and each studio and one- or two-bedroom condo is privately owned and decorated by the owner. There's a restaurant and bar on the premises, a heated outdoor pool, a Jacuzzi, sauna, shuttle, ski storage, ski valet, and laundry facilities. $180–1550. 595 East Vail Valley Drive, Vail, CO 81657; 800-950-8245, 970-476-5651.

Sonnenalp Resort of Vail is right in the heart of the Village, a short walk to the lifts. It's actually three separate lodges, each exuding European charm: Austria Haus, Bavaria Haus, and Swiss Haus. Individual rooms and two-bedroom units are available; all include breakfast. There are also restaurants, bars, Jacuzzis, a pool, a spa, a sauna, laundry facilities, and a game room. $240–$1450. 20 Vail Road, Vail, CO 81657; 800-654-8312, 970-476-5656.

Moderate
Evergreen Lodge is right on the bus route between Vail Village and the Lionshead area. Hotel-style rooms have a minirefrigerator, and condos have one to three bedrooms. Extras include a café, outdoor heated pool, sauna, hot tub, and ski storage. $140–260. 250 South Frontage Road West, Vail, CO 81657; 800-284-8245, 970-476-7810.

Vail Village Inn is a large Bavarian-style property that has hotel rooms and one- to four-bedroom condos. It's about a four-minute walk from the nearest lift. There are several restaurants and bars, a small market, a heated outdoor pool, and ski storage. Rooms $185–295, condos $375–1250. 100 East Meadows Drive, Vail, CO 81657; 800-445-4014, 970-476-5622.

Vail Cascade Hotel & Club is a ski-in-and-out resort close to the Cascade Village chairlift, about one and a half miles from the center of the Vail Village. It has the largest health spa and club in Vail (which also houses a nursery). Children enjoy the gym facilities, play games, and watch videos. The complex includes two movie theaters, restaurants, and an outdoor pool. Kids stay free in their parents' room, and rollaways are free for children. $199–335. 1300 Westhaven Drive, Vail, CO 81657; 800-420-2424, 970-476-7111.

Marriott's Mountain Resort at Vail is at the base of the new Lionshead gondola and has guest rooms, suites, and condominiums. Baby-sitting can be arranged during the evening. Within the resort are indoor and outdoor pools, a ski-rental shop, ski-storage facilities, a bar, a spa, and restaurants. Kids stay free in their parents' room and rollaways are free. $225–349. 715 West Lionshead Circle, Vail, CO 81657; 800-648-0720, 970-476-4444.

Budget
Homestake Condominiums are an excellent value just a half mile from Vail Village on the free bus route. Their units come in several configurations: studios with a loft, one-bedroom condos plus a loft, and two-bedroom condominiums. All feature fully equipped kitchenettes and cable TV. $100–190. 1081 Vail View Drive 81657; 970-476-3950.

Westvail Lodge offers standard hotel rooms and one-and two-bedroom condos. A skier shuttle ferries skiers to the slopes. There are two restaurants. Kids 13 and under stay free in their parents' room, and rollaways cost $10 per night. $129–279. 2211 North Frontage Road, Vail, CO 81657. 970-476-3890.

The Roost has functional rooms and offers a complimentary continental breakfast and evening snack. It's one block from the town bus stop. Within the facility is an indoor pool, a sauna, a Jacuzzi, and ski storage. $122–220. 1783 Frontage Road, West Vail, CO 81657. 970-476-5451.

Park Meadows has small condos at very low prices; as you might expect, they are reserved far in advance. All units have kitchens and living/dining areas. One-bedroom condos can sleep up to 4 in the bedroom and on day beds or sofa sleepers. Two-bedroom condos sleep more. Guests can use an outdoor Jacuzzi and laundry facilities on the premises. $75–240. 1472 Matterhorn Circle, Vail, CO 81657 (near chair 20); 970-476-5598.

Children's Ski School
The ski school has designed a clever "motivational tool" for students: Kids get big fat buttons as they enter ski school, with spots for flashy gold and black stickers they are awarded when they pass a learning landmark. This gimmick provides an incentive for even the most reluctant skier to progress. Because so many of Vail's visitors stay six or seven days, the ski school has a week's worth of theme days such as Race Day, Circus Day, and Treasure Hunt Day.

The Mini Mice program is for toilet-trained 3-year-olds who are introduced to skiing through group games. The Mogul Mice program is for 4- to 6-year-olds not yet able to stop on skis. Once 3- to 6-year-olds can stop, they graduate to the Super Stars program. Six- to 13-year-olds are always grouped by both age and ability for their lessons. Snowboarding lessons begin at age 6. Children's Ski Centers are located at Golden Peak (970-479-4440) and Lionshead (970-479-4450) base areas.

Day Care

The Small World Play School Nursery is located at the Golden Peak base. Children ages 2 months to 6 years are accepted, and separated into different playrooms depending on their age: infants to 15 months, toddlers 16 to 30 months, and preschoolers. In addition to indoor fun, children are taken out to play in the snow where they can sled and build snowmen and snowballs. Free pagers are available for parents. Reservations are required; 970-479-2044.

Kid's Night Out Goes Western: This fully supervised kids-only evening includes music, games, storytelling, a wagon-wheel pizza dinner, dessert, and a show by the Buckaroo Bonanza Bunch at the Golden Peak Children's Center (970-476-9090). It takes place on Thursdays for children ages 5 to 13.

Teens

A special teen hot line (970-479-4090) has recorded information about the latest teen activities. Below Zero is a teen nightclub in the Lionshead parking structure that has a big video screen, games, and nonalcoholic refreshments. Special teen ski classes for 14- to 18-year-olds are offered during peak holiday periods. Teen Guides is an all-day program for intermediate to advanced skiers ages 14 to 18 where kids ski together rather than work on specific skills. It's offered regularly throughout the year.

Snowboarding

Kids 6 years and up can enroll in snowboarding classes (970-476-3239). Eleven specially designed trails include half pipes, gullies, jibs, and other features. The TAG Heuer snowboard park includes tabletops and all kinds of bumps and hits; it's one of the largest snowboard parks in the world. It contains a long night-lit half pipe at the top of the gondola at Adventure Ridge. A free snowboarding trail guide—available at any activities desk and at on-mountain information kiosks—will help you find it.

Cross-Country Skiing

Vail Nordic Center (970-479-4391) has 15 kilometers of groomed tracks at the Vail Golf Course. A rental shop (with children's sizes) and ski school is on the premises. Private lessons are available for children or families. There are no children-only classes.

Golden Peak Ski School (970-845-5313) offers cross-country lessons and guided backcountry tours. Instructors take their group in a van to a forest-service trailhead. Rentals are available. Meet at the Golden Peak Lodge.

Other Activities

Adventure Ridge: This fun zone at the top of the gondola at Lionshead consists of a multitude of activities and a day lodge with four restaurants and a business center. Select from laser tag, snowmobiling, tubing, broomball, snowshoeing, and ice skating. It's open daily until midnight. Buy a footpass for the Eagle Bahn gondola to reach the Ridge during the day, or access it at no charge during the late afternoon and evening. For information contact the activity desk at 970-476-9090.

Bobsledding: Try the 2,900-foot twisting course just below mid-Vail on Lionsway near the Black Forest Trail. Each bobsled seats four riders and can reach speeds of more than 50 miles per hour. You ski or snowboard to the course and ride down while your equipment is separately transported to meet you at the bottom. Helmets are required, and riders are told what to expect. For reservations contact the activity desk at 970-476-9090.

Colorado Ski Heritage Museum (970-476-1876), on the third level of the Transportation Center, describes the 100-year history of the sport in Colorado. Committed to preserving the history of skiing, the museum is filled with old photos, vintage ski fashions, a ski Hall of Fame, and equipment that ranges from old wooden skis and cable bindings to the high-tech models of today.

Ice skating: Skates can be rented at a night-lit outdoor rink in the Adventure Ridge area at Lionshead. More ice skating is found at the Dobson Ice Arena (970-479-2220), an indoor skating arena east of the Lionshead parking structure, served by the free town shuttle.

The **Vail Public Library** (970-479-2184) has one of the most delightful children's rooms of any library in the country. In addition to shelves of colorful picture books, there are climbing structures, big pillows, toys, and a large playhouse. The perfect stop for a snowy day, it's located across from Dobson Ice Arena.

Laser tag: The Native American Village (970-479-4383), used by the ski school during the day, is turned into a laser-tag arena at night. Players dodge the teepees and obstacles as they run around under the lights in the snow.

Daylight **sleigh rides** are available, as well as a special nighttime excursion to the award-winning gourmet restaurant, Beano's Cabin at Beaver Creek. Get a baby-sitter for this one. Vail Golf Course 970-476-8057.

Snowmobiling: Nova Guides (888-949-6682, 970-949-4232) and Timber Ridge Adventures (970-668-8349) conduct tours that vary in length and include a guide familiar with the terrain and surrounding views for groups or private parties.

Snowshoeing is available through the Nordic Center (970-479-4391). The U.S. Forest Service also offers guided snowshoe tours through scenic forest trails.

Tubing hill: Tubes can be rented at Adventure Ridge (970-479-4383), where five different night-lit trails, from slow to superfast, are served by a lift. The steepest is at a 45-degree angle and is about 150 yards in length. Children must be 36 inches tall to participate.

Winter Park Resort

Address: 677 Winter Park Drive, P.O. Box 36, Winter Park, Colorado 80482

Telephone: 800-729-5813 (central reservations) 970-726-5514

Web site: http://www.skiwinterpark.com

Winter Park is the closest major ski resort to Denver, accessible by the two-hour-long Ski Train that whisks Denverites to the slopes every weekend. Its adaptive ski program (teaching people with disabilities to ski) is one of the finest and largest in the nation, and its adults' and children's ski schools are also highly regarded. The immediate base area and surrounding region look rather plain, but Winter Park offers a great value for families and has plans to create a small pedestrian village at the base. For now, there are a few accommodations at the base and more choices farther down the road in nearby towns.

The skiing extends over three interconnected mountains and an alpine bowl. Each of these four areas has a slightly different emphasis. Groswold's Discovery Park, on Winter Park Mountain, is an enclosed 20-acre learn-to-ski park, and the runs in the vicinity tend to be wide and nicely groomed. Vasquez Ridge is known for long intermediate trails, Mary Jane for endless bump runs and steeps chutes, and Parsenn Bowl offers above-timberline skiing and tree skiing from the 12,060-foot summit. Families can ski together or explore separate terrain individually.

The Children's Center is one large facility that houses the kids' ski school, day care for infants to 5-year-olds, the ski patrol, and a medical facility. The National Sports Center for the Disabled (http://www.nscd.org/nscd) is headquartered

MOUNTAIN STATISTICS
Base elevation: 9,000 feet
Summit: 12,060 feet
Vertical drop: 3,060 feet
Skiable acres: 2,581
Annual average snowfall: 355 inches
Snowmaking: 280 acres
Night skiing: none
Season: early November to late April
Lifts: 20 (7 high-speed quads, 5 triples, 8 doubles)
Terrain: 12% beginner, 30% intermediate, 17% advanced, 41% expert.
Lift tickets: adults $47, children 6 to 13 $15, seniors 62 to 69 $22, under 6 and over 70 free.

FAMILY STATISTICS
Day care: From two months to five years, 970-726-1551
Children's lessons: 970-726-1551
Baby-sitting: Kids Needs come to your lodging, 970-726-0707
Baby gear: Go Baby Go (970-726-9604) rents all kinds of equipment for babies, including cribs, high chairs, playpens, humidifiers, back packs, safety products, videos, and toys.
Medical: Seven Mile Medical Clinic, 970-726-8066

here as well, and in addition to teaching disabled adults and kids to ski, Winter Park now includes snowboarding, showshoeing, and cross-country skiing lessons in their adaptive program.

Most of the month of January is devoted to beginners, and first-timers are entitled to a free three-hour lesson with the purchase of an all-day adult lift ticket; second and third day lessons cost $15.

How to Get There

Winter Park is 85 miles from the Denver International Airport, and shuttles operate daily during ski season. Amtrak (800-USA-RAIL) stops in Fraser, and the Ski Train (303-296-I-SKI) from Denver's Union Station operates weekends beginning mid-December through late March. A free local shuttle service, The Lift, runs guests from lodging properties and activities in the valley to the ski-resort base area.

Where to Stay

Expensive

The Vintage Hotel, the only real full-service hotel in Winter Park, has hotel rooms and studios, and one- and two-bedroom units with kitchenettes. It's within walking distance of the slopes and has a large children's game room and swimming pool. Ski storage and laundry facilities are available. Hotel rooms $89–180, units with kitchens $105–535. 100 Winter Park Drive, P.O. Box 1369, Winter Park, CO 80482; 800-472-7017, 970-726-8801.

Iron Horse Resort Retreat, the area's sole ski-in-and out property, is a large complex with standard hotel rooms, suites, and condominiums. All of the condos have fireplaces, private balconies, and full kitchen facilities. There's ski storage, laundry facilities, a game room, a restaurant, a swimming pool, hot tubs, and a steam room. $109–579. 257 Winter Park Drive, P.O. Box 1286, Winter Park, CO 80482; 800-621-8190, 970-726-8851.

Moderate

Snowblaze Resort Condominiums & Athletic Club offers studios (sleeping up to four people), two-bedroom (up to six) and three-bedroom (up to eight) units. All except the studios have fireplaces and private saunas. A complimentary skier shuttle service operates every half hour, since the property is one mile from the ski area. Bonuses include an indoor heated pool, a hot tub, a sauna, and a Nautilus weight room. Most properties require a minimum stay of two to three nights. $87–395. Highway 40, Winter Park, CO 80446; 800-729-5813.

Crestview Condominiums are within walking distance of town and about one mile from the ski slopes, also serviced by the skier shuttle. Their one- and two-bedroom condos, some with a loft, have more lavish decor than some of the other condos in the area, along with full kitchens, whirlpool bathtubs, and underground covered parking. $120– 444. Highway 40, Winter Park, CO 80446; 800-729-5813.

Budget
Super 8 Motel is two miles from the ski area and within walking distance of the shops and restaurants in downtown Winter Park. It's a particularly well-kept budget property, with a free continental breakfast, microwaves and minirefrigerators in some rooms, and a hot tub. The skier shuttle picks up guests at the front door. Children under 12 stay free in their parents' room; $76–130. 8665 U.S. Highway 40, Winter Park, CO 80482; 800-800-8000, 970-726-8088.

Children's Ski School
Children are assigned to one of four age groups and then placed in a ski class appropriate to their ability.

The Ute program is for toilet-trained nonchairlift-riding 3- and 4-year-olds who are introduced to skiing in a fun, play-oriented environment. The Cheyenne program for 5- and 6-year-olds, the Navajo program for 6- to 8-year-olds, and the Arapaho program for 9- to 13-year-olds offer lessons that emphasize basic skills and fun on the snow. Kids first grade to 13-years old may also opt to take snowboarding lessons.

As soon as beginners are comfortable stopping on skis, they head to Discovery Park. More experienced skiers explore the big mountain, which has a hidden teepee village and a special video arena. Kids can check into ski school as early as 8 A.M., 970-726-1551.

Day Care
Day Care, located in the Children's Center, is for children 2 months to 5 years of age, who can stay full or half days. The program takes place in one big room that has partitions for various age groups. There's an infant area and play areas for toddlers and preschoolers with toys, activities, little slides, and small climbing gyms. Beepers are available for parents for $5 per day; 970-726-1551 (reservations required).

Teens
Teens can participate in an afternoon ski program that focuses more on high-intensity fun than formal instruction; 970-726-1551.

Snowboarding

Three terrain parks keep boarders happy. The newest, Knuckle Dragon on Winter Park Mountain, includes rail slides, quarter pipes, and a series of jumps. Another, Stone Grove, capitalizes on the natural features of the mountain: Trees have been cleared to create wider landing areas below the drop-offs, ramps, gullies, and rail slides built into the park. The resort's half pipe is on Winter Park Mountain.

Cross-Country Skiing

Devil's Thumb Cross-Country Center, about a 15-minute drive from the north of Fraser, has a network of 105 kilometers of groomed trails for both classic and skating techniques. There are lessons, a retail shop, and equipment rentals. 3530 Country Road 83, Tabernash, CO; 970-726-8231.

Snow Mountain Ranch has 100 kilometers of groomed trails, including three kilometers of lighted track for night skiing. It's about 15 miles away from Winter Park. Lessons and rentals are available. P.O. Box 169, Winter Park, CO 80482; 970-887-2152.

Other Activities

Dogsled rides: Dog Sled Rides of Winter Park (970-726-TEAM) cut a path through an area of national forest right outside of town (reservations required).

Hot-air balloon rides: Grand Adventure Balloon Tours (970-887-1340) floats you across the valley in splendor in a colorful hot-air balloon.

Ice skating: A small, free outdoor ice skating rink (970-726-4118) is located in Copper Creek Square in Winter Park. Skate rentals are available on the square at Sport Stalker (970-726-8874). Right outside of Fraser is a larger outdoor rink (970-726-8882) that has evening bonfires. Skate rentals are available at Ski Broker (970-726-8815).

Sleigh rides: Dashing Thru the Snow Sleigh Rides (970-726-5376), Dinner at the Barn (970-726-4923), and Jim's Sleigh Rides (970-726-0944) offer a variety of rides, some of which include hot chocolate or dinner and entertainment.

Snowmobiling: Mountain Madness (970-726-4529), between Winter Park and Fraser, offers smaller versions of snowmobiles—called snoscoots—that can be operated by children 11 years and older along a go-cart-style course.

Snowmobile dinner tours: (970-726-5514, ext. 1727). Head up Winter Park Mountain to Vasquez, through a closed area to Mary Jane, and then to a restaurant atop the mountain for a simple hot meal.

Snowshoeing: Guided snowshoe tours begin with a ride up the Gemini Express for a trek (all downhill) through forested trails. Guides introduce the basics of snowshoeing and talk about the history, plants, and animals of Winter Park; 970-726-5514, ext. 1727 (reservations required).

Tubing: Fraser Valley Tubing Hill (970-726-5954) is ten minutes away in the town of Fraser. It's open evenings, weekends, and holidays. Tubes are rented by the hour and the rope tow lift has handles to ride back up.

Deals and Discounts

Visit from January 5 to 31 to take advantage of the Learn for Free program that entitles skiers to a free three-hour ski or snowboarding lesson with the purchase of an adult lift ticket.

Need a couple of useful pointers to shake those bad habits? For $5, the Quick Tips Learning Lane offers a video analysis of your technique and suggestions for improvement from a certified ski or snowboard instructor in 15 minutes.

Inquire about the family package for accommodations and tickets, which is offered all season long. Early- and late-season packages are an excellent buy: April is a gorgeous skiing month, and prices drop considerably.

Utah

❄ Alta Ski Area

Address: P.O. Box 8007, Alta, Utah 84092
Telephone: 801-942-0404 (lodging reservations), 801-742-3333 (main office)

Unpretentious Alta is one of the granddaddies of skiing, and may be the only major resort that hasn't tried to change with the changing tide. The first chairlift was built using spare parts from the mining industry that dominated the area at the turn of the century. It was the nation's and the world's second ski lift—Sun Valley beat them by just a few years. Alta's purpose is to run a great ski mountain, not develop real estate or produce a stellar après-ski experience. It's quiet, tranquil, and safe.

The resort sits in Little Cottonwood Canyon, a glacier-cut canyon that gets some of the most—and the best—powder snow in North America. Wide, meandering runs will delight beginning and intermediate skiers, and steep chutes, bumpy vertical bowls, and ungroomed glades will please the most advanced skiers. There is a scattering of lodges next to the resort; most offer a modified American plan of breakfast and dinner, since there is only one restaurant in Alta. People come to ski in a low-key atmosphere (you won't see any fur coats here) and a lovely setting in the majestic Wasatch Mountains. Alta's visitors, many of whom are loyal repeaters, are happiest when nothing changes. Consequently, there are no snowboarders allowed (they can go to Snowbird next door), and even the lifts have a vintage feel as skiers mosey up the mountain, two by two. Lift-ticket prices are a throwback, too, at only $28 per person per day.

Nightlife at Alta is playing a game or reading a book by the fire in the lodge and getting to bed early so you can hit the slopes when the lifts open. It's a great place to spend uninterrupted time with your family.

MOUNTAIN STATISTICS
Base elevation: 8,550 feet
Summit: 10,650 feet
Vertical drop: 2,020 feet
Skiable acres: 2,200
Annual average snowfall: 500 inches
Night skiing: none
Season: mid-November through mid-April
Lifts: 12 (6 doubles, 2 triples, 4 surface lifts)
Terrain: 25% beginner, 40% intermediate, 35% advanced
Lift tickets: adults $28

FAMILY STATISTICS
Day care: Alta Children's Center, 3 months to 12 years, 801-742-3042
Children's lessons: Alf Engen Ski School, ages 4 to 12, 801-742-2600
Baby-sitting: Make arrangements at individual lodges
Medical: Alta View Hospital in Sandy, 801-576-2600

A day-care center cares for children as young as 3 months, and the children's ski school takes kids from ages 4 to early teens. Alta takes part in the Skecology program, which promotes environmental awareness. Special trail markers are placed throughout the mountain that teach children about the wildlife of the area.

How to Get There

Alta is 25 miles southeast of Salt Lake City at the top of Little Cottonwood Canyon. Salt Lake City International Airport is 45 minutes away and shuttle service is available from Canyon Transportation (800-255-1841). The Alta shuttle takes skiers around the Alta base area.

Where to Stay

Most of the accommodations in Alta are ski in and out and are on the modified American plan, which includes breakfast and dinner. There's virtually no nightlife except in the lodges themselves, where dinner and a quiet evening in the lounge around the fire cap off a great ski day. If you're on a tight budget, stay in one of the lodgings at the canyon's mouth in Sandy.

Expensive

Owner Bill Levit bought the **Alta Lodge** (http:www.skialta.com) in the 1950s and established it as a family resort. He had five children of his own and was frustrated by the difficulty in finding ski lodges that welcomed children. Now the same families come back year after year, many with the grandchildren in tow. Kids are served dinner an hour before the grown-ups eat, and planned children's activities during the adult dinner allow Mom and Dad to dine in peace. Dining is family style, and before and after meals children play games in the lobby while their parents catch up on their reading in comfortable chairs. The lodge sprawls over three levels and there is no elevator, but the bell service is good. Families can stay in a variety of room configurations. Adults double occupancy (includes breakfast and dinner) $288–375. Kids in their parents' room: ages 4 to 6 $39–46; 7 to 12 $64–72; over 12 $82–92. Alta Lodge, Alta, UT, 84092; 800-707-ALTA, 801-742-3500.

Rustler Lodge (http://www.rustlerlodge.com) offers ski-in-and-out convenience. After warming up with a morning stretch class before breakfast, you can ski from your doorstep to Alta's base lifts, or take the complimentary daily shuttle to Snowbird, just over the ridge. There's an outdoor heated pool, Jacuzzi, sauna, and full-service ski shop on the premise. Kids' programs are offered over the holidays. $185–235 per person. Little Cottonwood Canyon, Alta, UT 84092-8030; 800-451-5223 (reservations), 801-742-2200.

Moderate
Goldminer's Daughter Lodge at the base of two of the lifts has a large sundeck and sun-filled atrium. Lodge guests enjoy the use of the hot tubs, a game room, and a sauna. Rooms are simple, and the largest has two double beds. $95 per person. Goldminer's Lodge, Alta, UT 84092; 800-453-4573, 801-742-2300. children's rates available.

Alta Peruvian Lodge has a variety of accommodations, from a dormitory to a two-bedroom suite. Rates include breakfast, lunch, dinner and a lift ticket. Kids will appreciate the outdoor pool and the nightly movie showings. $177 per person; kid's rates vary. Alta, UT 84092-8017; 800-453-8488 (reservations), 801-742-3000.

Budget
Wasatch Front Ski Accommodations (http://www.wfsa.com) represents condos at the opening of Big and Little Cottonwood Canyons, near supermarkets and other conveniences. A ski shuttle stops at some of the properties. Most families fly in and rent cars. $120–225. 2020 East 3300 South, Suite 23, Salt Lake City, UT 84109; 800-762-7606, 801-486-4296.

Children's Ski School
Kids' programs at the Alf Engen Ski School are for children age 4 and up: Children under 4 must take private lessons. All-Day Adventures are for all level of skiers ages 4 to 12. The All-Day Mountain Explorers program is for 7-year-olds to early teens who are competent skiers. Children ages 4 and 5 who want a shorter two-hour lesson can participate in the All-Day Mini Adventure. Children eat lunch in Alta's pleasant day-care center. Half-day lessons are also available both morning and afternoons; 801-742-2600.

Day Care
The Alta Children's Center accommodates 46 kids ages 3 months to 12 years. Full-, half-, and five-day packages are available. The cheerful and sunny facility is filled with small climbing toys, fantasy play areas, and toy-filled corners. Ages are separated from one another by low partitions so the staff can supervise everyone; 801-742-3042.

Snowboarding
Snowboarders are not allowed at Alta, but can go to Snowbird next door.

Cross-Country Skiing
No cross-country skiing is available in Little Cottonwood Canyon. If you have your own car, try Solitude Nordic Center (see page 145) in Big Cottonwood Canyon. Park City Mountain Resort (see page 136) also has cross-country skiing.

Deals and Discounts
You can't beat Alta's ticket price at just $28. If you just ski the beginner lifts, lift tickets cost $21.

❄ Deer Valley Resort

Address: P.O. Box 1525, Deer Valley, Utah 84060
Telephone: 800-424-DEER, 801-649-1000 (central reservations);
801-649-2000 (snow report)
Web site: http://www.deervalley.com

Deer Valley's philosophy that details make the difference is reflected throughout the resort: Ski valets help you unload your skis before you park your car; the magnificent timbered lodges have flagstone floors, towering stone fireplaces, and plush furnishings; you can leave your ski boots overnight in a special drier; and a cap on the number of lift tickets sold each day keeps your ski experience civilized and uncrowded.

An overnight stay slopeside will definitely cost you more than Park City, just a few miles down the road. But the price of a lift ticket doesn't cost much more than those in most other ski areas, and the services offered for the extra price can be well worth it if you like to be pampered. With some of the best on-mountain food on the continent and a system of fast, efficient lifts, Deer Valley is popular for good reason.

Three mountains—Bald Mountain, Bald Eagle Mountain, and Flagstaff Mountain—comprise Deer Valley Resort. Each mountain has a different feel and offers something for all levels of skill with a strong emphasis on intermediates. Deer Valley will host some events for the 2002 Winter Olympic Games, including the slalom, the combined slalom, aerial and mogul events for men and women. Visitors can ski some of the Olympic runs already in place, such as Big Stick and Know You Don't. At press time, Deer Valley was planning to keep its resort closed to snowboarders.

MOUNTAIN STATISTICS
Base elevation: 7,200 feet
Summit: 9,400 feet
Vertical drop: 2,200 feet
Skiable acres: 1,100
Annual average snowfall: 300 inches
Snowmaking: 400 acres
Night skiing: none
Season: early December through mid-April
Lifts: 14 (3 high-speed quads, 9 triples, 2 doubles)
Terrain: 15% beginner, 50% intermediate, 35% advanced
Lift ticket: adults $54, children 12 and under $29, seniors 65 and over $38

FAMILY STATISTICS
Day care: Deer Valley Child Care Center, 2 months to 12 years, 801-645-6612
Children's lessons: Deer Valley Ski School, ages 3½ to 12 years, 801-645-6648
Baby-sitting: Guardian Angel Babysitting Service; 801-640-1229
Baby gear: Baby's Away rents cribs, high chairs, car seats, strollers, toys, and other gear; 801-645-8823
Medical: Park City Family Health and Emergency Center, 801-649-7640

Two base areas serve the guests. The lower area, Snow Park, houses the children's day-care and ski-school facilities, dining establishments, and shops, and is flanked by condominiums and lodges. The midmountain base, Silver Lake, has some of the finest ski-area lodging in the world, fine dining, and chic boutiques. It's the place to be for those with money to burn, as its location and amenities are truly first class. On sunny days you're likely to see guests midmountain soaking up the sun at McHenry's Beach—imagine a beach on the coast of France, deck chairs lined up in rows and sun worshipers facing the sun—that's McHenry's Beach except that it's snow, not sand underfoot.

Guests at Deer Valley can take advantage of the many recreational offerings in the Park City area in addition to Park City Mountain Resort (page 136) and The Canyons. Don't leave without visiting the Utah Winter Sports Park, which has public ski-jumping lessons, a bobsled ride, or stopping to take the Park City Silver Mine Tour.

If you plan to visit over Christmas or Presidents' weekend, be sure to reserve your lift tickets at the time you reserve your lodging.

How to Get There

Out-of-towners fly into Salt Lake City International Airport, a 40-minute drive from Deer Valley. Airline service includes Delta (Salt Lake is one of its hubs), American, America West, Continental, TWA, United, Northwest, Sky West, and Vanguard. Many shuttles travel from the airport to the ski resort. Park City Transit offers free shuttle service between Park City and Deer Valley.

Where to Stay

If you're feeling flush, stay midmountain near the Silver Lake Lodge, where a cluster of condos and hotels rooms, restaurants, shops, and delis create an upbeat buzz. If you're strapped for cash, stay in Park City and take the bus to Deer Valley. Deer Valley's accommodations fall into the price range of expensive, really expensive, and out of sight.

Expensive

Stein Erikson Lodge, midmountain, is reminiscent of a deluxe alpine chalet set in the Swiss Alps. Its location, just steps from the lifts, chic boutiques, and trendy bistros of the midmountain make it a convenient choice for families for whom budget is no concern. Get a baby-sitter the night you go to the lodge's famous restaurant, Glitretind, as it's one of the finest in any ski area anywhere. $300–2875. 7700 Stein Way, P.O. Box 3177, Park City, UT 84060; 800-453-1302, 801-649-3700.

Mont Cervin Condominiums are in the Silver Lake Village area, just steps from the lifts. The public and private rooms have solid-oak cabinetry and stone fireplaces, and the foyers and kitchens have flagstone floors. Units have two bedrooms, two bedrooms and a loft, or three bedrooms. All come with private hot tubs on an outside deck and two fireplaces, one in the living room and one in the master bedroom. $545–1275. Deer Valley Lodging, P.O. Box 3000, Park City, UT 84060; 800-453-3833, 801-649-4040.

Condominiums in the Snow Park Area

Snow Park is the lower mountain base lodge, and nearby accommodations range from one-bedroom condos to six-bedroom houses with all the amenities. The Lakeside units are two, three-, and four-bedroom townhouses that share a swimming pool, two Jacuzzis, and a sauna in the center of the complex. All units have fully equipped kitchens, jetted master bathtubs and steam showers in the master bedroom. All units have Berber carpets and cathedral ceilings. $295–890. Deer Valley Lodging, Park City, UT 84060; 800-453-3833, 801-649-4040.

Bristle Cone and *Deer Lake Village* are similar complexes that resemble deluxe mountain log cabins. Their two-, three-, or four-bedroom condominiums have lodgepole furniture, log railings on decks, and elegant rustic appointments. All come with private hot tubs. $270–1474. Bristle Cone is on Deer Valley Drive North and Deer Lake is located on Village on Deer Lake Village Drive. Deer Valley Lodging, Park City, UT 84060; 800-453-3833.

Children's Ski School

The Deer Valley Children's Center houses the ski school upstairs and the day-care site downstairs in a beautifully designed, modern building. Preschool-age children participate in programs integrated with day care. Children 3½ to 5 years participate in the Bambi Special with an hour of private ski instruction and indoor and outdoor activities in the children's center. The Reindeer Club, for kids age 4½ to kindergarten age, have their lessons combined with day care. The staff's goal is to teach kids to be as independent as possible and to get them to take one run on the lift before lunch the first day.

Adventure Club kids, age 6 to 12, are divided by age and ability. They get regular hot-chocolate breaks as they ski the mountain or visit a terrain garden called Snow Safari with its waves, bumps, and rolling embankments. A progress card keeps parents informed of their child's skill development.

All kids wear tickets around their neck so all staff members knows where children are supposed to be at all times. Snowboarding lessons are available at Park City Mountain Resort p. 136.

Day Care

The Deer Valley Children's Center offers child care for infants, toddlers, and preschoolers in special age-appropriate rooms, which can accommodate 32 infants and 65 children. But even at full capacity, this facility has a cozy feeling, since there are four different rooms for infants alone. Full- and half-day programs are available. The preschoolers can take ski lessons (see Children's Ski School above) and kids can take individual private lessons if they wish. Pagers are provided for parents.

Teens

Teen "Equipe" is a mountain experience for 13- to 18-year-olds of all skill levels that operates daily from 11 A.M. to 4 P.M. Teens socialize while they are coached in their skiing technique.

Snowboarding

Snowboarding is not allowed; send your boarders on the shuttle to Park City Mountain Resort (page 136) or The Canyons.

Cross-Country Skiing

Norwegian School of Nature Life has cross-country and snowshoe lessons for children and adults and overnight ski treks to a warm and cozy yurt with sleeping quarters for up to eight people; 800-649-5322, 801-649-5322.

White Pine Touring Company has guided tours, a groomed track, rentals, and lessons; 801-649-8701.

Other Activities

Sleigh rides of all types are available, the most popular of which is the dinner sleigh ride. Guests travel in wooden sleighs pulled by Belgian draft horses over the river and through the woods to a big barn where a western barbecue dinner is served. For information, call ABC Reservations Central (800-820-ABCD) or Snowdance (801-649-5713).

Hot-air balloon rides arranged by ABC Reservations Central (800-820-ABCD) go out early in the morning to avoid the thermal winds that kick up later in the day. Vans take you to the launch site and pick you up.

Snowmobiling tours with High Country (801-645-7533) and Snowest Snomobile Tours (800-499-7660) take you around the base of the Deer Valley area and into the woods.

Park City Silver Mine Tour: Put on your hard hat and yellow slicker and descend 1,500 feet into this former silver mine that became a tourist attraction when silver prices dropped. You'll hear real miners tell tales of fortunes found and lost and the ghosts and helpers who reportedly still live in these mines. Hwy 224, P.O. Box 3178, Park City, UT 84060; 801-655-7444.

Utah Winter Sports Park offers ski-jumping lessons for kids (no minimum age, but intermediate skiing ability is required) and adults, bobsled rides (minimum age 16) which speed up to 75 miles an hour along a mile-long track, and luge rides (kids must be 50 inches tall) which travel much slower but are equally thrilling. If you're lucky you'll see Olympic athletes training on these facilities, which will be used for the 2002 Winter Olympic Games. Be sure to call in advance to find the public-ride schedule. 3000 Bear Hollow Drive, Park City, UT 84060; 801-649-5447.

Deals and Discounts

Be sure to inquire about value season packages that can save you money on lift tickets and lodging. Multiple-day ticket purchases are also discounted; 800-424-DEER.

❄ Park City Mountain Resort

Address: P.O. Box 39, Park City, Utah 84060
Telephone: 800-222-PARK, 801-649-0493 (central reservations)
Website: http://www.pcski.com

The skiers speeding past you straight down the mountain at Park City may be U.S. Ski Team members in training. The U.S. team moved its headquarters here more than twenty years ago to take advantage of the easy access to the slopes (Salt Lake City Airport is a 40-minute drive), reliable snow, and variety of terrain.

Park City is the largest ski resort in Utah, and it's beginning to buzz with activity in preparation for the Winter Olympic Games in 2002, when the region will swell by hundreds of thousands of people and careers will begin and end on ice, snow, and in the air. The Park City Mountain Resort will host the giant slalom for both skiers and snowboarders and the snowboarding half-pipe competition. Other events will take place nearby: The Utah Winter Sports Park, four miles north of Park City, will be the site of the bobsled, luge, ski-jumping, and freestyle-aerial competitions; Deer Valley Resort (see page 131), just a few miles down the road, will host the slalom and mogul events. Olympic athletes will stay in Park City and around the Salt Lake City area.

Park City Mountain Resort has a variety of hotel rooms and condominiums right at the base, where you'll also find restaurants, ski shops, and gift shops. A short shuttle bus ride away, Park City—an old mining town that was once the largest silver mining camp in the country—is filled with charming western shops, cafés, and many other possibilities for lodging. Visitors who

MOUNTAIN STATISTICS
Base elevation: 6,900 feet
Summit: 10,000 feet
Vertical drop: 3,100 feet
Skiable acres: 2200
Annual average snowfall: 350 inches
Snowmaking: 475 acres
Night skiing: 35 acres, 2 chairs
Season: early November to mid-April
Lifts: 14 (3 high-speed 6-passenger chairs; 1 high speed quad; 1 quad; 5 triples; 4 doubles)
Terrain: 16% beginner, 45% intermediate, 39% expert
Lift tickets: adults $52, children 12 and under $23, seniors 65 to 69 $25, 70 and over free.

FAMILY STATISTICS
Day care: none
Children's lessons: Park City Ski School; 800-227-2SKI, 801-649-8111 (reservations required)
Baby-sitting: Guardian Angel Baby-sitting Service, 801-640-1229
Baby gear: Baby's Away rents strollers, cribs, high chairs, car seats, toys, and other gear; 801-645-8823
Medical: Park City Family Health and Emergency Center, 801-649-7640

stay in the town of Park City can take one of the frequent shuttles to the ski mountain, and guests who stay at the base can hop the bus to town in the evening for dinner and entertainment.

Park City's vast ski area is known mostly as an intermediate skier's mountain, and broad ribbons of smooth snow amble down from nearly every lift. Beginners will find their best ski turf at the top of the gondola, rather than the mountain base. The heart-pumping vertical, burly bump runs, and ungroomed steeps that keep the U.S. Ski Team happy will also please the advanced skiers and boarders in any group. Groomers know Park City skiers like powder, and they leave some of the runs un-touched after a big snow. Just a few miles down the road are The Canyons (formerly known as Wolf Mountain) and Deer Valley Resort, both worth exploring for a day. An excellent shuttle-bus system connects visitors to all three ski areas and the town of Park City.

Be sure to plan a day to visit the Utah Winter Sports Park, as you and your children can take a thrilling (or terrifying, depending on how you look at it) ski-jumping lesson. Lessons begin on small bumps in the snow and progress to a real ski jump by the end of the session. Older kids can try the high-speed bobsled run if they have the nerve.

There are no day-care facilities at the base of the mountain or in town. Parents with small children should arrange for private baby-sitting. The ski school takes children as young as 3.

How to Get There

Park City is 27 miles east of Salt Lake City and a 45-minute drive from Salt Lake City International Airport. Airport shuttle service is easily available. An excellent shuttle-bus system connects the resort with the town and nearby The Canyons and Deer Valley Resort.

Where to Stay
Expensive

Resort Center Lodge has ski-in-and-out condominiums right in the heart of the ski-area base. Steps away are rental shops, ski-fashion and accessories shops, restaurants, and a small grocery store. Accommodations range from hotel rooms to four-bedroom deluxe condos. Some of the units are clustered around an ice-skating rink, and guests enjoy a sauna, a steam room, whirl-pools, and a pool. $215–325. 1415 Lowell Avenue, Park City, UT 84060; 800-824-5331.

Snow Flower has a ski-in-and-out location and units range in size from studios to five bedrooms with a loft. All have fully equipped kitchens.

Within the complex are two heated outdoor pools, laundry facilities, and ski storage. $180–525. 400 Silver King Drive, P.O. Box 957, Park City, UT 84060; 800-852-3101, 801-649-6400.

Radisson Inn Park City serves a complimentary full breakfast to guests during ski season. Standard rooms contain one king-size bed or two queen-size beds and have a minibar, a sitting area, and a table and chairs. Suites have their own small refrigerator. Kids will enjoy the heated indoor pool that has a swim channel leading to an outdoor pool. There are Jacuzzis on both sides. Kids up to 17 stay free in their parents' room, and rollaways are $15 per night. $175–240. 2121 Park Avenue, Park City, UT 84060; 800-333-3333, 801-649-5000.

Moderate

The Inn at Prospector Square is near downtown Park City and is a five-minute shuttle bus ride from the ski resort. It's built around the Prospector Athletic Club and has one-, two-, and three-bedroom condos, studios, and hotel rooms. Guests can buy a daily membership ($7.50) in the athletic facility, making it a great choice for bad-weather days. The separately owned athletic facility has a day-care program, a gymnastics program in the winter, a lap pool, and a Jacuzzi; younger kids must be supervised. $99–199. 2200 Sidewinder Drive, P.O. Box 1698, Park City, UT 84060; 800-453-3812, 801-649-7100.

The Gables Hotel is located just steps from the lifts and the shops and restaurants of the ski-area base. One-bedroom condos all have fireplaces, jetted tubs, and fully equipped kitchens. $160–365 P.O. Box 905, Park City, UT 84060; 800-443-1045, 801-647-3160.

Budget

PowderWood Resort is a little far from the action, which brings the prices down. One- to two-bedroom units are available, all with patios, fireplaces, and fully equipped kitchens. The condos are six miles from Park City, three miles from The Canyons, and eight miles from Deer Valley Resort. Extras include an outdoor pool, indoor and outdoor Jacuzzis, and a free skier shuttle. $110–240. 6979 North 2200 West, Park City, UT 84060; 800-223-7829, 801-649-2032.

Best Western Landmark Inn has simple rooms spacious enough for families. Choices include rooms with a king-size bed and sleeper sofa or two queen-size beds and a sleeper sofa. A more expensive family suite has two bedrooms and two baths. Rollaways and cribs are free, and there's a large indoor heated pool, a game room, a Ping-Pong table, a hot tub, and a Denny's restaurant on-site. $89–250. 6560 North Landmark Drive, Park City, UT 84098; 801-649-7300.

Children's Ski School

Children ages 3 (toilet-trained) to 6 are placed in Kinderschule, which offers a fun-based skiing experience. Parents should note that this is a ski school, not a day-care program. Once children are enrolled, they have a snack and then spend the morning on the snow. At lunchtime they come in, eat, relax and watch a movie, and then go out again for their lesson. Some 3-year-olds may find this difficult, though half-day programs are available.

Youth School group lessons for 7- to 13-year-olds are tailored to both skiers and boarders, who spend most of their day on the snow. The all-day four- or six-hour lesson includes lunch. Half-day lessons are two hours in length; 800-227-2SKI, 801-649-8111 (reservations required).

Day Care

There is no on-mountain day care at Park City, but both Deer Valley Resort (see page 131) and The Canyons have day care at their bases. Creative Beginnings Daycare in Park City is a private facility that operates on weekdays only. They will take drop-ins if they have the space (801-645-7315). Private baby-sitting can be arranged through Guardian Angel Babysitting Service (801-640-1229).

Snowboarding

A terrain garden off the Payday lift is lit at night and open for both skiers and boarders. It features several tabletop jumps, bumps, and berms.

Cross-Country Skiing

White Pines Touring Company has guided tours, or skiers can use their groomed track. Rentals and lessons; 801-649-8701.

The Norwegian School of Nature Life leads guided tours but you must provide your own equipment; 800-649-5322, 801-649-5322.

Other Activities

Hot-air balloon rides arranged by ABC Reservations Central (800-820-ABCD) go out early in the morning to avoid the thermal winds that kick up later in the day. Vans take you to the launch site and pick you up.

Ice skating: The resort center at the mountain base has a small night-lit outdoor rink. Ice skate rentals are available in adjacent shops.

Park City Silver Mine Tour: Put on your hard hat and yellow slicker and descend 1,500 feet into this former silver mine that became a tourist attraction when silver prices dropped. You'll hear real miners tell tales of fortunes found and lost and of the ghosts who reportedly still live in these mines. An exhibition hall has interactive displays, dioramas, photo displays, and mining exhibits. 801-655-7444.

Sleigh rides of all types are available, the most popular of which is the dinner sleigh ride. Guests travel in wooden sleighs pulled by Belgian draft horses over the river and through the woods to a big barn where a western barbecue dinner is served. Reserve through ABC Reservations Central (800-820-ABCD) or Snowdance (801-649-5713).

Snowmobiling: Short guided tours, lunch and dinner tours, and twilight tours are available through ABC Reservations Central (800-820-ABCD) and Park City Snowmobile Adventures (800-303-7256).

Snowshoeing: The Norwegian School of Nature Life (800-649-5322, 801-649-5322) offers evening moonlight tours, intermediate snowshoe tours, and a half-day family tour that includes games and fun activities. Equipment may be rented from White Pine Touring Company (801-649-8701) on Main street in downtown Park City.

Utah Winter Sports Park offers ski-jumping lessons for kids (no minimum age, but intermediate skiing ability is required) and adults, bobsled rides (minimum age 16) that speed up to 75 miles an hour along a mile-long track, and luge rides (kids must be 50 inches tall), which travel much slower but are equally thrilling. If you're lucky you'll see Olympic athletes training on these facilities, which will be used for the 2002 Winter Olympic Games. Be sure to call in advance to find the public-ride schedule. 3000 Bear Hollow Drive, Park City, UT 84060; 801-649-5447.

Deals and Discounts

Park City offers early season rates from opening day (usually early to mid-November) to December 20.

Specials with reduced lift-ticket and lodging prices begin the first week of April and continue until closing.

Snowbird Ski and Summer Resort

Address: Snowbird, Utah 84092

Telephone: 800-453-3000 (central reservations: will book lodging, tickets and ski school), 801-742-2222.

Web site: http://www.snowbird.com

If you're looking for dramatic glacier-cut terrain covered in light, dry, fluffy powder, high-speed lifts, and above-the-treeline skiing, Snowbird is one of the best ski experiences you're likely to find. If you're looking for the alpine village charm of Aspen or the nonski activities of Lake Placid or Park City, strap on your skis and boards somewhere else. Snowbird is known for its awesome expert terrain, and its gravity-defying steeps, chutes, and verticals that challenge the most advanced skiers.

But Snowbird also has a good deal of satisfying intermediate terrain spread across the mountain and a high-speed 125-passenger tram that zips riders to the summit in eight minutes. The tram separates an enormous back bowl into two cavernous ski bowls, with numerous groomed and ungroomed trails leading down. You'll often find half a slope groomed to silky perfection and the other side left untouched for the powder hounds and mogul meisters. Recent masters of the snowplow may find Snowbird's terrain a bit too steep for comfort.

Located in Little Cottonwood Canyon, famous for its 500-plus inches of powder, Snowbird is just a mile down the road from Alta Ski Area (see page 127). The compact base village has condominiums and the Cliff Lodge, all a few steps from the slopes. The day-care center operates from inside the Cliff Lodge. Everything a skier might want

MOUNTAIN STATISTICS

Base elevation: 8,100 feet
Summit: 11,000 feet
Vertical drop: 3,240 feet
Skiable acres: 2,500
Annual average snowfall: 500 inches
Snowmaking: some
Night skiing: on one beginner run
Season: mid-November through early May
Lifts: 9 (1 125-person aerial tram, 1 high-speed quad, 7 doubles)
Terrain: 25% beginner, 30% intermediate, 45% advanced
Lift tickets: adults $47, kids 12 and under free on chairlifts.

FAMILY STATISTICS

Day care: Camp Snowbird, 6 weeks to 12 years; 801-742-2222, ext. 5026
Children's lessons: Camp Snowbird, ages 3 to 15, 801-742-2222, ext. 5170
Baby-sitting: Available through Camp Snowbird; 801-742-2222, ext. 5026
Medical: Alta View Hospital in Sandy 801-576-2600. Snowbird Medical clinic 801-742-2222 ext. 4195

can be found at the Snowbird Center: 12 restaurants, shops, a post office, the ski school, a medical clinic, and a pharmacy. You won't need a car. A shuttle system runs you around the resort; you can also shuttle to Alta.

Snowbird is a terrific buy for families. Two kids (under 12) ski free with each adult purchasing an all-day ticket and kids under 12 stay free in their parents' room. The day-care program takes care of children from 2 months to 12 years and a "Kids Club" held every Friday night from mid-December through March offers dinner, live entertainment, and craft activities for 3- to 10-year-olds.

How to Get There

The nearest international airport is the Salt Lake City International Airport, 29 miles away. Canyon Transportation (800-255-1841) runs regular shuttles from the airport. The resort is 25 miles from downtown Salt Lake City.

Where to Stay

Moderate to expensive

The Cliff Lodge dominates the base village with its imposing 11-story-high stone facade. It boasts 500 rooms, a 25-meter outdoor swimming pool for families, shops, restaurants, cafés, a day-care facility, a ski shop and ski storage, a lift-ticket office, a ski-school office, and valet parking. A glamorous full-service spa on the top story is enclosed by soaring glass windows that look out onto breathtaking views of the mountain peaks for those enjoying the swimming pool and hot tubs. The spa facility is for adults only. Spacious hotel rooms have two queen-size beds or one king-size bed, and some rooms connect; one-and two-bedroom suites are also available. All offer views of the slopes or the mountains. $209–879. P.O. Box 92900, Snowbird UT 84092; 800-453-3000, 801-742-2222, ext. 5000.

The Lodge at Snowbird, The Inn, and *Iron Blosam* are condo units within a few steps of the lifts. Ranging in size from studios to two bedrooms, all have full kitchens and stone fireplaces; many also have sofa sleepers in the living room. Families shop for groceries in Salt Lake before they arrive, or at the small market in the Snowbird Center, the main base area. The bellman will give you rides to the Cliff Lodge if you have little ones who are enrolled in the nursery or ski school. Each condo cluster has its own restaurant. $195–615. ext. 1000. P.O. Box 92900, Snowbird UT 84092; 800-453-3000, 801-742-2222.

Budget

Wasatch Front Ski Accommodations (800-762-7606) represents condos at the opening of both canyons, near markets and other convenient stores. The ski shuttle stops at some of their properties. Most families from out of town fly in and rent cars at the airport.

Children's Ski School

Children under 5 spend part of the day in Camp Snowbird at The Cliff Lodge and are picked up by ski instructors for their lesson. Chickadee lessons for 3- and 4-year-olds pairs two children of similar abilities with one instructor for a 90-minute lesson. Children ages 5 to 15 take Child and Teen Mountain Adventures, which include lessons, lunch, pizza parties, cookie races, and supervision from 9 A.M. to 4 P.M. Instruction is offered in both alpine skiing and snowboarding. Afternoon-only sessions are also an option. A three-hour beginners-only night lesson includes a lift ticket, instruction, and equipment rental; 801-742-2222, ext. 5170.

Day Care

The Cliff Lodge nursery can accommodate 35 infants and toddlers with a staff to child ratio of three to one for infants and four to one for toddlers. The cheerful and cozy infant area and nap rooms are separate from the several toddler rooms. Make reservations at the time you book your lodging, because this popular program fills up quickly; 801-742-2222, ext. 5026.

Camp Snowbird is for 3-to 12-year-olds who don't ski. Their activities—arts and crafts, parties, videos, and entertainment—take place in the same vicinity as the nursery; 801-742-2222, ext. 5026.

Snowboarding

The resort's terrain has natural snowboarding features with all kinds of hits and jumps. Snowboarders have access to all runs.

Cross-Country Skiing

No cross-country skiing is available in Little Cottonwood Canyon, but visitors with a car can drive to Solitude Nordic Center (see page 145) in Big Cottonwood Canyon next door or to Park City Mountain Resort (see page 136), a little farther down the road.

Other Activities

The Cliff Spa & Salon is a luxurious full-service indoor spa open to the public on the roof level of The Cliff Lodge. It offers every spa treatment imaginable, and there's a swimming pool overlooking a panoramic mountain vista, spas, hot tubs, and steam rooms; 801-742-2222, ext. 5900.

Explorer Utah is an adventure lecture series offered different nights throughout the season. Topics include avalanche control, mountaineering, and slide shows on a host of subjects. Schedules are posted throughout the resort; 801-742-2222, ext. 4080.

Warren Miller ski films are shown at the resort throughout the ski season. Check the schedules posted throughout the resort.

Deals and Discounts
Stay in budget lodging in Sandy (the town closest to the entrance to Little Cottonwood Canyon) or in Salt Lake City and take a shuttle to the resort. Since two kids ski free (except the tram, which costs $8 per child 12 and under) with one paying parent, large families love this resort.

A special package for visitors staying early in the season offers substantial savings on lift tickets, and ground transportation plus special air inclusive early week discount packages are also available.

Solitude and Brighton Ski Resorts

Address: Solitude: 1200 Big Cottonwood Canyon, Solitude, Utah 84121. Brighton: Star Route, Brighton, Utah 84121

Telephone: Solitude 800-748-4754, 801-534-5777; Brighton 800-873-5512, 801-532-4731

www address: http://www.skisolitude.com and http://www.skibrighton.com

Solitude and Brighton are a couple of miles away from each other in Big Cottonwood Canyon, about 25 miles from Salt Lake City and just over the mountains from Little Cottonwood Canyon where Snowbird and Alta are located. Both offer bountiful quantities of the fluffy dry powder snow for which these two canyons have become famous. They're smaller than some of the other Utah giants, but have plenty of excellent terrain for all levels of skiers and offer an excellent value for families.

Solitude is the larger of the two and has recently completed phase one of a sophisticated base village plan. A new condo/hotel, The Creekside at Solitude, and inn, The Village at Solitude, have been designed in the style of the great ski lodges of Vail. Virtually any size family can be accommodated in style with ski-in-and-out access to the slopes. Several restaurants (all with children's menus), shops, and a movie theater showing nightly films and offering complimentary popcorn are for Inn and Creekside guests' enjoyment. Solitude has a night-lit luge run.

Brighton is a bit quieter in the evening, although it offers excellent night skiing on 200 acres throughout most of the season. There is a small lodge a few steps from the lifts that has the lowest prices of any ski-in-ski-out accommodations anywhere.

MOUNTAIN STATISTICS: SOLITUDE
Base elevation: 7,988 feet
Vertical drop: 2,047 feet
Summit: 10,035 feet
Skiable acres: 1,200
Annual average snowfall: 470 inches
Snowmaking: 144 acres, 5 lifts
Night skiing: night-lit luge run
Season: early November through late April
Lifts: 7 (1 high speed quad, four doubles, 2 triples)
Terrain: 30% beginner, 50% intermediate, 20% expert
Lift tickets: adults $36; kids 10 and under and seniors over 70 ski free; seniors age 60 to 69, $29.

Both resorts allow children under 10 to ski free, and the lift ticket prices for adults are a throwback to the prices of several decades ago. Neither resort has day-care facilities, but both have children's ski and snowboarding schools.

MOUNTAIN STATISTICS: BRIGHTON
Base elevation: 8,755 feet
Vertical drop: 1,745 feet
Summit: 10,500 feet
Skiable acres: 850
Snowfall: 430 inches
Snowmaking: 200 acres
Night skiing: 200 acres from mid-December to early April, Monday through Saturday
Season: early November to late April
Lifts: 7 (2 high speed quads, 2 triples, 3 doubles)
Terrain: 21% beginner, 40% intermediate, 39% advanced
Lift Tickets: adults $29 (until 4 P.M.), $35 9 A.M. to 9 P.M.; kids under ten and seniors over 70 free. $20 for night skiing 4 to 9 P.M.

FAMILY STATISTICS
Day care: There is no day care at either resort
Children's lessons: Solitude Moonbeam Academy ages 5 to 12, 800-748-4754; Brighton Kinderski, ages 4 to 7, 801-532-4731, ext. 234.
Baby-sitting: At Solitude, the front desk at the inn keeps a list of baby-sitters. No baby-sitting is available at Brighton.
Medical: Alta View Hospital in Sandy, 801-576-2600

Brighton has become known as a snowboarders' mountain and has one of the continent's best natural snowboard park, Mount Millicent, with bumps, jumps, rollers, half pipes, and quarter pipes. Solitude is one of the few resorts to offer lessons for all ages in four disciplines, downhill skiing, snowboarding, Nordic and telemark skiing. Both offer tremendously varied terrain, immaculately groomed runs, and few lift lines.

How to Get There

Solitude is 33 miles from the Salt Lake International Airport and 23 miles from Salt Lake City, about a 45-minute drive from either place. Brighton is 2 miles farther down the road.

Where to Stay

Wasatch Front Ski Accommodations handles condo and private home rentals near the mouths of Big Cottonwood canyon where Solitude and Brighton Ski areas are found. Condos range in size from studios to four bedrooms and some are on the city's ski shuttle bus line. 2020 East 3300 South, Suite 23, Salt Lake City, UT 84109; 800-762-7606, 801-486-4296.

Expensive

The Creekside at Solitude has luxury condominiums with one, two, or three bedrooms; prices include continental buffet breakfast. Units have fireplaces, fully equipped kitchens, marble bathrooms, VCRs, wet bars, and underground parking. Video rentals are complimentary. Guests can use The Inn's spa and fitness facility. $310–580. 800-748-4754, 801-536-5704.

The Inn at Solitude is an elegant ski-in-and-out hotel designed with rough stone walls and flooring, rustic wood paneling and plush furnishings. Rooms have coffeemakers, VCRs, and mini refrigerators. A few suite-style rooms have kitchenettes. Guests enjoy the use of a library, heated swimming pool and Jacuzzi, ski lockers, child care, movie theater, complimentary video rentals and laundry rooms. $180–235. 12000 Big Cottonwood Canyon, Solitude, UT 84121; 800-748-4754.

Moderate
Silver Fork Lodge is one mile below Solitude; staying here allows you to sample both ski areas. It's a rustic log lodge with lumberjack-size breakfasts (espresso bar, too) and delicious dinners. A family suite with a queen in one room and bunks in the other has a private bath, and other rooms and rollaways are available. The downstairs "family room" has a TV, videos, and games. There are no TVs in guest rooms. $80–160. Star Route, Brighton, UT 84121; 801-649-9551.

Inexpensive
Brighton Lodge has 20 rather cozy rooms. Kids 10 and under stay free in a room with their parents. Star Route, Brighton, UT 84121; 800-873-5512, ext. 236.

Comfort Inn in Sandy, at the mouth of the Big and Little Cottonwood Canyons, offers free continental breakfast to guests. Rooms have two queen-size beds but no kitchens. Children under 18 stay free in their parents' room. $69–80. 8955 South 255 West, Sandy, UT 84070; 800-228-5150, 801-255-4919.

The Sleep Inn in South Jordan, a little farther from the canyon mouth, has rooms with two double beds; a few rooms have microwave ovens and small refrigerators. Children under 18 stay free in their parent's room, and guests enjoy the free continental breakfast and an indoor pool. $69–80. 10676 South 300 West, South Jordan, UT 84095; 800-627-5337, 801-572-2020.

Children's Ski School
Solitude: The Moonbeam Ski Academy combines fun on the snow with ski and snowboarding skills. Children can start at age 5 and up. Snowboarding starts at age 8. The 3- and 4-year olds have their own special programs. Children ages 5 and up are grouped by age and then ability. Kids adore the Norwegian Troll Theme terrain park and its little jumps and bumps, as well as the yurt stop for hot chocolate. Full-day and afternoon

classes are available. Teens are grouped together whenever possible, especially at holiday periods. 800-748-4754.

Brighton: The Kinderski program starts children as young as four and groups kids in classes of six or less. The resort tries to get children riding the lifts as quickly as possible—over 90% ride their first day on skis. The Kinderski Bear highlights lessons in selected locations on the learners' hill. Children over age 7 go into adult lessons. Kids over 7 go into regular adult group lessons. Children who want to snowboard and who are 8 and up take regular snowboard lesson. Younger ones may take private snowboard lessons.

Day Care

Not available at either resort.

Snowboarding

Both resorts welcome snowboarders. Brighton's snowboard park has a variety of hits and jumps.

Cross-Country Skiing

The *Solitude Nordic Center* offers 20 kilometers of trails and is the only cross-country skiing facility in the canyon. It has ski rentals (including children's sizes), lessons, and guided backcountry tours. If you have your own skis you can ski from the base lodge. Otherwise, complimentary transportation is offered to the center from the Main Lodge. You can cross country ski (or snowshoe) to the Yurt for a gourmet dinner; reservations required. 800-748-4SKI, ext. 5709.

Other Activities

Snowshoe or ski cross country through the woods to the Yurt for dinner. Equipment is available at the Solitude Nordic Center; 801-536-5709.

Dinner sleigh rides to the Roundhouse Restaurant mid-mountain are available at Solitude on selected evenings during the ski season; 801-536-5709.

Luge rides, really modernized sledding, are offered at Solitude at night off the Easy Street Run off the Link Lift; 801-536-5709.

Deals and Discounts

VIP lift tickets that can save you a little money on daily lift tickets are sold at ski shops and grocery stores in the Salt Lake Area.

   Great Snow Weeks at Brighton offer discounted lift tickets, lodging at the Brighton Lodge, and a continental breakfast if you stay four days or more.

The Rest of the West

Sun Valley Resort

Address: Sun Valley Road, Sun Valley, Idaho 83353
Telephone: 800-786-8259, 208-622-4111
Web site: http://www.sunvalley.com

Ever since Averell Harriman convinced Hollywood glitterati to visit in the 1930s and '40s, Sun Valley's pedigree as a resort of the rich and famous has continued. While many of the nouveau riche choose Aspen and Telluride, Sun Valley delivers the total ski experience with a sheen of understated elegance. Three stunning world-class day lodges have been added, two at the ski-resort base and one mid-mountain. The massive timber-beam-and-stone lodges are magnificent structures, and their stylish cafeterias offer the best food of its kind in the ski world.

Then there's the skiing. Sun Valley is the Energizer Bunny of ski areas: Its spectacular long, flowing runs keep on going and going and going. Lift systems are fast and efficient, and the fact that there are only 7,000 beds in the base area around Ketchum and an lift capacity of more than 28,000 skiers per hour means that lift lines are nearly nonexistent and the slopes aren't crowded. Broad-coverage snowmaking and more sunny days round it out.

Sun Valley is made up of several distinct areas linked by an efficient shuttle-bus system. The ski mountain has two base lodges; the largest one, River Run Lodge, accommodates the children's ski school, ski-rental shop, a restaurant and lounge, and has condos a short walk away. Warm Springs Lodge is several miles away from River Run by car, but accessible on skis; it's smaller and is flanked by a few condominiums. A third grand lodge, Seattle Ridge Lodge, is mid-mountain. Sun Valley Village, a few miles from the ski area, is a small community centered around

MOUNTAIN STATISTICS
Base elevation: 5,750 feet
Summit: 9,150 feet
Vertical drop: 3,400 feet
Skiable acres: 2,054
Annual average snowfall: 184 inches
Snowmaking: 630 acres
Night skiing: none
Season: late November to late April
Lifts: 17 (7 high-speed quads, 5 triples, 5 doubles)
Terrain: 36% beginner, 42% intermediate, 22% advanced
Lift tickets: adults $52, children 12 and under $29.

FAMILY STATISTICS
Day care: Sun Valley Playschool, 6 months to 6 years, 208-662-2288
Children's lessons: Ski School, 3 to 12 years, 208-622-2248
Baby-sitting: A list is available from the Sun Valley Playschool, 208-662-2288
Baby gear: Baby's Away rents cribs, high chairs, strollers, car seats, toys, and other items, 208-788-7852
Medical: Wood River Medical Center, Sun Valley, 208-622-3333

the still glamorous Sun Valley Lodge. Connected to the lodge by footpaths are the day-care center, an outdoor ice-skating rink, two heated outdoor swimming pools, a variety of condos, shops, and restaurants, a small movie theater, and the Sun Valley Inn. Dollar Mountain is the resort's separate beginner's ski area which has its own children's ski school. One mile away is the former cattle ranching and mining town of Ketchum, with a main street lined with restaurants, bars, and shops. Most guests stay in the Sun Valley Village or in Ketchum because there is more to do.

How to Get There

Visitors can fly into Friedman Memorial Airport, 11 miles south of Ketchum, or into Boise or Twin Falls. Driving times: Boise, 2.5 hours (160 miles); Twin Falls, 1.5 hours (85 miles).

Once you're there, Ketchum Area Rapid Transit (KART) offers free shuttle-bus service between the two Sun Valley bases, the Sun Valley Resort area, Dollar Mountain, and Ketchum.

Where to Stay

There are many private homes to rent throughout Sun Valley, but it can be more fun to stay in the Sun Valley Resort area so you can walk to the shops, restaurants, ice-skating rink, and movie theater. It's a safe and self-contained community that older kids can explore on their own.

Expensive

Sun Valley Lodge is the premier property in the Valley. Its rooms are sumptuously appointed with Laura Ashley fabrics, dark woods, and Oriental rugs. Hallway photo displays remind guests of the rich and famous who have stayed here, and create a timeline of ski fashions and equipment. Common rooms are large and elegant, and waiters in the lodge dining room even wear white gloves. Several room types are available, including a spacious suite for families. Amenities include a ski-storage room, sauna, beauty salon, and a bowling alley in the basement. $139–329. Sun Valley Road, Sun Valley, ID 83353; 800-786-8259, 208-622-4111.

Wildflower Condominiums are found right next door to the Sun Valley Lodge amid small groves of spruce and aspen trees. One- to three-bedroom units are available, and all have fireplaces, high ceilings, and fully equipped kitchens. The decor can vary from '70s "ski lodge" to French provincial, as these units are individually owned. There's convenient access to all Sun Valley Lodge amenities. $139–399. Sun Valley Road, Sun Valley ID 83353; 800-786-8258, 208-622-4111.

Sun Valley Inn was originally built in 1937 to handle the overflow from the Lodge. Its public rooms have a more utilitarian feel, and its cafeteria serves standard fare, but its guest rooms are attractively decorated with fine furniture and fabrics. $99–169. Sun Valley Road, Sun Valley ID 83353; 800-786-8259, 208-622-4111.

Penray's at River Run, at the base of the River Run ski area, has one- and two-bedroom units with modern furnishings. All units have their own fireplaces, one bathroom per bedroom, and—best of all—their own washer and dryer. $201–399. P.O. Box 1298, Sun Valley, ID 83353; 800-736-7503, 208-726-9086.

Warm Springs Resort Condominiums are within walking distance of the Warms Springs Lodge. Units are in several different buildings and vary quite a bit in size and layout. Studios and one-, two-, three-, and four-bedroom condos are available. All guests can use the outdoor heated pool and hot tub. $115–600. P.O. Box 10009, Ketchum, ID 83340; 800-635-4404, 208-726-8274.

Moderate
Tamarack Lodge is located in downtown Ketchum, and its rooms are spacious, clean, and contemporary. All standard rooms have microwaves, refrigerators, and coffeemakers, while the suites have complete kitchenettes. There's an indoor pool and an outdoor hot tub. $89–145. 491 Walnut Avenue, Ketchum, ID; Mailing address: Box 2000, Sun Valley, ID 83353; 800-521-5379, 208-726-3344.

Budget
Christiana Lodge: This Best Western in the middle of Ketchum has rooms with two queen-size or double beds and tiny kitchenettes. Larger suites have king-size beds, fireplaces, and larger kitchens. The shuttle bus stops right outside the front door. $64–95. P.O. Box 2196, 651 Sun Valley Road, Ketchum, ID 83340; 800-535-3241, 208-726-3351.

Children's Ski School
Sun Valley uses the SKIwee method of instruction for both young skiers and boarders. Children's Ski School instruction for beginners takes place at Dollar Mountain, 1.5 miles from the River Run base lodge. Intermediate and advanced lesson for kids meet at the main mountain at River Run. If you have children of different abilities, you can register them at the same

time at the River Run Lodge, and your beginners will be bused with their instructors the short distance to Dollar.

Day Care

Sun Valley Playschool (208-662-2288) is in the Sun Valley Resort area near the Lodge and Inn. Kids from 6 months to 6 years are cared for in a cozy setting that resembles a cottage. Toddlers enjoy indoor and outdoor play and sledding. Children 3 and 4 years old enjoy indoor and outdoor play, creative art, movies, sledding, and ice skating. Parents can opt for a one-hour Tiny Track ski lesson for an extra fee.

Snowboarding

The entire mountain is open to boarders with the exception of two runs in the Seattle Ridge area, which is for skiers only. There is no official snowboard park, but plenty of terrain features enable snowboarders to carve awesome turns and catch big air.

Cross-Country Skiing

Sun Valley Nordic Center (208-622-2250) near Sun Valley Lodge has 40 kilometers of groomed and marked trails. Its ski school offers lessons, ski rental, and a waxing room. Special children's tracks have been set throughout the children's terrain garden and alongside the adult tracks.

Other Activities

Bowling: There is an alley (208-622-4111) in the basement of the Sun Valley Lodge where the public is invited to play.

Paragliding: When the weather is good, glider rides take off over Bald Mountain and head into the surrounding backcountry. 208-788-3054.

Ice skating: The Sun Valley Skating Center (208-622-2194, general info; 208-622-2192, skating school) has a 180-by-90-foot outdoor ice rink open to the public over the winter. An indoor rink is open if it's not used for hockey games. Both are next to the Sun Valley Lodge.

Sleigh rides: Huge draft horses from Trail Creek Cabin Sleigh Rides (208-622-2319) pull riders snuggled in blankets to a lovely log cabin where dinner is served.

Snowshoeing: The Nordic Center rents snowshoes (kids size available) and feature trails that are designated for snowshoers only. 208-622-2250.

Deals and Discounts

The "Kids Stay and Ski Free Program" is offered early season, from Thanksgiving to Christmas during the month of January, and again late in the season mid-March to end of the season. Children can stay and ski free in a Sun Valley Company property as long as they stay in their parents' room and their parent purchases a lift ticket. The offer is limited to one child (15 years and under) per parent. 800-786-8259.

❄ Big Sky Ski and Summer Resort

Address: P.O. Box 160001, Big Sky, Montana 59716
Telephone: 800-548-4486 (central reservations), 406-995-5806
Web site: http://www.bigskyresort.com

Even on holiday weekends you hear the refrain, "Where is everybody?" at Big Sky. Despite the opening of the tram to the top of Lone Peak that put Big Sky in the gold-medal position for highest vertical drop in the United States, the ski area remains underpopulated and unspoiled. It doesn't hurt that Big Sky is surrounded by millions of acres of wilderness in southwestern Montana. Chet Huntley acquired Big Sky and another 10,000 acres of breathtaking wilderness in the early 1970s. The border of vast Yellowstone National Park is 18 miles away and its west-entrance gate is 47 miles away. Another huge stretch of land, the Spanish Peaks Wilderness Area, sits just to the resort's north. All work to protect Big Sky's remote quality.

Visitors fly in to Bozeman, about 50 miles away, and can shuttle or drive to Big Sky Mountain Village, which looks slightly utilitarian but has everything visitors might want—a hotel, condominiums, day care, restaurants, and a few shops—for a family ski vacation. As you move farther from the base of the mountain, the price of accommodations drops accordingly. A shuttle takes visitors who stay farther away to and from the ski area.

In addition to claiming fame as the new king of vertical, the installation of the Lone Peak Tram has opened up hundreds of acres of advanced, expert, and extreme terrain. Three above-the-treeline-bowls and a series of wicked chutes with pitches of 50 degrees

MOUNTAIN STATISTICS

Base elevation: 6,970 feet
Summit: 11,166 feet
Vertical drop: 4,180 feet
Skiable acres: 3,500
Annual average snowfall: 400 inches
Snowmaking: 220 acres (20% of trails)
Night skiing: none
Season: mid-November to mid-April
Lifts: 15 (1 tram, 1 gondola, 3 high-speed quads, 1 regular quad, 3 triples, 3 doubles, 3 surface lifts)
Terrain: 10% beginners, 47% intermediate, 43% advanced
Lift tickets: adults $47, juniors 11 to 16 $40, kids 10 and under free, seniors 70 and over $24.

FAMILY STATISTICS

Day care: Big Sky Playcare Center, 406-995-2828
Children's lessons: Ski Camp, ages 4 to 14
Baby-sitting: The concierge at 406-995-5806 can provide a list of names.
Medical: Bozeman Deaconess Hospital, 406-585-5000

thrill the advanced skier. If you find yourself at the top and don't want to ski down, you can always enjoy the view and take the tram. Intermediates may want to avoid the new chutes and nasty coloirs, but the overall mountain is designed to please middle-of-the-road skiers. Nearly 50 percent of the runs are ranked intermediate, many of them scrupulously groomed.

Children are catered to with a full range of lessons and day care. Youngsters 10 and under can ski free when an accompanying adult purchases a lift ticket. An excellent cross-country venue, Lone Mountain Ranch, is worth a stay in its own right.

Short lifts lines, fast lifts, and long verticals equal a lot of skiing in one day—better make sure your legs are ready. Maybe it's a good thing that the nightlife is on the sleepy side and restaurants are few. You'll be in bed with the babies.

How to Get There
Gallatin Field Airport in Bozeman is served by Delta, Northwest, Horizon, and Skywest airlines. Bozeman is about an hour's drive (48 miles) from Big Sky.

Where to Stay
Expensive
Huntley Lodge is right at the heart of the Mountain Village. All children 10 and under stay free at the Lodge. Guests enjoy a complimentary breakfast. Rooms have two or three queen-size beds, a wet bar, a small refrigerator, and a coffeemaker. Two lounge areas have fireplaces, and there's a dining room and a bar with live entertainment on most nights. Other features include heated outdoor pools, saunas, ski storage, a theater, a game room, and shops. $129–325. Lone Mountain Trail, Big Sky, P.O. Box 160001, Big Sky, MT 59716; 800-548-4486, 406-995-5000.

Shoshone Condominium Hotel, attached to the Huntley Lodge, is considered among the more luxurious of the ski-in-and-out condos around the base. One-bedroom and one-bedroom-with-loft units have fireplaces and full kitchens. The concierge can make arrangements for a variety of recreational activities, including your ski-lift tickets. $242–512. Lone Mountain Trail, Big Sky, P.O. Box 160001, Big Sky, MT 59716; 800-548-4486, 406-995-5000.

Beaverhead is another group of deluxe ski-in-and-out condominiums, ranging in size from two bedrooms to four bedrooms plus a loft. They're quiet since they're set back from the road. Each beautifully decorated condo (most have a western motif) has its own full-size Jacuzzi and washer and dryer. $341–755. Lone Mountain Trail, Big Sky, P.O. Box 160008, Big Sky, MT 59716; 800-548-4486, 406-995-4800.

Moderate
Stillwater condos are about a five-minute walk from the lifts. Studio units have a sleeper sofa or a Murphy bed, one-bedroom units can sleep up to four people, and both the one-bedroom-with-loft and the two-bedroom units can sleep up to six people. All come with fireplaces and full kitchens. $120–325. P.O. Box 160008, Big Sky, MT 59716; 800-548-4488, 406-995-4800.

Budget
Golden Eagle Lodge is in Meadow Village about six miles from the slopes and right on the shuttle-bus line. Formerly a hostel, two different room types offer simple comfort and great affordability. Families with very young children (under 7 or 8) can take a room with a queen-size or double bed and a set of bunks. These rooms are small, and no more than two adults are allowed in them, but one or two young children are permitted. Suites consist of three rooms: The center room is a sitting room and the two outer rooms are sleeping rooms, one with a double bed, the other with a combination of twin and bunk beds. All rooms have TVs and private baths but no telephone. A restaurant on the premises serves Mexican and Italian food. Children 10 and under stay free. $45–110. Little Coyote Road, P.O. Box 4800, Big Sky, MT 59716; 800-548-4488, 406-995-4800.

Silver Bow is in Meadow Village, about six miles from the slopes. Its rustic condos have one to three bedrooms with fireplaces and full kitchens. $105–675. Black Otter Road, P.O. Box 160008, Big Sky, MT 59716; 800-548-4488, 406-995-4800.

Children's Ski School
Ski Camp is for children ages 4 to 14 who are divided for their lessons by age and ability. Younger kids ages 3 or 4 may want to combine Ski Camp with the Handprints Daycare Center. Small Fry Try is an introductory program for 3 to 5 year olds who are trying skiing for the first time. Mini-camp is for 4 to 5 year olds. Ski Camp for 6 to 14 year olds takes place in morning or afternoon sessions. Because many of Big Sky's guests visit for a week, activities such as treasure hunts, ice cream socials, scavenger hunts, and a race day are planned throughout the week.

The Shredders Program is designed for 14 to 16 year olds who cruise the mountain with ski camp guides. Groups are divided by ability.

Day Care

Important!!! Montana State Law requires that all children in group care programs be inoculated. That means you MUST bring (or fax to 406-995-5848) your child's current immunization record. You can also request health record forms be sent or faxed to you in advance.

Handprints Daycare on the Mountain, located on the second level of the Snowcrest Lodge, takes children from infants to 6 year olds. Infants under 18 months require a five-day advance reservation and have a special room designed just for their needs. Children 18 months and older have their own special play room, plus an outdoor play area. They enjoy a small library, an art station and a quiet time corner plus lots of bright toys. 406-995-5847.

Snowboarding

Big Sky's natural terrain offers plenty of hits and jumps. The opening of the tram has given boarders access to vast stretches of untracked powder. A popular nature-made half pipe is found on Lower Morning Star. The resort's "Fun Park" featuring little jumps and dips is found under the Swift Current Quad chair.

Cross-Country Skiing

Lone Mountain Ranch is a cross-country skiers' paradise that offers 65 kilometers of professionally groomed trails. Guests stay in cabins and a ridgepole lodge. 800-514-4644, 406-995-4644.

The West Yellowstone Entrance to this national park has cross-country skiing as well. For information, call the National Park Office at 307-344-7381.

Other Activities

Bozeman Hot Springs Pool (406-586-6492) is a 90-foot indoor spring-fed swimming pool.

Yellowstone tours: Yellowstone Alpen Guides (406-649-9591) offers daily winter tours.

Dogsled rides, 406-995-3424.

Sleigh rides: Take a sleigh ride through the wilderness to a log cabin where meals are cooked on a 100-year-old stove. A fun singalong follows dinner at the Lone Mountain Ranch; 800-514-4644, 406-995-4644.

Snowmobiling: west Yellowstone: Rendezvous, 800-426-7669.

Winter fly-fishing: Grossenbacher Guides, 406-582-1760.

Deals and Discounts

Two kids under age 10 ski free with the purchase of one adult lift ticket.

Save up to 40% on lifts and lodging during Great Ski weeks and Super Saver Weeks from opening to December 24, and approximately March 30 to closing.

❄ Taos Ski Valley

Address: P.O. Box 90, Taos Ski Valley, New Mexico 87525
Telephone: 800-776-1111, 505-776-2291 (reservations)
Web site: http://www.taoswebb.com/skitaos

Desert-dry powder, legendary steeps, and strikingly sunny weather cast a spell on skiers who visit Taos, one of the southernmost ski resort in the United States. And it isn't just the skiing that makes Taos a draw: The history and culture that this area radiates brings visitors back again and again. Maybe it's the quality of the light and the way the sun falls on the Sangre de Cristo Range, the southernmost outcropping of the Rocky Mountains, that has attracted artists for over 100 years. Taos is cut off by these mountains from the high desert terrain surrounding it, and the arid climate and its special weather conditions create snow famed for its fluffy texture.

Ski-resort founder Ernie Blake created an alpine ski village like those he remembered from his native Switzerland. Taos has a distinctly Euro-alpine feel, but with a southwestern twist. The resort remains family owned and operated, and it's one of the last resorts that does *not* allow snowboarding—either a big bonus or disappointing omission, depending on your preferences.

Taos's ski school is consistently ranked one of the best in the country, partly due to the quality of the instructors. Because Taos's advanced terrain is so fierce, many highly experienced skiers take lessons when they arrive, in part to get ski tips for the mountain. More than half of the Taos terrain is advanced, and about half of those expert runs are double-black diamond, the steepest and bumpiest of all. Intermediates should ask a red-jacketed mountain host to point them in the best direction for trails they'll enjoy.

MOUNTAIN STATISTICS
Base elevation: 9,207 feet
Summit: 11,819 feet
Vertical drop: 2,612 feet
Skiable acres: 1,100
Annual average snowfall: 320 inches
Snowmaking: 95% of beginner and intermediate terrain
Season: late November to mid-April
Nightskiing: none
Lifts: 11 (4 quads, 1 triple, 5 doubles, 1 surface lift)
Terrain: 24% beginner, 25% intermediate, 51% advanced
Lift tickets: adults $40, teens 13 to 16 $30, children 3 to 12, and seniors 65 to 69 $25, over 70 and under 3 free.

FAMILY STATISTICS
Day care: Kinderkare, 6 weeks to 2 years; 505-776-2291, ext. 1332
Children's lessons: 505-776-2291, ext. 1334 (ages 3 to 5); 505-776-2291, ext. 1335 (ages 6 to 12)
Baby-sitting: Ski school and day care staff keep a list of employees who are willing to baby-sit; 505-776-2291, ext. 1332 or 1334
Medical: Holy Cross Hospital in Taos, 505-758-8883

Intermediate and beginner runs are smoothed and groomed, but they can sometimes be steeper than similarly ranked runs in other areas. There are beginner runs from the top of every lift, so the novices in your family will be comfortable no matter where they ski. A separate beginner's area is served by three different lifts, two small chairlifts, and a poma. Once you can ski Strawberry Hill, the most difficult of the beginner runs, you can head up the mountain and ski green runs anywhere.

The 18,000-square-foot children's center, Kinderkäfig, is right on the slopes. Here you will find the children's ski school, ticket counters, children's ski rentals, and a kid's ski-accessories shop. There's also a day-care program for children 6 weeks to 3 years old.

The town of Taos, 18 miles down the road from the ski area, was founded in the seventeenth century by Spanish settlers who headquartered near the Taos Pueblo. Native Americans have lived in the multitiered adobe Taos Pueblo for 1,000 years, and it is still much the same as it was centuries ago. Some of the traditional ceremonial dances performed here are open to the public.

Georgia O'Keeffe helped create Taos' legendary reputation as a haven for artists and art lovers. The town's 88 art galleries and seven museums featuring fine arts, fine crafts, and furnishings, showcase the town's artistic leanings. More than 50 restaurants range from simple pizza joints and Northern New Mexican cafés to sophisticated continental establishments.

Taos's historical district is centered on the town's main plaza, where you will see beautifully preserved homes and historic buildings, notably the original county courthouse and jail. If your family includes nonskiers, stay in town and shuttle to the ski area or if you have a car and need to save money, stay just outside of the historical district.

How to Get There

Albuquerque International Airport is 150 miles away, about a 2½-hour drive. Amtrak (from Chicago and Los Angeles) stops in Albuquerque. Shuttles are available, but rental cars are helpful in case you want to visit the fascinating city of Santa Fe on your way in or out. Shuttle service is available from The Pride of Taos (505-758-8340) or Faust's Transportation (505-758-3410). Driving times: Santa Fe, 1.5 hours (70 miles); Albuquerque, 2½ hours (130 miles).

Where to Stay
Expensive
Thunderbird Lodge and Chalet is just 100 yards from the main ski lifts and has special amenities for families. Every night a supervised dinner is

offered at 5:30 P.M. followed by a movie. Parents sit down for dinner at 6:30 P.M. at this American-plan resort (three meals a day are included in the rates). Lunch is served in the dining room, or you can arrange a picnic on the slopes. Each night offers different entertainment, such as country-western dance lessons, live country music, and talent nights for the kids. Families get rooms with a double bed and bunk bed or with a double bed and twin beds. Children under 13 stay free in their parents' room. Per adult: $101–185. #3 Thunderbird Road, P.O. Box 87, Taos Ski Valley, NM 87525; 800-776-2279, 505-776-2280.

St. Bernard Condominiums have a European flair and are some of the plushest condos around the ski area. All have two bedrooms and two baths, fireplaces and full kitchens, and are a five-minute walk from the lifts. The restaurant in their sister hotel (Hotel St. Bernard) has a children's menu and entertainment for the kids. By the week only, $1,800–2,600. #15 Twining Road, P.O. Box 676, Taos Ski Valley, NM 87525; 888-306-4135, 505-776-8506.

Alpine Village Suites features elegant one-bedroom suites that can sleep up to four people. They have small kitchenettes, balconies, fireplaces, and hand-carved furniture. In addition there's covered valet parking, ski lockers, massage facilities, and an outdoor hot-tub deck. The property is two minutes from the lifts and tucked into a private cluster of evergreens between two mountain streams. $145–269. P.O. Box 917, Taos, NM 87571; 800-576-2666, 505-776-8540.

Kandahar Condominiums have ski-in-and-out access via Strawberry Hill, a beginners' run. Two-bedroom, two-bath condos that sleep up to six have fireplaces and fully equipped kitchens. Guests can use the steam room, large hot tubs, Jacuzzi, and exercise room. Its location can't be beat, as the children's center and ski school are directly below. $350. P.O. Box 72, Taos Ski Valley, NM 87525; 800-756-2226, 505-776-2226.

Moderate

Taos East Condos are right on the Hondo River in a secluded area four miles from Taos Ski Valley. Fully equipped units accommodate two to ten people, all with kitchens, fireplaces, and room service if you desire. $90–195. Highway 150, 1074 Taos Ski Valley Road, P.O. Box 657, Taos Ski Valley, NM 87525; 800-238-SNOW, 505-726-2271.

El Monte Lodge has standard motel rooms with small refrigerators, and a few have kitchenettes. Its room decor has a southwestern theme, making this place a cut above many other chain motels. A complimentary continental breakfast is served daily, and the property is within walking distance of downtown Taos. $95. 317 Kit Carson Road, P.O. Box 22, Taos, NM 87571; 800-828-TAOS, 505-758-3171.

Holiday Inn Don Fernando de Taos, 18 miles from Taos Ski Valley, is one of the nicest Holiday Inns in the country. Rooms are in one of six different adobe buildings, and its restaurant has a children's menu and great free hors d'oeuvres. Complimentary shuttles to and from town are available, and there's an atrium-style pool and hot tub on the property and a movie theater next door. Kids 19 and under stay free in their parents' room; rollaways are $10 per night. $95–165. 1005 Paseo del Pueblo Sur, P.O. Drawer V, Taos, NM 87571; 800-759-2736, 505-758-4444.

Budget

Quality Inn, 2½ miles south of Taos Plaza and a half hour from the Taos Ski Valley, has a ski shuttle for $5 per person round trip. Its motel captures the southwestern charm and atmosphere of the area in the hand-carved furniture and appointments in otherwise ordinary rooms (two queen-size or one king-size bed). Half of the rooms have microwaves and refrigerators, and two suites have full kitchens and can sleep four people. In addition there is an indoor hot tub, outdoor heated pool, and a restaurant. Kids under 18 stay free in their parents' room. $69–150. 1043 Paseo del Pueblo Sur, P.O. Box 2319, Taos, NM 87571; 800-845-0648, 505-758-2200.

Sagebrush Inn, three miles from the historic downtown district, is a Taos landmark built in 1929. Georgia O'Keeffe lived here during the 1940s, and the walls sport treasures of southwestern art. All rooms and suites have Navajo-style rugs, tin light fixtures, and hand-carved furniture. A full complimentary breakfast is served to all guests. Most rooms have small refrigerators and a few have microwave ovens. The inn has 2 indoor hot tubs. Kids 12 and under stay free in their parents' room. $85–150. 1508 Paseo del Pueblo Sur, P.O. Box 557, Taos, NM 87571; 800-428-3626, 505-758-2254.

El Pueblo Lodge, a short walk from Taos Plaza, is a complex of six adobe-style buildings surrounding a lovely green courtyard. Standard rooms have two queen-size beds, efficiency units have a small kitchenette, and condos have one, two, or three bedrooms, with a complete kitchen and a large stone fireplace. Each bedroom has its own bathroom. Rates include continental breakfast. Laundry facilities, an outdoor pool, and a hot tub are on the premises. There is a $10 extra-person charge for condominiums. $65–215. 412 Paseo del Pueblo Norte, P.O. Box 92, Taos, NM 87571; 800-433-9612, 505-758-8700.

Children's Ski School

The Junior Elite Ski School is for children 3 to 12 who are divided into two age groups: Junior Elite I, for toilet-trained 3- to 5-year-olds, takes a game-oriented teaching approach that combines skiing with snow play and indoor activities. Reservations (505-776-2291, ext. 1334) are required for this group: Enrollment is capped to preserve a ratio of one instructor per six kids. Junior Elite II (505-776-2291, ext. 1335) includes kids from 6 to 12 years who spend more time on the mountain. Lunch is provided for both groups in the Kinderkäfig, as are hot-chocolate breaks. Children enrolled in multiday lessons have cubbies and ski storage for the week in the facility.

Day Care

Kinderkare (505-776-2291, ext. 1332) for children 6 weeks to 2 years has all-day and half-day programs in a cheerful upstairs room separated for different age groups. Toddlers can go outside for snow play, take walks, play games, enjoy free play, experiment with arts and crafts, and watch movies. Reservations are strongly suggested, as only 30 toddlers and 15 infants can be accommodated.

Teens

Certain weeks throughout the year are designated as teen (ages 13 to 16) ski weeks. Teens are evaluated by ability and placed in morning classes with the same group each day. In the afternoons they are free to ski with their family or new friends.

Snowboarding

Snowboarding is not allowed, but Angel Fire Resort (800-633-7643), 26 miles east of Taos, welcomes boarders.

Cross-Country Skiing

Enchanted Forest Cross Country Ski Area (505-754-2374) has ski rentals and 30 kilometers of groomed trails.

Los Rios Whitewater Ski Shop (800-544-1181, 505-776-8854) offers backcountry guided tours and lessons.

Shadow Mountain Guest Ranch (800-405-7732, 505-758-7732) has equipment rentals, lessons, and guided ski tours.

Other Activities

Fly-fishing: Guided trips on mountain lakes and streams are offered through Wild River Canyons (800-748-1707) year-round.

Ice skating takes place at the Taos Ice Arena in Kit Carson Park (505-758-8234) from December through February.

Snowmobiling can be arranged through Native Sons Adventures, 715 Paseo del Pueblo Sur, P.O. Box 6144, Taos, NM 87571; 800-753-7559, 505-758-9342.

Snowshoeing: Enchanted Forest Cross Country Ski Area has ski rentals and groomed trails (505-754-2374). You can also rent snowshoes from the Los Rios Whitewater Ski Shop (800-544-1181, 505-776-8854).

Deals and Discounts

Super Saver days offer discounted lift tickets in the early and late season. Special rates are available for beginners if they stick to certain lifts. Multiday lift tickets let you buy four out of five days so you can take a day off to visit Taos or just relax.

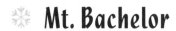

Mt. Bachelor

Address: 355 Southwest Century Drive, Bend, Oregon 97702;
Mailing address: P.O. Box 1031, Bend, Oregon 97709
Telephone: 800-829-2442, 541-382-2442 (central reservations)
Web site: http://www.mtbachelor.com

You can ski in the morning and play golf in the afternoon for more than half of Mt. Bachelor's nine-month ski season, which runs through July 4th of each year. Starting in early March (and often before), two 18-hole golf courses are open in the nearby town of Bend, and many guests wield skis and poles in the morning and clubs in the afternoon.

The ski resort is situated in the Deschutes National Forest and operates with a permit that prohibits construction of on-mountain overnight lodging. That lack of development has preserved the area around the mountain in a wild and natural state, but it means that accommodations and most services are a 20-minute drive away in the town of Bend or in Sun River, a planned community of homes and condominiums. Shuttles to the mountain are available from both places, but it's more convenient if you have your own car.

The skiing is on an extinct 9,065-foot symmetrical cinder cone—Mt. Bachelor—which features 360-degree skiing on its sides. Seven high-speed lifts allow you to spend most of your time on the slopes rather than on the chairlift or waiting in lines. Several chairlifts service a beginner's area next to the main children's ski-school headquarters. Once first-timers are comfortable on skis, they can ski in a number

MOUNTAIN STATISTICS
Base elevation: 5,700 feet
Summit: 9,065 feet
Vertical drop: 3,365 feet
Skiable acres: 3,368
Annual average snowfall: 250–300 inches
Snowmaking: none
Night skiing: none
Season: mid-November to July 4th
Lifts: 13 (7 high-speed quads, 3 regular triples, 1 double, 2 surface lifts)
Terrain: 15% beginner, 25% intermediate, 35% advanced, 25% expert
Lift tickets: adults $38, kids 7 to 12 and 65 and over $22, and 6 and under free.

FAMILY STATISTICS
Day care: Mt. Bachelor Daycare Center, 6 weeks to 7 years, 800-829-2442 or 541-382-2442 ext. 2138
Children's lessons: Mountain Masters, ages 4 to 12, 800-829-2442 or 541-382-2442, ext. 2108
Baby-sitting: Desert Country Nannies 541-388-9269
Baby gear: none
Medical: St. Charles Mountain Medical Clinic, 541-382-4321

of different areas that have both beginning and intermediate trails. Advanced skiers tend to stick to the summit, an above-the-treeline area of steep slopes and breathtaking views of the Cascade Mountains and other extinct volcanoes in the distance. Mt. Bachelor's location in the high desert of central Oregon means that the snow is light, fluffy, and dry, and grooming is ranked among the finest in the West.

The children's ski school is rated highly by families who have experienced Bachelor's friendly service and low-key attitude. There are two daycare and children's ski-school centers: one in the main lodge, West Village, and a smaller facility in the Sunrise area.

Cross-country aficionados will find 56 kilometers of trails starting right next to the main base lodge, making it easy to meet family members for lunch or to rendezvous later in the day. There are a few activities for nonskiers on the mountain, namely dogsledding and snowshoeing, but most of the rest, including a highly-regarded natural-history museum about the high desert, are located in Bend.

How to Get There

Tiny Redmond Airport is 20 minutes away from Bend and is serviced by Horizon Air (800-547-9308) and United Express (800-241-6522). Many people fly into Portland, 168 miles away. Super Shuttles (800-829-2442, 541-382-2442) travel from the town of Bend to the ski resort. Drive times: Portland 3 hours (168 miles), Eugene 2.5 hours (128 miles), Boise, Idaho 5.5 hours. (346 miles), Seattle, Washington 6 hours (365 miles).

Where to Stay

Expensive

Sunriver Resort (http://www.sunriver-resort.com) is central Oregon's largest destination resort, packed with skiers in the winter and mountain bikers and golfers in the summer. Fifteen miles south of Bend, the 3,500-acre collection of guest rooms, homes, and condominiums accommodate both full-time residents and vacationers in units of all possible sizes and shapes. Recreational facilities include an ice rink, tennis courts, 54 holes of championship golf, swimming pools, restaurants, and shops. Guest rooms $89–139, condos $149–189, houses $259–350. Ski packages are available. P.O. Box 3609, Sunriver, OR 97707; 800-801-8765, 541-593-1000.

Mount Bachelor Village Resort, on the Deschutes River, has one- to three-bedroom condominiums and townhouses. The resort includes a year-round pool and spa and river nature trails. It's situated next to the new Athletic Club of Bend. $97–320. 19717 Mount Bachelor Drive, Bend, OR 97702; 800-452-9846, 541-389-5900.

Moderate

The Inn of the Seventh Mountain (http://www.7thmtn.com), 14 miles
from Mt. Bachelor, has hotel rooms and condominiums tucked in between
groves of ponderosa pine trees. Condos range in size from studios to three-
bedroom units and hotel rooms contain one or two queen-size beds. A
laundry list of activities is available: a covered ice-skating rink, a year-round
heated swimming pool and a second pool that opens at the end of March
and features a 65-foot waterslide, hot tubs, sauna, and horse-drawn sleigh
rides. Certain recreational features are open when the weather permits:
horseshoes, miniature golf, sand volleyball, mountain biking, horseback
rides, and outdoor tennis courts. In addition there are two restaurants, a
small market, and a ski-apparel shop on the premises. A shuttle to Mt.
Bachelor costs extra. Kids stay free in their parents' room. Rollaways cost
$8 per night. Condo, $99–299, hotel, $59–99. 18575 Southwest Century
Drive, Bend, OR 97702; 800-452-6810, 541-382-8711.

The Riverhouse (http://www.riverhouse.com) overlooking the Deschutes
River is the only four-diamond resort in Bend. Its golf course is highly rated
by *Golf Digest*, and it's open for play nearly year-round. Twenty-two different types of rooms are available, from simple doubles to two-level, two-
bedroom suites with a kitchen and private hot tub accommodating up to
ten people. On-site amenities include a restaurant, a lounge with nightly
live music, an indoor pool and spa, an indoor sauna, a jogging trail along
the river, and tennis courts. Children under 7 stay free in their parents'
room while ages 7 and older are charged an additional $6 per night. Certain
times of year the hotel offers a "kids ski and stay free" package; be sure to
inquire. $55–175. 3075 North Highway 97, Bend, OR 97701; 800-547-
3928, 541-389-3111.

Budget

Sonoma Lodge is an older, family-owned property with renovated rooms
and one of the best deals in any ski town anywhere. Nine different room
types are available, from simple rooms with a queen-size bed to a unit
sleeping up to eight with a full kitchen. Most have some kind of kitchen
facility; either a microwave and refrigerator or something more elaborate.
Rates include a continental breakfast with fresh fruit, homemade bread,
juice, coffee, tea, and cocoa. Ski packages are available, and the Lodge is
near the access road to Mt. Bachelor. $30–89. 450 Southeast Third Street,
Bend, OR 97702; 541-382-4891.

Motel West: Several of this clean and simple motel's 39 units have kitchenettes. Rooms have one or two queen-size beds. It's basic but an excellent value. $30–42. 228 Northeast Irving, Bend, OR 97701; 800-282-5577, 541-389-5577.

Children's Ski School

The Mountain Masters program is for children ages 4 to 12. The program operates out of both base lodges, but West Village has the more extensive program. Children age 4 to 6 are separated from the 7- to 12-year-olds, and full-and half-day lessons are available. There are nine different levels of instruction, from absolute beginner to advanced. Snowboard lessons start at age 7; 800-829-2442 or 541-382-2422, ext. 2108.

Day Care

Mt. Bachelor has two day-care facilities for children from 6 weeks to 7 years of age. The largest facility is at West Village (the main lodge), and another is at Sunrise Lodge. Parents who are skiing the lifts near Sunrise use that facility, which is also used for overflow on busy weekends and holidays. West Village's facility is on the ground floor of the main lodge in three spacious and colorful rooms. The largest room is for preschoolers and contains all kinds of toys, a small slide, a dress-up area, a truck area, a kitchen area, and an area with balls and a basketball hoop. The toddler room for 13 months to 2 ½ years has a slide, fantasy play areas, and cribs and mats. The infant room for 6 weeks to 13 months has cribs, swings, and mats for them to lie or crawl on with toys overhanging. Sunrise Lodge has a much smaller, but similar facility; 800-829-2442 or 541-382-2422, ext. 2138 (reservations strongly recommended).

Snowboarding

Two half pipes are kept in good shape by the resort's pipe dragon. One is designed for a World Cup event and is in view of the lodge; the other, for intermediate boarders, is in the snowboard park along with hits, jumps, and rolls. The Snowboard Park is near the Skyliner Chair.

Cross-Country Skiing

Mt. Bachelor's Cross Country Center (800-829-2442 or 541-382-2422, ext. 2209) is at the base of the ski area. Its 56 kilometers of trails are groomed daily and meander through exquisitely beautiful National Forest wilderness. The center has its own restaurant and offers lessons and equipment rentals for children and adults.

Other Activities

Golfing is available starting in early spring at two different courses: Eagle Crest Resort (541-923-4653) and River's Edge Golf Course (541-389-2828).

Guided nature tours: The U.S. Forest Service (541-388-5664) gives nature walks and talks on alpine and geological subjects. Guests must be 10 or older and can wear snowshoes or boots.

The High Desert Museum is a wonderful stop on a bad weather day. It has outdoor animal habitats and a wide variety of excellent interactive exhibits and children's activities. 59800 South Highway 97, Bend, OR 97702; 541-382-4754.

Ice skating: The Inn of the Seventh Mountain (800-452-6810, 541-382-8711) 18575 Southwest Century Drive, Bend, OR 97702) has a covered outdoor rink.

Dogsled rides (800-829-2442, 541-382-2442) take you on backcountry tracks. There are three different types of rides: the standard (about 90 minutes), the marathon trip (26 miles and about 5 hours), and Elk Lake Lodge overnight trips (adults only).

Snowshoeing tours can be arranged through the Cross Country Center (800-829-2442 or 541-382-2442, ext. 2209).

Wanderlust Tours offers half-day or overnight guided snowshoe trips; 800-962-2862, 541-389-8359.

Deals and Discounts

Children 7 to 12 receive free lift tickets during the Kids Ski and Stay Free program offered in late season. At the end of April, reduced-price lift tickets become available. The last Friday is always a free skiing day.

Jackson Hole Mountain Resort

Address: P.O. Box 290, 7658 Teewinot, Teton Village, Wyoming 83025

Telephone: 800-443-6931 (central reservations), 888-DEEP-SNOW (snow report), 307-733-4005

Web site: http://www.jacksonhole.com/ski

With the Grand Tetons, Yellowstone National Park, and the National Elk Refuge just minutes away, Jackson Hole is truly a winter dream vacation spot. Skiers and boarders who can't get enough of the steeps find true happiness here for weeks at a time—the resort has one of the longest vertical drops and some of the most extreme skiing on the continent. Families who want to spend time exploring our nation's spectacular natural wonders can wander on snowshoes, cross-country skis, snowmobiles, horse-drawn sleighs, and dogsleds. There are enough activities off the slopes to keep nonskiers busy for days.

Don't let Jackson Hole's reputation as an experts-only mountain keep you from visiting this terrific western-style resort. Unless you are a family of beginners or timid intermediates, you'll find plenty of intermediate terrain—some of the best in the country. If you or your kids want to learn how to maneuver in Corbets Couloir, a legendary site where skiers jump off a cliff into a tiny chute 20 feet below and make a sharp turn as soon as they hit, attend one of the steeps camps for intermediate and advanced boarders and skiers during the year. Central reservations can give you dates.

The ski resort, called Jackson Hole, and its base area, called Teton Village, sit 12

MOUNTAIN STATISTICS

Base elevation: 6,311 feet

Summit: 10,450 feet

Vertical drop: 4,139 feet

Skiable acres: 2,500

Annual average snowfall: 33 feet

Snowmaking: 110 acres

Night skiing: 110 acres

Season: late November through April

Lifts: 10 (1 aerial tram, 1 8-person gondola, 1 high-speed quad chair, 2 quads, 1 triple, 3 doubles, 1 surface lift)

Terrain: 10% beginners, 40% intermediate, 50% advanced

Lift tickets: Adults, $48, children 14 and under, $24.

FAMILY STATISTICS

Day care: Kids Ranch (at the ski-resort base), 2 months to 5 years, 307-739-2691 (reservations required)

Children's lessons: Kids Ranch, 3 to 5 years, 307-739-2691; Ski School, 6 to 13, 800-450-0477, 307-739-2663

Baby-sitting: Kids Ranch supplies a list of employees who are available for baby-sitting, 307-739-2691

Baby gear: Baby's Away rents cribs, strollers, car seats, high chairs, toys, and other gear; 307-733-0387

Medical: St. John's Hospital in Jackson, 307-733-3636

miles out of Jackson, a round 'em up Wild West town where dusty Stetsons mix with electric-colored ski pants. Lodging in all budget categories is available right at the base, outside of town, or in Jackson itself, which is small enough to walk around yet large enough to offer much to do.

Thanks to a $14 million capital improvement campaign, all skier services—day care, kids' ski school, ticket office, and rental shops—are now housed under one roof. A brand new gondola whisks skiers from the resort base to the base of the headwall in minutes.

How to Get There

Jackson Hole Airport is 10 miles from the town of Jackson and 22 miles from the ski resort. Delta, American, United, United Express, HorizonAir, and Skywest airlines fly in. Shuttle service to the resort is available. Drive times: Salt Lake City, 6 hours (275 miles); Denver, 10 hours (500 miles).

Where to Stay

Expensive

Spring Creek Hotel & Conference Center (http://www.springcreek resort.com) is situated at the crown of East Gros Ventre Butte looking out over the spectacular Grand Teton Mountain Range. This luxury cabin resort is about four miles north of Jackson between the town and the ski area in a 1,000-acre wildlife refuge. Rooms, suites, studios, one- to three-bedroom condos, and four-bedroom homes all include fireplaces, balconies, and refrigerators or full kitchens. The resort offers horse-drawn sleigh rides, ice skating, snowshoeing, and cross-country skiing. Shuttles to town and the ski area are provided. Hotel rooms and suites are on a plan that includes breakfast. Children 12 years and under stay free in their parents' room; packages are available. Hotel rooms $120–275, condos $280–775, homes $700–1200. 1800 Spirit Dance Road, P.O. Box 3154, Jackson, WY 83001; 800-443-6139, 307-733-8833.

The Alpenhof Lodge, an Austrian chalet–style luxury hotel has hand-carved Bavarian furniture and down comforters. Its elegant restaurant, known for deliciously rich entrees and even richer desserts, has a children's menu. Its bar and bistro are more informal and serve breakfast, lunch, and dinner on an outdoor deck when the weather is good. The Alpenhof is the closest lodge to the lifts. Rooms have one king-size bed, two doubles, or two queen-size beds. Suites are larger, and some have fireplaces and balconies. Amenities include an outdoor pool, hot tub, sauna, massage services, and game room with pool, Ping-Pong, and video games. $130–398. P.O. Box 288, Teton Village, WY 83025-0288; 800-732-3244, 307-733-3242.

Teton Pines Resort and Country Club (http://www.tetonpines.com) is a luxury golf resort in summer, and in winter the prices drop. There's indoor tennis, cross-country trails, and a hot tub. A health club next door is free for guests, plus there's a free shuttle to the lifts and the airport. Standard rooms and suites are available. $160–355. 3450 North Clubhouse Drive, Jackson, WY 83001; 800-288-3866, 307-733-1005.

Moderate

Snow King Resort has hotel rooms, full suites for four to six people, and 50 condominiums with one to four bedrooms. The standard hotel-style rooms have one king-size or two queen-size beds. Skiing (and even night skiing) is a few steps away, and there's an indoor ice-skating rink next door where the local hockey team plays, plus a heated outdoor pool, game room, whirlpools, and even a hair salon.Hotel rooms $100–175, condos $120–500. $10 charge for rollaways. 400 Snow King Avenue, Jackson Hole, WY 83001; 800-522-KING, 307-733-5200.

Best Western Inn at Jackson Hole, just 100 yards from the tram at Teton Village, has comfortable slopeside accommodations and a restaurant with a children's menu. Families will find the loft suites most spacious. Many rooms come with a kitchen and a few with a fireplace. Within the hotel are three hot tubs and a sauna. Standard rooms have two double beds; suites have a king-size bed and either a sleeper sofa or two queen-size beds. $110–240. 3345 West McCollister Drive, Teton Village, WY 83025; 800-842-7666, 307-733-2311.

Best Western Lodge at Jackson Hole is in downtown Jackson (with shuttle service to the lifts) and is a lodge in the Old West sense of the word. Its massive log walls, elaborately carved timbers, log staircase, and antler chandeliers set it apart from Best Western accommodations elsewhere. It's one of the best hotels for families thanks to its indoor/outdoor pool, Wild West decor, game arcade, and free continental breakfast. Two kinds of minisuites are available, one with two queen-size beds, a sleeper sofa, and kitchenette, the other with a king-size bed, sleeper sofa, kitchenette, fireplace, and Jacuzzi. $79–149. 800 Scott Lane, P.O. Box 30436, Jackson Hole, WY 83001; 800-458-3866, 307-739-9703.

Budget

The Hostel in Teton Village has four-person bunk rooms with private bathrooms. For accommodations so close to the lifts (100 yards), the price is an astonishing $60–70 for four people. There are two game rooms and a small library within the hostel. Guests have kitchen privileges. 3325 McCollister Drive, Box 546, Teton Village, WY 83025; 307-733-3415.

Forty Niner Inn by the Jackson town square has spacious suites and standard rooms with pine furniture and marble framed fireplaces. Suites also have kitchenettes and living areas. Rates include continental breakfast, and the hotel's Mexican restaurant has a children's menu. The hotel features an outdoor hot tub, sauna, and fitness room. $58–120. 330 West Pearl Street, Jackson, WY 83001; 800-451-2980, 307-733-7550.

Children's Ski School

The Explorers program offers kids ages 6 to 13 snowboard and ski lessons for half or full days (half days are mornings only). Kids who stay for all-day lessons eat lunch at the rustic Solitude Cabin, where the dinner sleigh rides travel to later in the day.

Private one-hour ski lessons are available to teach basic skills to 3- to 5-year-olds. Child care, lunch, and snacks are included (see Day care below).

Day Care

The Kids Ranch (307-739-2691) at the base area takes little ones ages 2 months to 5 years. Tenderfoots (ages 2 through 18 months) have their own special play area and a separate crib room; only six slots are available in this age group, so be sure to make reservations when you book your lodging. Wranglers (19 months through 5 years) can select a variety of activities in a main playroom that has a separate area for arts, crafts, and lunch. The structured day-long program offers an array of arts and crafts projects, snow playtime, sledding, lunch, singing, dancing, games, and nap or quiet time. If they can turn and stop consistently, 3- to 5-year-olds can participate in their own group lesson that runs two hours in the morning and two hours in the afternoon. Private lessons are available for kids who can't turn and stop. All programs are half or full day.

Teens

Mountain Experience Camp for teens is offered during winter and spring breaks. Teens, grouped by age and ability, explore Jackson Hole with an instructor who teaches them about racing, steeps, and skiing or boarding the bumps. Evening activities such as pizza parties and ski videos are scheduled throughout the week. Movies are shown in the Pepi Stiegler Sports Building throughout the week in the evening. Look for the schedule posted around the resort.

Snowboarding

The natural snowboard features at Jackson Hole—the steeps, rocks, chutes, and drop-offs—appeal to snowboarders who have free reign to snowboard anywhere in the resort. One of the most popular runs has a groomed half pipe.

Cross-Country Skiing

Jackson Hole Nordic Center (307-739-2629) offers tours into Grand Teton National Park, along with instruction and rentals of cross-country gear. Nordic skiers can glide along a trail at the base of the Tetons or skate on a network of 15 kilometers of groomed trails. Instructors are available to take visitors into backcountry powder bowls.

Other Activities

Dogsledding: The Jackson Hole Iditarod Sled Dog Tour (307-733-7388) is led by a veteran dogsledder who takes guests to a local hot-springs area and back. If you visit in February, you can see the end of a dog race that starts at the other end of the state and finishes in Jackson Hole.

Grand Teton National Park: Winter activities start at the Park Headquarters Visitors Center (307-739-3399) in Moose, just 12 miles north of Jackson. Activities include ranger-led snowshoe hikes (reservations a must), snowmobiling, cross-country skiing, and ice fishing.

Ice skating: The indoor ice skating at the new Snow King Center has public skating, skate rentals and instruction. 100 East Snow King Avenue, Jackson, WY 83001; 800-522-KING, 307-733-5200.

National Elk Refuge: Sleigh ride tours of the National Elk Refuge (307-733-9212) take you through the largest herds of elk in North America. Sleighs depart from the National Museum of Wildlife Art (2820 Rungis Road, Jackson WY 83001) and last about 45 minutes; rides run every 20 to 30 minutes from late December through March.

The National Museum of Wildlife Art: This new museum is right across from the Elk Refuge. As you might guess from its name, it's devoted to exhibiting all kinds of wildlife art—painting, sculpture, prints, photos—and hosts visiting exhibitions, speakers, and slideshows. A special kids' discovery center has hands-on activities, and there are special kids programs throughout the year. 2820 Rungis Road, Jackson, WY 83001; 307-733-5771.

Sleigh rides: Solitude Cabin Winter Sleigh Rides (307-733-6657) heads to hearty dinners at Solitude Cabin on Apres Vous Mountain.

Snowmobiling: More than a dozen snowmobile concessionaires in the Jackson Hole area take vacationers into Yellowstone National Park. They'll pick you up at your hotel and drive you to the park, where you'll hop on a snowmobile for an unforgettable tour of steamy Old Faithful all covered in snow. Other tours take you to Granite Hot Springs' natural warm pools or into the Gros Ventre Mountains. Lists of outfitters are available from hotels and condos.

Wildlife tours: Tour with a wildlife biologist from the Great Plains Wildlife Institute (307-733-2623) to view and learn about local moose, bighorn sheep, bald eagles, and more.

Yellowstone National Park: Access to Yellowstone's southern entrance is about 55 miles away from Jackson. Much of the park is closed in the winter but there is still much to see and do. One of the most popular activities is a snowmobile trip to visit Old Faithful (see above).

Deals and Discounts

Life tickets for the beginner's terrain on Teewinot and Eagles Rest are free for kids five and under, $5 for kids 6 to 14, and $10 for adults. Discounted ski packages are available throughout the year from Jackson Central Reservations, 800-443-6931.

THE EAST

Middle Atlantic

Whiteface Mountain Ski Area

Address: Administrative Offices Olympic Regional Development Authority, Olympic Center, Lake Placid, New York, 12946. Mountain location: Route 86, Wilmington, New York.

Telephone: 800-44PLACID (central reservations), 518-523-1655 (general information)

Website: http//www.lakeplacid.com

The steeps of Whiteface Mountain experienced the glory of Olympic gold in 1932 and 1980, when Lake Placid hosted the Winter Olympic Games. Its 3,216 feet of vertical, the greatest in the East, still serve up excellent skiing, but these days Lake Placid really takes the gold off the slopes. Here and nowhere else can your kids learn to drive a bobsled or luge, take a ski-jumping lesson, skate in an Olympic ice rink, and try a six-story toboggan ride.

If you're a family who likes to combine cross-country and downhill skiing, the Lake Placid region has hundreds of kilometers of trails. The area still hosts national cross-country ski competitions and is regularly named the best cross-country ski center in the nation by the readers of *Snow Country* magazine.

The village of Lake Placid is actually on Mirror Lake, separated from larger Lake Placid by a narrow strip of land. Most of the shops, restaurants, and hotels are found between the Olympic speed-skating rink at one end of town and Mirror Lake Inn at the other. The ski mountain is about nine miles from the village in Adirondack Park, a natural area that is protected by the state of New York. As a result, the over-development—motels, fast-food joints, and strip malls—found at some ski resorts is pleasantly absent here.

Because of the Olympics and the fact that it is a popular summer resort,

MOUNTAIN STATISTICS

Base elevation: 1,220 feet
Summit: 4,436 feet
Vertical drop: 3,216 feet
Skiable acres: 170
Annual average snowfall: 168 inches
Snowmaking: 95% of trails
Night skiing: none
Season: late November to early April
Lifts: 10 (2 triples, 7 doubles, 1 surface lift)
Terrain: 35% beginner, 37% intermediate, 28% advanced
Lift tickets: adults $39, juniors 7 to 12 $19, seniors ages 64 to 69 $25, 6 and under 70 and over free.

FAMILY STATISTICS

Day care: Bunny Hutch Nursery, ages 1 to 6, 518-946-2223
Children's lessons: Kids Kampus, ages 4 to 12, 518-946-2223
Baby-sitting: Lake Placid Community Daycare, 518-523-2166
Medical: Adirondack Medical Center, 518-523-3311

Lake Placid has scores of moderately priced accommodations, making it a great value ski vacation. Since Whiteface Mountain is a government-owned property, its lift tickets cost less than ski resorts in Vermont and New Hampshire. If you have preteens or teens, plan to splurge on bobsled and luge rides; they offer the thrill of a lifetime.

At Whiteface Mountain, the "Kids Kampus" has its own base lodge, ski lifts, a full-service nursery, ski school, and a shuttle bus to and from the main base lodge. Young Olympic hopefuls can test their mettle as often as they wish at the coin-operated ski racing run. Just drop the money in the slot and go; times are monitored electronically and displayed at the bottom of the hill.

The mountain offers skiing for all abilities, with plenty of good beginner and intermediate terrain in addition to the steeply pitched Olympic down-hill-type runs. Its snowmaking covers nearly 100 percent of the trails, giving Whiteface consistently good early-morning skiing that can last into the afternoon, but on a windy winter day it can turn rather hard, icy, and cold.

A great value for families is the Gold Medal Vacation Package, a three-, four-, or five-day ticket that includes unlimited downhill skiing, cross-country skiing, public skating on the speed-skating oval, and admission to Olympic venues. The adult ticket includes a ride on a luge or bobsled, which costs an extra $12 to add onto a child's ticket.

How to Get There

Adirondack Airport, 16 miles from Lake Placid, has USAir (800-428-4322) flights from many Eastern cities. Albany County Airport, 2.5 hours away, is the closest major airport, and Logan International Airport is the nearest international airport to the area, 5.5 hours away by car. Driving times: Albany, 2.5 hours (130 miles); Boston, 5 hours (300 miles); Montréal, 2 hours (120 miles); New York City, 5 hours (280 miles).

Amtrak (800-USA-RAIL) ski trains run daily from New York City and other points on the Eastern corridor and stop in Westport, 40 miles from Lake Placid. Shuttle-bus service (518-523-4431) to Lake Placid requires a reservation.

Lake Placid is small enough to walk around in, but you'll need a car to get to Whiteface Mountain or you'll be stuck paying the premium price that the shuttle services charge.

Where to Stay

Expensive

Mirror Lake Inn (http://www.mirrorlakeinn.com) is the town's best luxury lodging and it's easy to see why. From the chandeliers and mahogany walls, private ice rink and fine collection of antiques, to its full-service spa and salon, it will delight those who love to be pampered. Children under 18 stay free, and the children's "Stay and Eat Free" package can be a good deal. $115–575. 5 Mirror Lake Drive, Lake Placid, NY 12946; 518-523-2544.

Lake Placid Resort Holiday Inn (http://www.lpresort.com) overlooks the Olympic arena and has a spectacular 360-degree view of the surrounding peaks. It has a shuttle service, laundry facilities, and a game room with video games and a virtual-reality skiing game. It's about eight miles from the downhill lifts, and an hourly shuttle takes guests to and from the slopes. There's also an enormous indoor pool and a wide selection of accommodations including hotel rooms, minisuites sleeping six, and chalets, which are minihouses with complete kitchens. A cross-country resort is on-site. $50–200. 1 Olympic Drive, Lake Placid, NY 12946; 800-874-1980, 518-523-2556.

Moderate

Howard Johnson Resort Lodge is suitable for small families who can stay in standard rooms that have two double beds, or for larger families willing to take two rooms. Eight miles from Whiteface Mountain, it has a large indoor swimming pool and Jacuzzi with rock grottos and a small waterfall. Many sports teams visiting Lake Placid stay here. There's skating on the lake and cross-country ski trails that start next door. Children under 18 stay free in their parents' room. $85–145. 90 Saranac Avenue, Lake Placid, NY 12946; 800-858-4656, 518-523-9555.

Budget

Mt. Van Hoevenberg Bed-and-Breakfast and Cottages is situated on five acres next to the Olympic cross-country skiing center and the luge and bobsled runs. It has several rooms in a natural wood farmhouse, and simple but comfortable cabins that come in varying sizes, accommodating two to ten people. All have complete kitchens. $120–300. Route 73, HCO1 Box 37, Lake Placid, NY 12946; 518-523-9572.

Wildwood on the Lake has standard rooms with two double or queen-size beds. Some rooms have kitchenettes. Several cabins are on the property; one sleeps six and has a complete kitchen. Children under 12 stay free, but rollaway beds cost $8. A sauna, whirlpool, and swimming pool are on the premises. Rooms $48–98, cabins $130–150. 88 Saranac Avenue, Lake Placid, NY 12946; 800-841-6378, 518-523-2624.

Children's Ski School

All of Whiteface Mountain's children's programs operate from the Kids Kampus, (518-946-2223) which has its own base lodge, ski lifts, beginner runs, snow playground, and shuttle bus. Whiteface uses the SKIwee program of instruction and separates learners into two age groups: children age 4 to 6 combine indoor and outdoor play with skiing instruction. Children 3 to 6 can also take a ski lesson through the day care. Kids 7 to 12 spend most of their time on the snow perfecting their skiing technique. Full- and half-day programs are available. Director Ed Kreil is a former Austrian Ski Team member. Snowboarding lessons start at age 6.

Day Care

The Bunny Hutch Nursery at Kids Kampus (518-946-2223) is for ages 1 to 6 who enjoy indoor and outdoor play, arts and crafts, story time, group activities, games, and quiet time. Hourly, half-day, and full-day programs are available. It's first-come, first-served, so show up early, especially during holiday periods. Children ages 3 to 6 can take a Play and Ski class which introduces them to skiing in a playful manner.

Teens

Every Friday night from December through March, kids ages 8 to 17 can participate in junior bobsledding and luge programs. The best part is that kids learn to drive themselves. For $30 all equipment and instruction is provided, including helmets.

Snowboarding

All terrain at Whiteface is open to snowboarding. The snowboard park on the mountain was designed by professional riders and features jumps, spines, a variety of other hits, and a quarter pipe.

Cross-Country Skiing

Olympic Sports Complex at Mt. Van Hoevenberg (800-462-6236, 518-523-2811) seven miles south of Lake Placid, has 50 kilometers of trails for all levels of Nordic skiing. Ten miles from Lake Placid Village, it's the main cross-country center for the Lake Placid area, which has been rated by readers of *Snow Country* magazine as the best place in North America for cross-country skiing for two years in a row. Some of its runs have snow-making, and its warming lodge has waxing rooms, equipment rentals, a ski shop, and a snack bar.

The Jack Rabbit Trail connects different cross-country centers throughout the area; some are groomed and some are not. Covering more than 50 kilometers of wilderness, you can access the trail from a number of places in and around Lake Placid Village. The Lake Placid Visitors Center in the Olympic Center (518-523-2445) can give you details.

Other Activities

Airplane tours: The Adirondack Flying Service (518-523-2473) offers 20-minute flights over the breathtaking Adirondack wilderness area. Family discounts are available.

Bobsled rides: You're the passenger on a bobsled piloted by a professional driver down the Olympic track at Mt. Van Hoevenberg. (518-523-4436). Half-mile rides twist and turn around some pretty hairy curves, but if you're on the full-mile course, expect some real heart pounding and adrenaline pumping. The bobsled attracts athletes from around the world for training and competition. You must be at least 48 inches tall to ride it. Half-mile rides cost $30 per person; one-mile rides cost $100 per person. Closed Tuesday. The one-mile run is open by appointment only.

Dogsled rides with XTC Ranch & Resort (800-613-6033, 518-891-5684) and Thunder Mountain Dog Sled (518-891-6239) take you across Mirror Lake or Lake Placid or on day trips into the back country.

Sleigh rides are offered during the evening all winter long by XTC Ranch & Resort (800-613-6033, 518-891-5684).

Ice skating: Take your own gold-medal lap (just like Eric Heiden did) around the Olympic Speed Skating Oval (518-523-1655). Skate rentals are available. Open evenings during the week, and midafternoon on Saturday and Sunday.

If spectator sports are more your speed, visit the indoor ice rinks at Olympic Center in Lake Placid (518-523-1655). The public can observe figure skaters, hockey players, and speed skaters practicing their sport free of charge. Keep an eye out for listings of special skating events that take place at this venue.

Luge Rocket Rides: More thrilling than any roller-coaster your kids will experience, the luge ride (518-523-4436) lets them race down the track by themselves in their own fiberglass Luge Rocket. The track was built for the 1980 games and is still used for training and competition.

Olympic Ski Jumping Complex: Admission includes an elevator ride to the top of the 26-story jump which offers some magnificent views of Lake Placid and the surrounding mountains. The complex is home to the U.S. Freestyle and Ski Jumping Teams (through 1998), has two ski jumps and a freestyle-jumping complex, and is open daily. Learn-to-ski jump clinics sponsored by the New York Ski Education Foundation (518-523-2202) take place on weekends for anyone age 6 years and up.

Snowmobiling through Adirondack Park is offered by Adirondack Snowmobile (518-523-1888) and XTC Ranch (800-613-6033, 518-891-5684).

Snowshoeing is possible on the hiking trails that meander through the Adirondack wilderness; rentals are found in a variety of shops around Lake Placid and at XTC Ranch (800-613-6033, 518-891-5684).

Toboggan chute: The town of Lake Placid operates this unusual toboggan experience (518-523-2591). Climb a 50-foot tower, get on your toboggan, race down a chute to the frozen surface of Mirror Lake, and careen across the lake as far as you can go. Sledders can reach speeds of about 40 miles per hour, and some sledders have rocketed as far as 2,000 feet across the lake. The chute is a toboggan-width wooden trough lined with ice. Toboggans can seat four people. Open Wednesday, Friday, and Saturday evenings, Saturday and Sunday afternoons, and more often during holidays.

Winter Olympic Museum: View exhibits, video highlights, athletes' uniforms and equipment, memorabilia, and historical information about the 1932 and 1980 Olympic games at the Olympic Center in Lake Placid (518-523-1655). Open daily.

Deals and Discounts
The Gold Medal Vacation Package (see page 182) is the best way to save money if your family wants to ski and sample some of what Lake Placid has to offer. Pre-season and late season packages offer discounts.

Seven Springs Mountain Resort

Address: Champion, Pennsylvania 15622
Telephone: 800-452-2223, 814-352-7777 (reservations)
Website: http://www.7springs.com

With more skiable acres and the greatest uphill capacity of any mid-Atlantic ski resort, the Seven Springs Mountain Resort draws families from Washington, D.C., Pittsburgh, and surrounding communities. The resort's convenience—the hotel, ski lodge, childcare facility, and loads of recreational activities are all under one roof—makes it a solid choice for families with young children. On bad weather days you can go bowling, miniature golfing, or roller skating without ever having to step outside.

Many of the resort's chair lifts are lighted for night skiing, making Seven Springs a good buy with older kids who never seem to tire. Lift ticket options include full day tickets, twilight tickets which are good from 1 P.M. to 10 P.M. and evening passes for night skiing. Or, send them out on the resort's lift-served tubing run for a different kind of snowy thrill. There's also a NASTAR race course and a snowboard park with a groomed half pipe and various jumps and hits.

A variety of accommodations are clustered around or near the enormous base lodge/hotel building: chalets, cabins, and condominiums. More condominiums are a short shuttle bus ride away, and budget lodging is available in the nearby town of Somerset.

MOUNTAIN STATISTICS
Base elevation: 2,240 feet
Summit: 2,990 feet
Vertical drop: 750 feet
Skiable acres: 500
Annual average snowfall: 105 inches
Snowmaking: 95%
Night skiing: four to six chairs operate nightly until 10 P.M.
Season: December 1 through March.
Lifts: 18 (3 quad chairs, 7 triple chairs, 8 surface lifts)
Terrain: 50% beginner, 33% intermediate, 17% advanced
Lift ticket: adults $39, children 6 to 11 $32, 70+ and under 6 free.

FAMILY STATISTICS
Daycare: Kids Korner for kids walking and older 814-352-7777, ext. 7488
Ski School: Tiny Tot Ski School ages 4 to 7, Junior ski school ages 7 to 14 814-352-7777, ext. 7589
Babysitting: 814-352-777, ext. 7629 (guest information desk); on Friday and Saturday nights call the child care center for reservations; 814-352-7777, ext. 7488
Medical: Somerset Community Hospital, 814-443-5000

How to Get There

Driving times: Pittsburgh, 1 hour (60 miles); Washington, D.C., 3.5 hours (210 miles); Columbus, 4 hours (299 miles); Cleveland, 3 hours (174 miles).

Where to Stay

Seven Springs Hotel has rooms with two double or two queen-size beds. Guests enjoy the complimentary use of the swimming pool and outdoor hot tubs, and all of the resort's recreational activities for a small fee. Rollaways are available at no additional charge. Rooms $165–$185 per night: children 6 to 11 $10 per night, 12 and up $30 per night, under 6 free. 800-452-2223.

Condominiums: The Villages Condominium complex is the newest group of condo units and are situated on the ski slopes, offering ski-in-and-out convenience. The Swiss Mountain and Mountain Village condos are ¾ to two miles away from the ski area and on a free shuttle line. All have one to four bedrooms and fully equipped kitchens. They're rented for a minimum of two nights. Two-night stay, $430–$1135. 800-452-2223.

Chalets sit side by side and have a living area and equipped kitchens. Medium chalets can sleep up to ten people. They have one bedroom downstairs with three sets of bunks, a bedroom upstairs containing two double beds, and two bathrooms. The Tyrol and large chalets can sleep up to twelve people. These units have two bedrooms downstairs with two sets of bunks in each, a bedroom upstairs with two double beds, and two baths. Chalets are within walking distance of the hotel. Two-night stay, $600–840. 800-452-2223.

Cabins accommodate both families and groups; all have kitchens. One cabin sleeps up to six people; the rest can accommodate fourteen to twenty-five guests in a dormlike lodging. All are within walking distance of the lodge. Two-night stay, $600–$840. 800-452-2223.

Day's Inn in Somerset, about 15 miles away, offers plain and simple rooms at a low price. Kids under seventeen stay free in their parents' room, and most rooms have two double beds. A complimentary continental breakfast is served daily $48–60. 220 Waterworks Drive, Somerset, PA 15501; 800-325-2525, 814-445-9200.

Children's Ski School

Youngsters 4 to 7 take their classes in the Tiny Tot Ski School. Kids are placed into small groups based on their age and ability. Full- and half-day programs are available, and supervised indoor playtime, snacks, and lunch are included. Prices include equipment for this age group.

Junior Ski School is for youngsters 7 to 14 and ranges from beginner to expert level instruction. Kids ski for five hours, taking a midday break for lunch, which is included in the price. Equipment is not included in the price for this age of skier.

Day Care

Kids' Korner Child Care Center, on the third floor of the main lodge building, is available for children of walking age through age 12, but most are under age 7. In addition to enjoying games, free play, and story time, children who are old enough take advantage of the recreation opportunities at the resort such as roller skating, swimming, and miniature golfing. Half- and full-day sessions are available and are first come first serve but reservations are strongly suggested. Friday and Saturday night care is available by appointment only.

Snowboarding

Seven Springs Snowboard Park is 400 by 500 feet and includes a halfpipe and a quarter pipe groomed to perfection by a pipe dragon, and various tabletops, hits, and jumps that change week to week.

Other Activities

Indoor swimming pool: Located on the second level of the Main Lodge, the pool is open every day and evening. Guests staying at the resort can swim free of charge; kids under 12 must be accompanied by an adult.

Miniature golf: An indoor mini golf course is located on the second level of the Main Lodge and is open daily; ext. 7626.

Sleigh rides are offered daily, weather permitting, from 10 A.M. to dusk; ext. 7285.

Bowling: A bowling alley is located on the ground level of the Convention Center and is open daily; ext 7922.

Rollerskating: The fourth level of the Convention Center in the Exhibit Hall has roller skating during the winter. Roller skates and in-line skates are available; ext. 7941.

Snow tubing park offers fast thrills. Riders speed down one of several 400-foot long chutes. A handle bar tow whisks riders back to the top again.

Deals and Discounts

Inquire about the low-priced midweek lodging package that includes a Wednesday night.

During two weeks of the season, usually in January and March, a bargain package is offered in which guests pay $77 per night per person, which includes both lodging and a lift ticket. Children ages 6 to 11 pay $37.50; under six are free.

A special weekend lift ticket package allows you to ski Friday night, Saturday day and night, and all day Sunday: adult $72, children 6 to 11 $55.

Vermont

Killington

Address: Killington Road, Killington, Vermont 05751

Telephone: 800-621-MTNS (information and reservations), 802-422-3333, 802-422-3261 (snow report)

Web site: http://www.killington.com

Killington reads like a Guinness Book of East Coast Ski Records: the largest ski resort, the highest-capacity lift system, the longest ski season, the longest alpine ski trail in the United States, the largest grooming fleet, the most on-mountain places to eat, and the best party scene in the East. Known as "The Beast of the East," Killington consists of seven mountains six of which are interconnected by a system of trails.

There's something for everyone: strictly beginner's hills (with their own lodge at the base), thigh-shattering bump runs with moguls the size of Airstream trailers, snowboarders' half pipes, glade trails that meander through the trees, and wide intermediate cruisers.

The size of the place can seem overwhelming at first. Spend your first morning taking one of the complimentary mountain tours that leave from the Snowshed Base Lodge. These tours ski over easy terrain and will give you a better picture of the mountain.

To counter its image as a resort for hard-partying singles, Killington recently created a "family mountain" at Rams Head and installed a new high-speed quad chairlift to replace an older, slower double model. All of Rams Head's trails are beginner or intermediate and lead down to

MOUNTAIN STATISTICS
Base elevation: 1,045 feet
Summit: 4,241 feet
Vertical drop: 3,150 feet
Skiable acres: 1,200
Annual average snowfall: 250 inches
Snowmaking: 722 acres
Night skiing: none
Season: mid-October to late May or early June
Lifts: 33 (3 gondolas, 3 high-speed quads, 6 quads, 3 doubles, 6 triples, 8 surface lifts)
Terrain: 36% beginner, 32% intermediate, 32% advanced
Lift Tickets: adults $49, children 6 to 12 and seniors $29, under 6 free.

FAMILY STATISTICS
Day care: Friendly Penguin Child Care Center, 6 weeks to 6 years, 802-733-1330
Children's lessons: Rams Head Family Center, ages 2 to 12, 802-422-3333
Baby-sitting: Evening baby-sitting can be arranged through the Friendly Penguin Child Care Center, 802-733-1330
Medical: Rutland Medical Center, 802-775-7111

the 2,550-square-foot Family Center, which houses the ski school, day-care center, kids' rentals, and cafeteria. The entire Rams Head area has been designated a family-ski area, which means that fast skiers and party types will steer clear of that part of the mountain. The ski patrol cruises the area to make sure the environment is just right for little ones.

Older kids and experienced skiers have a never-ending variety of turf elsewhere on the mountain where most runs are covered by snowmaking and smoothed to silky perfection by an army of grooming machines.

Most accommodations are in condominiums scattered along Killington Road and within walking distance, or a short shuttle ride to the lifts. Rutland, the nearest town, has many chain motels for the budget conscious.

Because Killington's season goes so late, value packages from early April until the end of the season can save a lot of money. Winter Magic Family Weeks, offered four times per year, allow kids 12 and under to ski for free and teens pay a discounted rate when their parents purchase a five-day midweek ticket.

How to Get There

The closest airports are in Albany, a 2 ¼-hour drive, and in Burlington, about a two-hour drive away. Small commuter planes fly into an airport just south of Rutland, 20 minutes from the resort.

Driving times: Boston, three hours (158 miles); Montréal, 3.5 hours (187 miles); New York City, 5 hours (250 miles).

Once you're there, a shuttle-bus service runs up and down Killington Road between the resort and Rutland.

New Yorkers can take Amtrak's Ethan Allen Express (800-USA-RAIL) from Penn Station to Rutland, fifteen miles west of Killington, with a transfer service available (call 800-621-MTNS to arrange transfer).

Where to Stay
Expensive

Mountain Green Resort is a condominium hotel within a few short steps of the slopes. Units range in size from studios to four bedrooms; all have kitchens and fireplaces, and guests can use the health club which includes a racquetball court, weight room, and a pool. $102–750. Killington Road, RR 1, Box 2841, Killington, VT 05751; 800-336-7754, 802-423-3000.

Trail Creek condos have one- to three-bedroom units with full kitchens, their own washers and dryers, and TVs with VCRs. Three-bedroom units have their own saunas and Jacuzzis in the bathroom. Anyone who stays can use the Activities Center, which has an indoor pool, whirlpool, sauna, and game room. The condos are within walking distance of the Snowshed lift and your own ski-home trail. $145–450. Killington Resort Village, Killington Road, Killington VT 05751; 800-621-MTNS, 802-422-3101.

Moderate

Inn at Long Trail, six miles from Killington's base lodge, is a rustic country inn/ski lodge with pine paneling and pillars that still have the bark on them. Families will be most comfortable in one of the family units, which are two rooms—one with a double bed and the other with two twin beds—with a bathroom in between. Fireplace suites have a bedroom and a living room with a couch that pulls out into two twin beds or a queen-size bed and has a small refrigerator. During the week, stays include breakfast, and on weekends and holidays, rates include breakfast and dinner. The Inn's lively and legendary Irish pub features rousing weekend entertainment. $68–$220. Route 4, Sherburne Pass, Killington, VT 05751; 800-325-2540.

Glazebrook Townhouse Resort's one-, two- and three-bedroom units can sleep up to ten. All have a fully equipped kitchen, their own sauna, a whirlpool, and most important, their own washer/dryer. The complex has two restaurants and a bar. The townhouses are one mile from the lifts, and require a two-night minimum stay. $62–788. Killington Road, P.O. Box 505, Killington, VT 05751; 800-544-8742, 802-422-4425.

Budget

If you've seen one **Econo Lodge**, you've seen them all—except that this one delivers the standard clean and basic motel room, free continental breakfast, and discount prices in a shell that looks like a classic New England inn. Kids 17 and under stay free in their parents' room. Box 7650 Route 4 West, Rutland, VT 05701; 800-922-9067, 802-773-6644.

Comfort Inn at Killington Center has studio suites, and two and three room suites with kitchenette facilities. Standard rooms have either one king or two double beds; some have microwave ovens and small refrigerators. A free continental breakfast is included in the rates. Children under 18 stay free in their parents' room. $72–$495. Killington Road, P.O. Box 493, Killington, VT 05751; 800-257-8664, 802-422-4222.

Children's Ski School

Rams Head Family Center (802-422-3333) contains all of the kids' facilities and easy-to-ride beginner lifts right outside the back door in the Snow Play

Park, including a conveyor belt on the snow, called the Magic Carpet. The high-speed quad slows for loading and unloading, and the center has a food court and lockers. All children's learn-to-ski programs are full- or half-day.

The First Tracks program introduces kids age 2 and 3 to skiing through special games on the snow. You can opt for a lesson only, or combine the lesson with time in the Friendly Penguin Child Care Center.

Ministars, for 4- through 6-year-olds, receive ski instruction using the Perfect Turn teaching techniques, as well as play time indoors and out. Full days include two hours of lessons in the morning and two hours in the afternoon, plus lunch and some indoor rest time.

Superstars (ages 6 to 12) are placed in small groups according to age and ability. Two-hour group lessons for this age group are also available.

Snowboarding lessons for ages 6 to 12 include a two-hour group lesson, rental equipment, and tickets.

Day Care

The Friendly Penguin Child Care Center (802-773-1333) has half- and full-day sessions available for children 6 weeks to 6 years. Advance reservations are required. It's a multi-age facility, which means children are all in one room, grouped by age and interest areas, with a closed nap area for infants. Children age 2 and 3 can sign up for a short ski lesson (extra fee) where they spend about 30 to 45 minutes on the snow in both the morning and afternoon. Children enjoy circle time, singing, arts and crafts, blocks, and toys. Parents can call the facility to inquire about evening babysitting and the staff will try to arrange it.

Teens

Teen Ski and Snowboard Weeks are offered four times a year, with special daily activities, ski and snowboard races, and ski and snowboard clinics. Evening events include teen-only dance parties and mixers. It's free to any teen enrolled in a five-, six-, or seven-day Perfect Turn Clinic (800-621-MTNS).

Snowboarding

The 1,300-foot snowboard park on Snowdon Mountain has tabletops, different-size hits, and some unusual berms and rails. Snowdon Mountain has a regulation 12-foot half pipe and a 9-foot learning pipe, both groomed every other night. A half pipe and park are located at Pico Mountain as well.

Cross-Country Skiing

Mountain Meadows Lodge ski touring center (Thundering Brook Road, Killington, VT 05751; 802-775-1010) has 60 kilometers of trails, rentals, and instruction.

Mountain Top Inn Cross Country Ski Resort (Mountain Top Road, Chittenden, VT 05737; 800-445-2100, 802-483-2311), a 15-minute drive from Killington, has 100 kilometers of trails, snowmaking capabilities, and a log warming hut.

Other Activities

Ice skating at Killington takes place at an outdoor rink (802-422-3970) next to the Grist Mill Restaurant that operates while the weather is cold enough to keep the pond frozen. Skate rentals are available and the rink is lit for night skating. Box 119 Killington Road, Killington VT 05751.

Maple sugaring takes place in March and April at Sugarbush Farm in Woodstock, RRI, Box 568, Woodstock, VT 05091; 802-457-1757.

Snowmobiling is available through Back Country Snow Mobile Tours (802-422-8744) and Killington Snowmobile Tours (802-422-2121).

Snowshoeing: Killington offers naturalist-guided snowshoeing tours. Meet at the skyeship, take the gondola, and walk around the top of the mountain learning about the natural history of the area and enjoying views of five states and Canada. Reservations are required (800-621-MTNS). Mountain Meadows Lodge (802-775-1010) also offers snowshoeing on its groomed cross-county trails.

Deals and Discounts

Special value packages are offered throughout the season: Call general reservations (800-621-MTNS) for an update each year. Weekend packages that combine lodging and lifts with on- and-off-slopes events are also available.

Killington is part of the American Skiing group of companies and offers lift ticket discounts through its Magnificent 7 card (800-543-2SKI), which is good for skiing at Sunday River (see page 250), Sugarloaf USA (see page 245), Sugarbush (see page 225), Mount Snow (see page 198), Haystack (see page 198), and Attitash Bear Peak (see page 233).

Mount Snow (including Haystack)

Address: Mount Snow Resort, P.O. Box 2810, Mount Snow, Vermont 05356

Telephone: 800-245-SNOW (reservations and guest information), 802-464-3333 (information and guest services)

Web site: http://www.mountsnow.com

 With a location close to major Eastern metropolitan areas, Mount Snow is Vermont's second largest ski area. Families of all ages find this a great place for a weekend or midweek ski visit, and families with teens and preteens, especially those who love to board, will find that Mount Snow offers more than many other resorts.

If you visit over a weekend, head to the Planet 9 family area after dinner. Mom and Dad can sit in the warmth and comfort of the lodge, sipping something hot, while their inexhaustible youngsters try crazy snowboard tricks on the night-lit competition half pipe in full view out the lodge's picture windows. Settle back with a good book while the kids try a few spins around the outdoor ice rink next door, or put on your mittens and watch them speed down (and hike up!) the night-lit sledding run. They may pause to join you for a steaming mug of hot chocolate before they throw themselves along the half pipe one more time.

If your kids are older, there is an alcohol-free supervised teen nightclub in this area, known as Planet 9 After Dark. Another club for 10- to 14-year-olds, The Cave Club, has games and contests. If your children are younger and you can get away midweek, you can save money by

MOUNTAIN STATISTICS

Base elevation: 1,900 feet
Summit: 3,600 feet
Vertical drop: 1,700 feet
Skiable acres: 768 (including Haystack)
Annual average snowfall: 155 inches
Snowmaking: 537 acres
Night skiing: snowboarders 460-foot half pipe
Season: early November to late April or early May
Lifts: 26 (3 high-speed quads, 1 quad, 9 triples, 6 doubles, 7 surface lifts)
Terrain: 20% beginner, 60% intermediate, 20% advanced
Lift tickets: adults $49, teens 13 to 17 $41, children 7 to 12 and seniors 65 and up $31, under 6 Free.

FAMILY STATISTICS

Day care: 6 weeks to 5 years, 800-245-SNOW
Children's lessons: ages 3 to 17, 802-245-SNOW, ext. 4316
Baby-sitting: Day-care facility has a list of baby-sitters, 800-245-SNOW ext. 8251
Medical: The Deerfield Valley Health Center, 802-464-5311

visiting over special Teddy Bear Ski Weeks, which offer bargain-price mid-week packages and teddy bear–themed programming that will please the younger set.

The skiing takes place on five different mountain faces with 51 miles of varied trails and two different base areas. Haystack, about three miles from Mount Snow's main base, has one of the five mountain faces, and a shuttle connects the two areas. If you buy your lift tickets at Mount Snow, you can ski Haystack, and there is also another, less expensive Haystack-only ticket. Some families prefer Haystack on busy weekends because it's smaller and not as crowded.

Intermediate skiers are true kings of the mountains in both places. Over half of the terrain is devoted to them, but advanced and beginners are catered to as well. The North Face, known for its bone-rattling steeps, has sheer-faced cruisers, gnarly bump runs, and places to catch some air. Big, wide beginner hills are found at the base of Mount Snow near the learn-to-ski area, and another favorite beginner run, Outcast on Haystack, wanders through the woods. You can schedule a mountain tour in advance by calling the general number and they'll set someone aside for you. A solid kid's ski school employs the Perfect Turn method of teaching, and a cheerful day-care center takes kids as young as 6 weeks.

Accommodations at the base tend to be condominiums, with the rest of the lodging along uninspiring Route 100 and in nearby Wilmington.

How to Get There

Albany County Airport and Bradley International Airport are both about two hours away.

Driving times: Albany, 1.5 hours (68 miles); Boston, 2.5 hours (127 miles); Montréal, 5.5 hours (257 miles); New York, 4 hours (213 miles).

The Moover provides free shuttle service between Haystack and Snow Mountain every hour. It also takes guests between Snow Lake Lodge and other base lodges at Mount Snow and Haystack and up and down Route 100.

Where to Stay

Expensive

The Hermitage is a 24-acre country retreat with 50 kilometers of cross-country ski trails out the back door. Guests stay in antique-filled rooms with fireplaces and enjoy a fine dining experience in the elegant dining room (full dinner and breakfasts are included in the rates). Some of the guest rooms are in the main building, an imposing white farmhouse; some are in a converted carriage house, and the rest are in the Wine House. The

Hermitage is known for its elegance, its extensive wine cellar, and its original Delacroix artwork. There's also a hunting preserve and a sugar house where maple syrup is made. $200–245; children over 7 $70; 2 to 7 $10 (breakfast only); under 2 free. P.O. Box 457, Coldbrook Road, Wilmington, VT 05363; 802-464-3511.

Brookbound, about a mile from the Hermitage, has fourteen rooms, and offers several room configurations especially for families, such as two rooms that connect with a double and twin bed in one room and two twins in the other. Smaller families will be comfortable in one of the larger rooms that have both a double and a twin bed. The hotel has a comfortable great room with a large stone fireplace and TV. The hotel serves a complimentary continental breakfast. The property is about one mile from Haystack, and cross-country trails start right outside the door. $80–125. Rollaways available for $10 per person age two and over. P.O. Box 457 Coldbrook Road, Wilmington, VT 05363; 802-464-3511.

Seasons Condominiums have ski-in-and-out convenience and are some of the nicest and most spacious condos in the area. Choose from one-, two-, or three-bedroom units, all of which have a fireplace and sofa bed in the living room and a washer and dryer, and are distinctly decorated by their individual owners. A sports center on the premises has a pool, hot tubs, a rec room with Ping-Pong, a basketball game, Foosball, and shuffleboard. A small skating rink is a short walk away. $120–180. 299 Mountain Road, Mount Snow, VT 05356; 800-451-4211, 802-464-7788.

Moderate

Kitzhof, one of the many small hotels and motels along Route 100, offers a bit more charm than most and has a number of rooms and suites suitable for families. Some rooms have a queen-size or double bed and two twins, and there are three suites with a queen-size bed in one room and a door connecting to a second room with bunk beds. Rates include a full breakfast and a two-minute shuttle ride to the lifts. There is a lounge area with fireplace and TV. $100–130. Route 100 HCR 63, Box 14, West Dover, VT 05356, Route 100 800-388-8310, 802-464-8310.

Austrian Haus along Route 100 offers simple rooms for families: Their economy room is divided by a partition into two rooms that share a bathroom. Other rooms have two or three double beds. A complimentary breakfast comes with the rooms. Kids under 4 stay free. A fireplace lounge and game room have board games, and a pool and sauna are on-site. Valley transportation stops out front. $28–68 per person 12 and older, reduced rates for ages 4 to 11. P.O. Box 335, West Dover, VT 05356; 802-464-3911.

Snow Lake Lodge offers a location 300 yards from the lifts, but if you're too exhausted to walk you can ride the shuttle. The property has a huge lobby lounge, game room, restaurant, pub, and a sauna and gym. Its standard rooms have two double beds, and suites have a king-size bed and a living room with a pull-out sofa. $120–180. 199 Mountain Road, Mount Snow, VT 04356; 800-451-4211, 802-464-3333.

Budget
Snow Creek Inn is a simple motel 1½ miles from the ski resort. Families with one child can stay in efficiencies with a kitchenette, but all rooms have a small refrigerator and TV. One room has a queen-size bed and a connecting door to a room with twin beds. Laundry facilities are on-site. $60–95. Route 100, P.O. Box 1008, West Dover, VT 05356; 802-464-5632.

Old Red Mill Inn, in the village of Wilmington about 15 minutes from the slopes, recalls Vermont of the past. The building was originally a nineteenth-century sawmill and still has many of the original touches. It's a good buy even though the rooms are small—ideal for families with kids over the age of 6 or 7. Two family rooms have four twin beds in one large room. $80–160. Route 100, Wilmington, VT 05363; 802-464-5632.

Children's Ski School
All kids' programming is headquartered in the same base area, making it easy for nervous parents to take a few runs and check back on their kids. Pre-Ski programs are available for 3-year-olds enrolled in Mount Snow's child-care program (see day care below).

Snow Camp, for 4- to 6-year-olds, combines indoor and outdoor snow games with lessons. The staff is known for encouraging children to have a good time; half- and full-days are available.

Haystack has its own separate ski school facilities for the kids. Mountain Camp and Mountain Riders are for children age 7 to 12 who receive half-day or all-day clinics in skiing or boarding; each group gets two sessions of personalized coaching, plus lunch and a snack. 800-245-SNOW, ext. 4316 (reservations required).

The Teen Extreme program, ages 13 to 17, includes coaching during the day for skiers and riders and social activities in the evening.

Day Care

Mount Snow offers child care for youngsters 6 weeks to 5 years; a total of 75 kids can be accommodated. Babies and toddlers are grouped by age and have sleep rooms for nap times. Cooking and music projects are specialties: A musician comes in four days a week, and the kids bake cookies, pretzels, or Play-Doh. In the outdoor play area, kids build snowmen. Babies go for a ride in a four-seater buggy. Reservations are required; 800-245-SNOW.

Teens

The entire Planet 9 area is a center for teen activities thanks to its night-lit half pipe, and skating and sledding venues. Planet 9 After Dark is a teen nightclub for ages 15 to 20 that has a DJ, soft-drinks bar, snacks, and jukebox. It's open from 8 P.M. to midnight.

The Cave Club, in the main base lodge, is open from 7:30 to 10 P.M. for kids ages 10 to 14 (kids have to be signed in by their parents). Kids play trivia games and have silly contests where they can win prizes. Both nightclubs feature DJ entertainment, adult supervision, and refreshments. On Saturdays, participation in the Teen Extreme program includes admission to programs in these clubs.

Snowboarding

The Gut is a 460-foot competition-size half pipe with lights for night riding, open Friday and Saturday and holidays. If you want to watch your youngsters catch big air, you can see straight up this pipe from the Carinthia Base Lodge. Un Blanco Gulch is a snowboard only park on the main mountain for more advanced boarders only with approximately 25 different freestyle elements. Its total length of 2,700 feet and average width of 80 feet makes it highly popular. El Diablo is a terrain park on the Exhibition Trail with all different sizes of terrain features for all levels of skiers and snowboard riders.

Plenty of other snowboard and ski elements are clearly marked throughout the resort. "Mount Snow's Greatest Hits" are jumps and terrain features scattered all over the mountains. Haystack has a rider cross course with banks, jumps, etc; it's like a timed motor cross course for advanced snowboarders.

Cross-Country Skiing

Timbercreek Cross Country Center (802-464-0999) is right across from the entrance to Mount Snow and has instruction, rentals, and groomed trails.

The White House Ski Touring Center has 43 kilometers of trails. Equipment and snowshoes rentals are on-site. Lodging is available in an elegant country inn. Route 9, Wilmington, VT 05363; 800-541-2135.

The Hermitage (802-464-3551) has 50 kilometers of trails through the backcountry. Coldbrook Road, Box 457, Wilmington, VT 05363.

Advanced cross-country skiers can take the **Ridge Trail** between Mount Snow and Haystack. Pay $10 to ride the lift up at Haystack and ski to Mount Snow, taking a shuttle back.

Other Activities

A *petting zoo* at Adams Farm (802-464-3762) gives little ones a hands-on animal experience.

Snowmobiling tours are conducted throughout the area and the backcountry by High Country Snowmobile Tours (800-627-7533) and Rock Maple Snowmobile Tours and Rentals (800-479-3284). Reservations are suggested.

Sleigh rides: Adams Farm (802-464-3764) has sleigh rides through wooded areas, at night or during the day. Wrapped up in big blankets, riders are regaled with a fascinating history of the farm and countryside and treated to a stop at a warming hut for hot chocolate and board games, then serenaded by a player piano, before returning to the farm.

Winter walks are led by naturalist Lynn Levine. The Owl Moonwalk (for ages 5 and up) meanders through the woods on a winter night. Walkers learn to imitate the call of a barred owl on their trip through the woods, and are taught how to listen to the sounds of the night. Animal Tracking Winterwalks take walkers through the Green Mountain National Forest where walkers can see (and maybe follow) the footprints of fox, fisher, porcupine, mink, and squirrels. Snowshoes are supplied. Book the walks through guest services (802-464-3333).

Deals and Discounts

During Teddy Bear Ski Weeks (there are five weeks scheduled intermittently each season), kids ages 6 to 12 ski free and receive an ice-cream sundae and admission to family-oriented events throughout the resort when their parents purchase at least one five-day lift ticket. The week runs Sunday through Thursday. Children will be thrilled with the many charming activities offered: photos with teddy, a meeting with Smokey Bear, grooming-machine rides, a breakfast with pancakes shaped like teddy bears, a theater presentation, races, an ice-cream party, and the teddy-bear parade, where kids make their own teddy bears and march in the parade.

Some other good-value packages are offered midweek, and designated special-value weeks offer half-price lodging and tickets (Sunday arrival required).

Mount Snow is part of the American Skiing Company and offers lift ticket discounts through its Magnificent 7 card (800-543-2SKI), which is good for skiing at Sunday River (see page 250), Sugarloaf (see page 245), Sugarbush (see page 225), Killington (see page 193), and Attitash Bear Peak (see page 233).

Okemo Mountain Resort

Address: 77 Okemo Ridge Road, Ludlow, Vermont 05149
Telephone: 800-78-OKEMO (central reservations), 802-228-4041 (information)
Web site: http://www.okemo.com

"A great family mountain" is how loyal skiers describe the Okemo experience. This resort has somehow managed to combine a cozy environment for families whose younger children are just learning to ski with enough high-energy flash to please the teen crowd. Parents appreciate the huge selection in trailside condominiums and a mountain layout where all trails lead to one central base area.

Okemo is known as an intermediate's mountain since more than half of the terrain consists of easy-going impeccably groomed cruisers. Most of the mountain is covered by artificial snow when nature doesn't provide the real thing, and Okemo's snowmaking equipment knows just how to shoot out the light stuff. It has the best snowmaking coverage in the East.

Snowboarders rave about The Park, an enormous snowboard playground with an ear splitting 600-watt sound system and a 420-foot half pipe. Okemo was the only North American stopover for the International Snowboard Federation Master World Cup Pro Tour in 1997.

Okemo offers some attractive discounts. Beginners can use two surface lifts free of charge; children 12 and under stay free at resort properties (sharing a unit with their parents); 3- and 4-year-olds can take an introductory ski lesson for just $15; and college students get substantial discounts on lift tickets.

Kids' Night Out takes place on selected weekends and holidays, offering Mom and Dad a night off while the kids have pizza, movies, and games.

MOUNTAIN STATISTICS
Base elevation: 1,194 feet
Summit: 3,344 feet
Vertical drop: 2,150 feet
Skiable acres: 500
Annual average snowfall: 200 inches
Snowmaking: 95% of terrain
Night skiing: none
Season: early November through late April
Lifts: 13 (3 high-speed quads, 4 regular quads, 3 triples, 3 surface lifts)
Terrain: 25% beginner, 50% intermediate, 25% advanced
Lift tickets: adults $50, young adults 13 to 17 $42, children 7 to 12 and seniors over 65 $31, under 7 free.

FAMILY STATISTICS
Day care: Penguin Playground Daycare Center, 6 weeks to 8 years; 802-228-4041, ext. 105 and 261.
Children's lessons: SkiWee ages 4 to 7 and Young Mountain Explorers ages 7+; 802-228-4041 ext. 10.
Baby-sitting: List available at Penguin
Medical: Rutland Hospital 802-775-7111

A good selection of lodging is available right at the base, and in the charming New England town of Ludlow, which is just a mile from the resort.

How to Get There

The closest international airports—Albany, Manchester, and Burlington—are all about a two-hour drive away. Driving times: New York, 4.5 hours (225 miles); Albany, 2.25 hours (105 miles); Boston, 2.75 hours (120 miles). A shuttle service runs between Ludlow and the ski base, but a car is helpful.

Where to Stay

Expensive

Okemo Trailside is located mid-mountain; some units are on the ski trails while others are on the shuttle service. The one- to four-bedroom luxury houses have fireplaces, master bedrooms, Jacuzzi tubs, and saunas. $313–550. Westhill Road, Ludlow, VT 05149; 800-829-8205, 802-228-8255.

Solitude Village Condominiums offer ski-in-ski-out convenience. They'll ultimately consist of over 175 spacious and elegant condos, townhouses, and single-family homes. Amenities include a day lodge, cafeteria, and a recreation center with pool. $145–850. 77 Okemo Ridge, Ludlow, VT 05149; 800-78-OKEMO, 802-228-5571.

Moderate

Best Western/Ludlow Colonial Motel has modern units connected to an 1825 Colonial home. Rooms range from standard motel rooms with one king- or two queen-size beds to kitchenette and family units. All have coffee makers. The village of Ludlow and its restaurants and shops are a short walk away. The property is on the Okemo Village Shuttle Bus route. $80–275. 93 Main Street, Ludlow, VT 05149; 802-228-8188.

Ludlow Colonial Condominiums Condo units range from efficiencies to one- and two-bedroom condominiums. All have full kitchens. Some of the condo units are adjacent to the Best Western/Ludlow Colonial Motel and the others are closer to Okemo Mountain. All are on the shuttle route. $95–275. 30–32 Pond Street, Ludlow, VT 05149; 802-228-8188.

Budget

Cavendish Point offers some very attractive midweek packages. Kids stay free with their parents, and facilities include a restaurant, an indoor pool, a hot tub, and a game room. A shuttle runs to and from the mountain, and the big lobby has country charm. Most popular with families are rooms with two queen- or king-size beds and bunks. $89–149. Route 103, Cavendish, VT 05142; 802-226-7688.

Children's Ski School

The SKIwee program is for ages 4 to 7; MINIriders snowboard program is for ages 5 to 7, and the Young Mountain Explorers program is for ages 7 to 12, as is the YOUNGriders snowboard program. The TEENriders snowboard program for 13- to 18-year-olds operates primarily on weekends and holiday periods. The Get Altitude program for 13- to 18-year-old skiers operates on weekends and holidays.

Parent and Tots private lessons allow parents to tag along and share in their children's learning experience. Little ones ages 3 and 4 who just want to sample skiing can try the Introduction to Skiing program through the daycare (below).

Day Care

Penguin Playground Daycare Center inside the base lodge has care for children 6 weeks to 8 years. Children are separated into age-appropriate groups. All kids have the opportunity to go outside for snow play when the weather is good. An Introduction to Skiing option for 3- and 4-year-olds costs $15 and is a good way to give your child a positive first skiing experience. Indoor activities during the day include arts and crafts, games, circle and story times, quiet time, and puppet shows. Reservations are recommended.

The Kids Night Out Program (802–228–4041) takes place at the center every Saturday evening from 6 to 10 P.M. starting Christmas week and continuing through late March.

Teens

Altitude After Dark, open Saturday nights and midweek during selected holiday periods, is a teen nightspot for ages 13 to 18 and features dancing to a professional DJ, outdoor volleyball, and other fun activities.

Snowboarding

Okemo has The Park, The Pipe, and The Pull for boarders. The Park is a gigantic snowboard playground that features a variety of jumps and hits. The Pull is a J-bar lift that carries riders to the top of the Park 'n Pipe zone. The Pipe is 420-foot half pipe that is groomed to perfection by a pipe dragon. Terrain features include big hits, tabletops, rails, and rolling knolls. Lessons are available for all ages and abilities.

Cross-Country Skiing

Fox Run, two miles from Okemo Mountain, offers 20 kilometers of trails through forests and meadows along streams and ponds. Rental equipment and lessons are available. 802-228-8871.

Other Activities

Snowmobiling: Guided tours are available from Okemo Snowmobile Tours (800-328-8275) and Snow Country Snowmobile Tours and rentals (802-226-7529).

Ice skating: Dorsey park in downtown Ludlow has a free public rink (802-228-2849) that is lit for night use. Bring your own skates.

Deals and Discounts

Beginners can use two surface lifts free of charge. Children 12 and under stay free in their parents' rooms at resort properties. Introductory ski lessons for ages 3 and 4 cost only $15. College students who purchase a $39 college card get their first midweek lift ticket free, and get half-price lift tickets midweek (non-holiday) and discounts of $10 per lift ticket on weekends.

❄ Smugglers' Notch Resort

Address: Route 108, Smugglers' Notch, Vermont 05464-9599
Telephone: 800-451-8752, 802-644-8851
Web site: http://www.smuggs.com

Smugglers' Notch continues to capture the top spot for family programs from the readers of *Snow Country* and *Skiing* magazines. Its innovative and comprehensive children's and teen activities and highly ranked kids' ski-and-snowboard school back up its promise of guaranteed family fun for all ages. It's the summer camp/ cruise ship of ski areas, with so many choices of how to spend your days and evenings that you can't possibly pack them all in. Every night of the week has a different theme and different activity. During the day, if your aching muscles need a break from the pounding of the slopes, you can head out on a variety of day trips or take an art class. Five nights a week at the Alice's Wonderland Child Enrichment Center, a Parents' Night Out program enables parents to leave kids between the ages of 3 and 12 for the evening so that parents can get some time alone. On Thursday, often the last full day for week-long guests, a cookie race is held, followed by a delightful skit by ski instructors, a torchlight parade, and fireworks.

Hard-to-please teens are offered special ski and snowboard programs that don't start until the afternoon; the resort staff found that teens had a tough time falling out of bed for a 9 A.M. class. Their fun heads into the evening with activities such as snow volleyball and a pizza party.

Skiing is on three different mountains and beginners get one mountain and one lift system all to themselves. They'll find terrain features and a

MOUNTAIN STATISTICS
Base elevation: 1,030 feet
Summit: 3,640 feet
Vertical drop: 2,610 feet
Skiable acres: 1,000 (250 groomed)
Annual average snowfall: 272 inches
Snowmaking: 60%
Night skiing: night snowboarding lesson for beginners: handle-tow lift
Season: late November to mid-April
Lifts: 8 (5 doubles, 3 surface lifts)
Terrain: 21% beginner, 56% intermediate, 18% advanced, 5% extreme
Lift tickets: adults $44, youth 17 and under $28, seniors 65 to 69 $22, 6 and under and 70 and over free.

FAMILY STATISTICS
Day care: Alice's Wonderland Child Enrichment Center, ages 6 weeks to 6 years; 802-644-1180 (reservations required)
Children's lessons: Snow Sport U., ages 3 to 17; 802-644-1148
Baby-sitting: Alice's Wonderland has a list of baby-sitters and will arrange bookings for you; 802-644-1180
Medical: The Cambridge Regional Health Center, 802-644-5114

special terrain park with bumps, rolls, and spines designed just for them. The second-highest vertical drop in Vermont after Killington gives Smugglers' Notch some steep descents for the intermediate and advanced skier, and new snowmaking has improved much of the mountain. The number of groomed trails remains consistent, but the resort has opened up the area between groomed runs to give powder hounds something to crow about. Chairlifts are mostly slower double models, which can result in long lift lines on weekends and holidays.

Anyone who stays two nights or more receives a one-day ticket to ski Stowe Mountain Resort (see page 214) next door. The connection between the two ski areas is worth the trip alone: One trail leads over and one trail leads back. To get to Stowe, skiers cross over Sterling Pond, Vermont's highest natural trout pond, then ski down a little path dotted with birch trees, which opens up to reveal Stowe Mountain. Going back, the trail follows the line of the Notch through the woods until it reaches Sterling Pond.

Smugglers' Notch is a largely self-contained village with lodging, restaurants, ski lifts, an outdoor ice rink, tubing hill, sleigh rides, a well-stocked store, nightclub, and parties for kids and adults all within walking distance. Many parents feel comfortable letting their older kids roam around by themselves.

How to Get There

USAir, Continental, United Airlines, Northwest Airlink, and Delta's Business Express fly into Burlington International Airport, 30 miles away. Driving times: Boston, 4 hours (225 miles); New York City, 6 hours (342 miles); Montréal, 2 hours (91 miles).

Where to Stay

Smugglers' Notch Condominiums consist of 415 units in several dozen buildings scattered throughout the Village. All units are privately owned but are managed by the resort, which puts strict requirements on owners, insuring a uniformity of quality and condition. Ranging in size from studios to five-bedroom units, all come with kitchenettes or kitchens. Guests have complimentary access to the ice-skating rink, tubing hill, swimming pool, and all evening entertainment. Accommodations are sold as a package that includes ski tickets and lessons. The longer you stay, the lower the rates drop per night. $158–845. Route 108, Smugglers' Notch, VT 05464; 800-451-8752.

Children's Ski School

Ski-school programs operate from several different areas, depending on a child's ability. Discovery Dynamos Ski Camp for 3- to 5-years-olds combines ski lessons with interactive games, sleigh rides, storytelling, and other supervised activities. The ski portion of the day starts at 9:30 A.M. and runs until 2 P.M., with entertainment from 2 to 4 P.M. Two-year-olds can take private lessons with the Mom and Me . . . Dad and Me Program.

Adventure Rangers Ski Camps for ages 6 to 12 offer full-day ski instruction, guided ski treks, races, mountain-adventure games, and a hot lunch. Adventure Rangers Snowboard Camps, also for ages 6 to 12, use a coaching style to meet all levels of ability.

The afternoon Mountain Explorer Ski and Snowboard Programs (802-644-1148) for ages 13 to 17 feature challenging instruction and race development. The program starts at 1 P.M. and continues on into the evening with activities off the slopes.

Day Care

Alice's Wonderland Child Enrichment Center (802-644-1180) offers day care for children 6 weeks to 6 years of age in a bright and cheerful 6,900-square-foot facility that can accommodate up to 97 kids. All on one floor, it's divided so that kids are grouped by ages. A special crib room allows for quiet nap times. Rooms are filled with toys, giant Legos, climbing structures, and some popular six-foot-tall teddy bears. Reservations required.

Teens

The Outer Limits Teen Center is open daily from 5 P.M. to midnight. It's equipped with music, videos, snacks, and a pool table. Special on-mountain teen activities take place during the afternoon and evening. The center's activities include snow volleyball, a pizza party, tub club party in the spa, a tube sliding party, moonlight treks, DJ dancing, and Karaoke.

Snowboarding

The terrain park has spines, tabletops, a quarter pipe, and other hits; it's designed primarily for snowboarders but is open to skiers. A nighttime beginner's snowboarding lesson (ages 6 and up) is available Tuesday, Wednesday, and Saturday evenings at Sir Henry's Learning & Fun Park. It lasts three hours and includes rental equipment and use of a handle-tow lift ride to the top of the night-lit hill. It's perfect for those who don't want to give up their ski day to learn a new sport. After an intensive hour of instruction, boarders are allowed to try their skills while instructors station themselves around the hill and offer helpful tips.

Cross-Country Skiing

The Nordic Ski Center (802-644-1173) has 23 kilometers of groomed track and trails, a base lodge with a warming stove, hot drinks, rental equipment (including kids' sizes), and group lessons in traditional skiing, ski skating, and telemark skiing. Don't miss the moonlight trip exploring the winter woods. Guided backcountry tours ski off the beaten track and explore the meadows and forests of the region. Other cross country resorts in the area can be found on page 218.

Other Activities

Smugglers' Notch offers many activities as part of their vacation package. Call 800-451-8752 for information on activities unless another phone number is indicated

Craft classes: The "Artists in the Mountain" program features ten different crafts such as dried-flower arranging, bronze powder stenciling, Colonial tin punch, and creative beading. One to two classes are held daily and last two to three hours. Classes require an extra fee that covers supplies.

Day trips: Visit Montréal for the day, search for antiques and collectibles, or make a Vermont excursion that includes tours of the Ben and Jerry's Ice Cream Factory (802-244-TOUR), the Cold Hollow Cider Mill, and the Trapp Family Lodge.

Horseback riding and sleigh rides: Right next door across from the entrance to Smugglers' Notch is a private concession, the Vermont Horse Park (802-644-5347), which offers trail rides, pony rides, and sleigh rides.

Ice skating: Smugglers' outdoor rink is lit at night. Rental skates are available, including kids' sizes.

Maple sugaring: If you visit in March or April, take a trip to a maple-sugar house; the resort can help you make arrangements. Many are open to the public, so you can see maple syrup in the making and taste it while it's still warm.

Snowshoeing: Snowshoes can be rented from the Nordic Center (802-644-1173), and trekkers can walk the centers groomed trails or head out into the backcountry.

Tennis: Two indoor tennis courts are right next to the Nordic Center.

Tub Club has two outdoor hot tubs, a sauna, a steam room, and exercise equipment. Massages can be arranged for an extra fee.

Tubing hill: Organized tube sledding down a 400-foot night-lit hill takes place every evening from 4 to 9 P.M. Tubes are supplied.

Deals and Discounts
During selected weeks throughout the winter, the resort offers specials that kick in something extra for free, such as child care, rental skis, or the FamilyFest Kids' all-day camp program.

Stowe Mountain Resort

Address: 5781 Mountain Road (Route 108), Stowe, Vermont 05672-4890

Telephone: 800-253-4SKI, 802-253-3000 (central reservations)

Web site: http://www.stowe. com

Stowe is one of the few Eastern resorts whose authentic village center rivals the quaintness and character of western resorts like Crested Butte Mountain Resort or Telluride. But Stowe's personality is distinctly New England in character, with steepled churches, white clapboard buildings, covered bridges, and red barns. Downtown streets are lined with specialty shops, galleries, antique stores, inns, and restaurants in addition to small-town businesses like the pharmacy and hardware store. It boasts more AAA three- and four-diamond lodges and restaurants than any other town in New England except Boston.

Stowe's first trails were cut by the Civilian Conservation Corps up the sides of Mt. Mansfield, Vermont's highest peak. Workers labored with axes, handsaws, and plenty of sweat to cut trails in the natural fallline of the mountain. The first rope tow, powered by a car engine, was installed in 1936, making Stowe the birthplace of New England skiing. In 1940, Stowe's first chairlift, a single, was installed; it broke down on its first run. Today a gondola and six chairlifts distribute skiers all over the two main peaks that make up the resort, Mt. Mansfield and Spruce Peak. Cross country skiers headquarter in Stowe to enjoy an excellent and expansive trail system special tickets are available that combine downhill and cross country skiing.

MOUNTAIN STATISTICS

Base elevation: 1,280 feet
Summit: 4,393 feet
Vertical drop: 2,360 feet
Skiable acres: 480
Annual average snowfall: 260 inches
Snowmaking: 73%
Night skiing: Wednesday through Sunday
Season: mid-November to late April
Lifts 11: (1 gondola, 1 high-speed quad, 1 triple, 6 doubles, 2 surface lifts)
Terrain: 16% beginner, 59% intermediate, 25% advanced
Lift tickets: adults $49, children 6 to 12, seniors over 64 $29, under 6 free.

FAMILY STATISTICS

Day care: Cub's Day Care, 6 weeks to 6 years, 802-253-3000, ext. 3686
Children's lessons: Children's Adventure Center, ages 3 to 12, 802-253-3000, ext. 3685
Baby-sitting: The Stowe Area Association publishes a comprehensive list of baby-sitters, 800-24-STOWE
Medical: Copley Hospital is ten miles away, 802-888-4231

Spruce Peak is dedicated to intermediate and beginning skiers, while Mt. Mansfield has terrain for all abilities. Mansfield's legendary and fearsome Front Four are double-black-diamond trails that should sport a sign reading: SKIING THESE RUNS CAN BE HAZARDOUS TO YOUR HEALTH. But you'll most likely be meandering along some of the East's longest cruising runs: Of the 11 lifts on both mountains, five are more than a mile long. Skiers in the know about Stowe recommend you rise early and hit the gondola at 7:30 to 8 A.M. to take advantage of the best light and fewest crowds. Night skiing takes place at Stowe up the gondola run Wednesdays through Sundays and nightly during holiday weeks. The children's ski school and day-care center operate from the same building at the base of the mountain.

Very few of the accommodations at Stowe are ski-in-and-out, but many are in Stowe or along Mountain Road, which starts in the Village and wanders along to the slopes. Lodgings for every taste and budget, from motels to country inns, are connected by the convenient shuttle system.

Smugglers' Notch Resort (see page 209) is just over the mountain from Stowe, and the two resorts have joined forces and built a two-way interconnect for skiers: One trail leads over and one trail leads back to insure that skiers will not have to do any climbing. Lift tickets to one entitle guests to ski the other.

How to Get There

Burlington International Airport, 40 minutes away, has nonstop flights from major airports through the U.S. The Amtrak "Vermonter" (800-USA-RAIL) stops in Waterbury, about 15 minutes away; shuttles can be arranged from your hotel. Driving times: Albany, 3.5 hours (170 miles); New York, 6 hours (325 miles); Boston, 3.25 hours (205 miles); Montréal, 2.25 hours (140 miles). The Stowe trolley and intermountain bus system takes skiers to and from the lodging, the Village, and the base of the ski area.

Where to Stay
Expensive

Trapp Family Lodge (http://www.trapfamily.com) is an elegant Austrian-style lodge and one of Stowe's premiere lodgings. Its cross-country center is the oldest in the nation and features trails that amble through 2,200 acres of rolling meadows and woodlands. A small children's program operates over the winter with arts and crafts and indoor activities, usually for one to two sessions a day. Named after a relative of *The Sound of Music*'s Trapp family, the resort is four miles from the downhill slopes of Stowe and has sleigh rides, snowshoeing, a lovely restaurant, and a tea room. It offers a free shuttle to the slopes, an indoor pool, and a weight room. Rooms, all luxuriously furnished in dark woods and goose-down comforters, have a variety of bed configurations. $90–225. 42 Trapp Hill Road, Stowe, VT 05672; 800-826-7000, 802-253-8511.

Topnotch at Stowe Resort and Spa (http://www.topnotch-resort.com) is another terrific establishment for families of varied interests. Nonskiers can amuse themselves with the four indoor tennis courts, sleigh rides, extensive spa facilities, and fine dining. Cross-country aficionados will find 100 kilometers of ski trails starting out the back door. Attractive bedrooms are furnished with antiques and original art. Townhouse decor varies according to their owner's taste. Children's programs operate over holiday periods. The full-service spa is adults only and has massages, herbal wraps, and the works. $165–325. Mountain Road, P.O. Box 1458, Stowe, VT 05672; 800-451-8686, 802-253-8585.

Moderate

The Golden Eagle Resort, a half mile from Stowe Village, offers family packages that include lodging, breakfast, ice skating, and a sleigh ride. Two nights a week "kids' night out" operates from 6 to 8 P.M. with a movie, activities, and snacks, so parents can eat a leisurely dinner. Within the resort are a whirlpool, indoor swimming pool, sauna, weight room, and fitness center. Accommodations range from hotel rooms and suites to two-bedroom apartments and three-bedroom houses. A shuttle to Stowe is available. $85–350. Mountain Road, P.O. Box 1090, Stowe, VT; 800-626-1010, 802-253-4811.

Innsbruck Inn has hotel rooms, suites, and efficiencies as well as one five-bedroom chalet. Fireside breakfasts are included (children's menu) in the price, and there's an outdoor spa. The property is 1½ miles from the lifts, and a skier shuttle is available for a dollar per person each way. $69–139. 4361 Mountain Road, Stowe, VT 05672; 800-225-8582, 802-253-8582.

Budget

Country Village Rentals handles 140 private homes in Stowe and they match houses with people's family size and budget. 800-320-8777, 802-253-8777.

Commodores Inn is right on the trolley line that whisks guests to the ski area and back. Some of its simple, clean rooms connect; most have two queen-size beds. Facilities include a lounge area with a massive fieldstone fireplace, a restaurant, a game room with Ping-Pong, pool, and video games, an indoor swimming pool and Jacuzzi, and a small health club. Stowe Village is about a mile away. Kids 18 and under stay free in their parents' room, and cots and cribs are available. $92–112. Route 100 South, P.O. Box 970, Stowe, VT 05672; 800-44-STOWE, 802-253-7131.

Inn at Little River is a charming restored (circa 1825) manor house in the heart of Stowe Village. A number of its guest rooms have kitchenettes, and all units have quilts, antiques, and country-style furnishings. A restaurant is open for lunch, dinner, and Sunday brunch. Children 12 and under stay free, and ski packages are available. $85–270. 123 Mountain Road, Stowe, VT 05672; 800-227-1108, 802-253-4836.

Children's Ski School

The Children's Adventure Center (802-253-3000, ext. 3685) offers skiing and snowboarding lessons for kids 3 to 12. Beginning classes are held in a 1,200-square-foot outdoor snow play area and on the gentle slopes of Spruce Peak. Children age 3 to 5 have up to four hours of ski activities as well as snow play and indoor fun. Mini-Mountain Adventure is for 6-to 8-year-olds and Mountain Adventure is for 9- to 12-year-olds; both offer instructor-led trail exploration and ski tips. Prices include lunch, coaching, and a lift ticket. Two-hour group lessons are also available for kids. Snowboarding pros teach boarders as young as 7.

Day Care

Cub's Day Care (802-253-3000, ext. 3686), at the base of Spruce and separated by a few buildings from the kids' ski school, is for nonskiing children from 6 weeks to 6 years old. The homey center was originally a private residence and its floor-to-ceiling windows offer views of the mountain and of the birds and squirrels who come to dine from the feeder outside. Infants (up to 16 months) have a playroom and nap room all to themselves, and toddlers and preschoolers enjoy music, arts and crafts, singing, puppets, climbing equipment, and quiet time. The older groups have an enclosed play area—a big "snow box" filled with pails, shovels, trucks, and other toys. Hot lunch and snacks are served daily. Reservations strongly suggested. Personal pagers are available for $5.

Teens

Teen Extreme is an all-day program in a fun, social setting for 13- to 16-year-olds who are intermediate and advanced skiers and boarders. Some night skiing is offered during holiday weeks.

Snowboarding

Four different terrain parks entertain boarders of all abilities. There are 3 half pipes; the Jungle terrain park, which is a double-black diamond with jumps, hits, and obstacles; a park for intermediate boarders and skiers, too; and another designed with beginners in mind. The Stowe Ski and Snowboard Training Center guarantees improvement for riders of all abilities. In addition to beginning, intermediate, and advanced clinics, you can arrange for private coaching and freestyle minicamps. Kids 7 to 12 get special lessons.

Cross-Country Skiing

Stowe has four interconnected cross-country ski centers and a large trail system.

Trapp Family Lodge Touring Center (800-826-7000, 802-253-8511), the first commercial ski center in the U.S., is the centerpiece of the cross-country system. Features include a rental shop, lessons, and groomed beginner and intermediate trails. Trails link Trapp Family Lodge to Stowe Mountain Resort Cross Country Center.

The Stowe Mountain Resort Cross-Country Center (800-253-4SKI, 802-253-3688) has 35 kilometers of groomed terrain and another 40 kilometers of country trails.

Topnotch at Stowe Resort and Spa (800-451-8686, 802-253-8585) also has a cross-country ski center that is connected to Stowe's 5.3-mile recreation path, a rather flat trail that connects Topnotch to the other ski areas and Stowe Village.

Edson Hill Manor Touring Center (800-621-0284, 802-253-7371) is the fourth cross-country center from which skiers can access Vermont's Catamount trail, a 300-mile route that runs the spine of the Green Mountains from Massachusetts to Québec.

Other Activities

Snowshoeing: Rentals are available from a variety of shops in Stowe and at all of the cross-country centers (see above).

Sleigh rides are available for the public at Topnotch at Stowe Resort and Spa; 800-451-8686, 802-253-8585.

Ice skating is available in the Jackson Arena, an open-air rink covered by a roof; skate rentals are available. Depot Street, Stowe VT 05672; 802-253-4402.

Ben and Jerry's Ice Cream tours: After being shown around this Vermont success story (800-244-TOUR) in nearby Waterbury, linger over the free samples.

Deals and Discounts

Lift ticket prices drop considerably early and late season. Order ski tickets in 72 hours advance and you'll save 10 percent off the window rate (888-253-4TIX). Place your order at least three days before you plan to ski. Other discounts are added when you pick up your tickets.

Call central reservations (800-235-4SKI) and ask for the best current discount offer that will be available when you plan to come.

Stratton Mountain Resort

Address: RR1 Box 145, Stratton Mountain, Vermont 05155

Telephone: 800-STRATTON, 802-297-4000 (central reservations)

Web site: http://www.stratton.com

 Stratton is heralded as the birthplace of snowboarding: It opened its trails to boarders back in 1983 after snowboard pioneer Jake Burton convinced Stratton management that this was a new sport whose time had come. The resort has been home to the U.S. Open Snowboarding Championships for a number of years. The same regulation half pipe, scrupulously groomed to glassy perfection, that is used for the Championships can be used by your young champions. Snowboard equipment and instruction is available for kids as young as 5, as long as they weigh at least 40 pounds.

The alpine-style base village is a smartly planned community that has every convenience a skier or nonskier could want—restaurants, cafés, chic boutiques, gift shops, and bars and taverns. Accommodations are clustered around the town square, and no accommodation is farther than three quarters of a mile away. Convenient shuttles operate regularly, so you can leave your car behind.

Stratton is one big mountain, which makes it easy to master. The entire family can take the gondola up the mountain together, ski off in different directions, and meet up again at the bottom. Beginners can ski easygoing Mike's Run, while the more advanced skiers in the group can duck off and ski the moguls. An entire section of the mountain has been fenced off and designated as a slow-skiing family zone. Dubbed the Learning Park, it consists of 40 acres of gentle terrain and trails where kids can ski safely on their own. The narrow

MOUNTAIN STATISTICS

Base elevation: 1,876 feet

Summit: 3,875 feet

Vertical drop: 2,003 feet

Skiable acres: 563

Annual average snowfall: 190 inches

Snowmaking: 75% of terrain, all lifts

Night skiing: yes

Season: mid-November to May

Lifts: 12 (1 high-speed 6-passenger lift, 1 12-passenger gondola, 4 quads, 1 triple, 3 doubles, and 2 surface lifts)

Terrain: 35% beginner, 37% intermediate, 28% advanced

Lift tickets: adults $52, juniors 7 to 12, seniors 70+ $31, young adults 13 to 17 and seniors 65 to 69 $42.

FAMILY STATISTICS

Day care: Child Care Center, 6 weeks to 5 years, 800-STRATTON

Children's lessons: KidsKamp, for ages 4 to 12, 800-STRATTON

Baby-sitting: Welcome Center keeps a list, 802-297-2200

Medical: Mountain Valley Health Center in Londonderry, 802-824-6901 winding-through-the-trees trails are popular with kids, but parents may need to duck every now and then. Terrain parks for both skiers and snowboarders are scattered around the mountain. Intermediates can cruise gladed runs and long sweeping stretches of mountain groomed to perfection. Many of the advanced-level black diamond runs at Stratton are easily managed by strong intermediate skiers, it's only the *double*-black diamonds here that get steep enough to challenge expert skiers.

How to Get There
Albany, New York, and Hartford, Connecticut, both have major airports about two hours away. Driving times: Boston, 3 hours (150 miles); Montréal, 4.5 hours (260 miles); New York, 4.25 hours (220 miles). If you stay in the Village, park your car for the week once you arrive, as shuttle-bus service runs daily throughout the Village base area.

Where to Stay
Stratton Mountain Village consists of hundreds of condos for rent, all individually owned. Ranging in size from one to four bedrooms, all offer the basics: kitchen, fireplace, and comfortable bedrooms. Some are on the mountainside within walking distance of slopes and Village, which are priced slightly higher. All condominiums are within three quarters of a mile of the mountain. Guests get the use of the sports center, a separate complex near the Valley Side Units. $170–530. 800-STRATTON.

Expensive
Equinox Hotel in Manchester is an elegant Colonial-style structure whose walls are hung with oil portraits and where guests tread on fine Oriental rugs and sink into rich upholstered chairs. Despite its luxuriousness, it's actually quite informal and comfortable for families. There are three restaurants, a health club, and an indoor pool. Room service is also available. The hotel hosts sleigh rides on designated weekends during the year. $170–309. Route 7A, Manchester Village, VT 05155; 800-362-4747, 802-362-4700.

Stratton Village Lodge offers the closest slopeside accommodations at Stratton. Guests receive privileges at (and a free shuttle ride to and from) the Stratton Mountain Inn, its sister property, where facilities include a spa and restaurant. Hotel-style rooms have either one queen-size or two double beds. Loft rooms offer families more space. All rooms have microwave ovens, coffeemakers, and small refrigerators. $99–269. Middle Ridge Road, Stratton Mountain, VT 05155; 800-777-1700, 802-297-2260.

Moderate

Stratton Mountain Inn is a full-service hotel with two restaurants, room service, a sauna, a workout area, and a shuttle to the slopes. Most rooms are standard hotel style, attractively decorated, clean, and comfortable— one notch up from a chain hotel. Middle Ridge Road, Stratton Mountain, VT 05155; 800-STRATTON, 802-297-2500.

Birkenhaus is a charming Austrian chalet–style property within walking distance of the slopes. It offers the ambience of a European inn with lovely restaurants, après-ski cookies and tea, and a cozy common room with a fireplace. Rooms come in a variety of configurations including several rooms with bunk beds. $74–149. Middle Ridge Road, Stratton Mountain, VT 05155; 802-297-2000.

Budget

Chalet Motel has 43 rooms all with in-room coffeemakers and small refrigerators. Families like the price and the extras such as the sauna, hot tub, game room, and the full-service restaurants. Rooms have two queen-size or one king-size bed. $55–105. RR1 Box 740, Manchester Center, VT 05255; 800-343-9900, 802-362-1622.

Dostal Resort Lodge, about 15 minutes from Stratton, has an indoor pool and a game room. Basic rooms have two double beds. Rollaways can be added. $69–125. RFD 1, Box 31, Londonderry, VT 05148; 802-824-6700.

Red Sled Resort Motel is in the Manchester area, about 20 minutes from the mountain. All rooms have a small refrigerator, and some have microwave ovens and coffeemakers. Unremarkable standard rooms have two double beds or one queen-size bed. As a bonus, there's an indoor pool. $68–98. P.O. Box 1925, Route 1130, Manchester, VT 05255; 802-362-2161.

Children's Ski School

KidsKamp ski school (800-STRATTON) is for children ages 4 to 12. Children age 4 to 6 participate in the Little KidsKamp program and are grouped by age and ability in classes offering play-based instruction on the slopes. Children age 7 to 12 participate in an all-day learning adventure for both skiers and snowboarders. Kids as young as 5 or 6 can take snowboarding lessons if they weigh 40 pounds or more. All programs combine the challenge of skiing and boarding with fun, age-appropriate playtime activities.

Day Care

The ChildCare Center (800-STRATTON) for children ages 6 weeks to 5 years is conveniently located at the skier drop-off area, so you can unload and register the kids while your spouse parks the car. Each age division has its own bright and cheerful room. All but the infants enjoy outdoor play, sliding, videos, painting, games, and toys. Children age 2 and 3 play on Nordic skis to get the feel of sliding on the snow.

Teens

The Late Risers program for teens operates on weekends and during holiday periods. Groups meet at 11 A.M., and kids ski with an instructor who can offer tips on improving their technique in relaxed, informal sessions. The purpose of the day-long sessions is to allow teens to meet some of their peers and ski together in an instructive, fun, and noncompetitive atmosphere.

The Nightrider program, held weekends and during holiday weeks from 6 to 10 P.M., offers a snowboard clinic and gives teens free time to board down the night-lit parts of the mountain.

Snowboarding

A groomed-to-perfection competition half pipe 380 feet long is the centerpiece of snowboard activity on the mountain. It's lit at night and has a sound system to send jumpers into the stratosphere. Snowboard park features can change over the season, but they generally include tabletops, spines, and quarter pipes. The resort has constructed other terrain parks for both skiers and riders, and individual hits and jumps are found throughout the mountain. Little extras like benches for buckling up make it clear that snowboarders are a welcome group.

Cross-Country Skiing

Grafton Ponds Cross Country Ski Center (802-843-2231), about 30 minutes away from Stratton Mountain, has 30 kilometers of trails, five kilometers of which are covered with snowmaking, a rarity in the cross-country world. Kid's equipment is available and children may take private lessons or join the adults for a group lesson. The Old Tavern, Grafton, VT 05146.

The Stratton Country Club Nordic Center (802-297-4114) is a half mile from the Stratton mountain and has groomed trails that meander around property that is a golf course in the summer.

Other Activities

Ice skating takes place in a lovely outdoor rink, right in the base area, near the lodge. Skate rentals are available for all sizes, and the rink is lit for night skating. Certain evenings feature bonfires, singing, and hot-chocolate treats.

Outlet centers: A 20-minute drive from Stratton, Manchester is an extensive outlet center featuring clothing from such popular designers as Armani, Tommy Hilfiger, and Ralph Lauren.

Snowshoeing: Both Nordic centers (see Cross-Country Skiing above) offer snowshoe rentals, guided tours, and the use of their groomed trails.

Sports center: All guests staying at the Stratton Mountain Village can use this facility free of charge. Options include tennis, racquetball, squash, exercise equipment, aerobics, and yoga classes. The center has an indoor pool, hot tubs, and saunas.

Deals and Discounts

Midweek packages are an excellent buy, and late- and early-season packages include weekend stays.

If you plan to ski Stratton for more than four days during the season, consider buying a discount card called the Express Card ($79). It allows you to save 50 percent on midweek and 25 percent on weekend and holiday lift tickets.

Sugarbush

Address: R.R. 1, P.O. Box 350, Warren, Vermont 05674-9500
Telephone: 800-53-SUGAR, 802-583-2381
Web site: http://www.sugarbush.com

Set in the idyllic Mad River Valley, Sugarbush reflects the same unspoiled character as the classic New England villages and pastoral farms surrounding it. This is the Vermont of postcards and magazines—steepled churches, covered bridges, and clapboard buildings. There are no fast food restaurants, no traffic lights, and very little of the kind of sprawling development that brushes up against other ski areas.

Long continuous runs from top to bottom make some skiers compare Sugarbush to Sun Valley, Idaho, where the long and lanky runs seem to spread out endlessly before you. Sugarbush is often referred to as two mountains—Sugarbush North and Sugarbush South—although there are over 100 trails on six different interconnecting mountain peaks. The addition of the Slide Brook Express Lift connects the South to the North and now the two mountain areas that used to ski as two separate resorts are united, virtually doubling the skiable terrain.

An area called Family AdventureLand is a designated safe skiing and boarding zone where fast skiing and snowboarding are monitored, and all of the trails are rated intermediate or novice. There are many clever and entertaining terrain features such as a castle the kids can ski

MOUNTAIN STATISTICS
Base elevation: 1,535 feet
Summit: 4,135 feet
Vertical drop: 2,650 feet
Skiable acres: 432
Annual average snowfall: 282 inches
Snowmaking: 285 acres
Night skiing: none
Season: early November to mid-May
Lifts: 18 (4 high-speed quads, 3 regular quads, 3 triples, 4 doubles, 4 surface lifts)
Terrain: 22% beginner, 46% intermediate, 32% advanced
Lift tickets: adult $49, children 7 to 12 $29, under 7 free.

FAMILY STATISTICS
Day care: Sugarbush Day School, ages 6 weeks to 3 years; 802-583-2385, ext. 378
Children's lessons: ages 4 to 16, 802-583-2385, ext. 340
Baby-sitting: The day-care center can provide a list of baby-sitters for nighttime use; 802-583-2385, ext. 378
Medical: Mad River Valley Health Center, Waitsfield; 802-496-3838

through, bumps, tunnels, twists, turns, and various snow sculptures. Be on the look out for Sugarbear, the resort's cuddly mascot, who skis throughout AdventureLand waving and playing with young skiers. Two beginner lifts and one high-speed quad service this area.

Experts have always had plenty to pick from at Sugarbush, and powder hounds who aren't familiar with the back country can hire guides to take them through the trees and bowls and educate them on the region's flora, fauna, and geological history. Many of Sugarbush's original trails, cut when the resort first opened, remain intact. The Castlerock area of the mountain was first developed in 1959, and it is exactly the same today with its numerous twists and turns, gnarly bumps, cliffs, steeps, and boulders. Terrain for intermediates and beginners comprises nearly 50% of the trails, and in addition to smooth wide-open meadows, there are gently sloped trails that meander through the woods and wind their way down the mountain.

How to Get There

Burlington International Airport is an hour's drive away. Driving times: Albany, 2.5 hours (135 miles); Boston, 3.5 hours (190 miles); Burlington, 1 hour (50 miles); Montréal, 3 hours (150 miles); New York, 6 hours (300 miles). A free daily shuttle-bus service runs between the two base areas during the day, but if you're staying off the mountain you most likely will need a car.

Where to Stay

Expensive

One of the most luxurious properties in the area, the **Sugarbush Inn** is the only true full-service hotel in a country inn. All its rooms accommodate two adults but many rooms connect. The Inn also has contemporary New England–style condos that are most comfortable for families and have one to four bedrooms. All guests who stay at the Inn or the condos can use the Sugarbush sports center about ½ mile way that has three indoor tennis courts, racquetball, massage, pool, and hot tub. A children's dinner menu is available in the Inn. Ski and lodging packages can be a good value; be sure to ask, Inn $115–185, condos $150–690. RR1, Box 350, Warren VT 05674; 800-537-8427, 802-583-2301.

The Bridges Resort & Racquet Club offers the most deluxe condominiums in the area. All feature full kitchens, fireplaces, decks, and attractive decor in their one-, two-, and three-bedroom units, some of which come with lofts. Six different floor plans accommodate groups of all sizes. There is an indoor pool, two indoor tennis courts, a Jacuzzi, a sauna, a fitness center, and a game room. $180–435. Sugarbush Access Road, Warren, VT 05674; 800-453-2922, 802-583-2922.

Sugarbush Resort's condominiums come in a variety of sizes and shapes, but all have complete kitchens and most have their own washer/dryers, saunas, or Jacuzzis. Small families can fit in a one-bedroom studio suite while families wanting to share a unit will find the four-bedroom villas spacious and comfortable. Ski-in-and-out condo clusters are Snow Creek and Mountainside. Glades and Paradise are not right on the mountain, but are very nice; both are within walking distance of the Sugarbush Sports Complex. $115–675. Sugarbush Resort RR1, P.O. Box 350, Warren, VT 05674; 800-537-8427. 802-583-3333.

Moderate

Tucker Hill Lodge, about two miles from the slopes, has 22 rooms in three buildings. Its main lodge has suites with a king-size feather bed and fireplace and a connecting room with twin beds. Its restaurant has a children's menu and serves a complimentary continental breakfast. Children under 10 are free in their parents' room. $60–115. Marble Hill Road, Waitsfield, VT 05673; 800-543-7841, 802-496-3983.

The Sugar Lodge (http://www.sugarlodge.com) is about a quarter-mile from the mountain. Its package deal is a good buy, including lift ticket and lodging with a five-night stay. $70–95 per person. Sugarbush Access Road, P.O. Box 652, Warren, VT 05674; 800-982-3465.

Budget

The PowderHound Inn and Condominiums, three miles from Sugarbush parking lot, has one-bedroom condo units that sleep four; the living room has twin beds made up as daybeds and a tiny kitchen unit outfitted with a stovetop and minirefrigerator, while the bedroom has two twins or a king-size bed. In front of the condos, a nineteenth-century farmhouse houses the breakfast room (on weekends) and a family-style pub with a pool table, dart board, and jukebox. There's also a hot tub. Children under 6 stay free. This is an excellent value midweek. Four people $100–130. Route 100, P.O. Box 369, Warren, VT 05674; 800-548-4022, 802-496-5100.

Hyde Away Inn has family suites and dorms that can sleep up to eight, in addition to more standard hotel rooms. There's cross-country skiing and ice skating right out the door. Snow shoes and cross country skis can be rented at a shop about a mile away, but bring your own skates. $39–89. Route 17 Waitsfield, VT 05673; 800-777-HYDE, 802-496-2322.

Children's Ski School

The Minibears program for 4- and 5-year-olds includes four hours of ski time, lunch, and a slate of fun activities in the Gate House Lodge Bear Den in the Lincoln Peak area. Children younger than 4 who want to ski can participate in the Microbears program through the Sugarbush Daycare Center.

Sugarbears, for ages 6 to 12, has its own 2,400-square-foot facility in the Valley House Lodge, but if families have kids in both Minibears and Sugarbears, they can drop everyone off at the Minibear facility. Four-hour group clinics are available for children of all abilities.

Snowboarding lessons start at age 7.

Teenagers (13 to 16 years) have their own program, Catamounts, which operates during school breaks and includes all-day supervision, ski clinics, and lunch.

All kids' programs (802-583-2385, ext. 340) include ski equipment; snowboard equipment is available for an extra charge.

Day Care

Sugarbush Day School (802-583-2385, ext. 378) accepts children from 6 weeks to 3 years and offers parents complimentary beepers. In a large, sunny nursery and playroom in Sugarbush Village, kids enjoy music, toys, games, books, and nap time. There's a special toddler room for two- to three-year-olds.

If you want your toddlers to ski, enroll them in the Microbears program, a combination of day care, snow play, and an introduction to skiing.

Kids' Night Out, held every Wednesday and Saturday from 6 to 9 P.M. for ages 3 to 10, features puppet shows, movies, games, group activities, and pizza.

Teens

Teen nights, held over holiday weeks and vacation periods, feature music with DJs or bands and pizza parties, all in Sugarbush Sports Center. 802-583-2391.

Snowboarding

The Mountain Rage Snowpark is the rage with young snowboarders. Its centerpiece is a precision-cut half pipe sculpted by the resort's pipe dragon, a mechanical device that cuts, reshapes, and maintains the pipe at least once a week. Other terrain features include a quarter pipe, tabletops, spines, rails, jumps, and hits; the half pipe is at the bottom.

Cross-Country Skiing

Sugarbush Nordic Center (802-583-2601) offers 25 kilometers of groomed cross-country terrain, ten kilometers of which include a skating track on the golf course and through the woods.

Blueberry Lake Cross Country Ski Center (802-496-6687) is up on a higher mountain plateau above the valley and also offers cross-country trails.

Inn at the Round Barn Farm (802-496-6111) has a cross-country center.

Other Activities

Snowshoe tours traverse the Long Trail between Lincoln Peak and Mount Ellen. Naturalists are on hand to educate participants on the region's animal and plant life and geological history. It's four hours long and offered when snow and weather conditions permit. Tips on snowshoeing are given, too. Arrange a tour through Sugarbush (802-583-2385, ext. 470) or Clearwater Sports (802-496-2708).

Icelandic horse farm: This farm (Common Road, Waitsfield, VT; 802-496-7141) has small and sweet Icelandic ponies. Visitors can ride them over the snow on a trail system, or can try *skijöring*, in which a horse pulls skiers behind.

Ice skating: The Skatium (802-496-9199) is a skating rink in Waitsfield, a ten-minute drive from Sugarbush.

Night sledding during holiday weeks takes place on the Easy Rider trail in the Lincoln Peak area from 6 to 8:30 P.M.

Luge course: Riders each get their own Laser Luge sled, a special plastic sled that is designed to run on a luge track. Kids 10 and above can ride down the 800-foot course on Thursdays, Fridays, and Sundays.

Ben and Jerry's Factory Tour: In Waterbury, about a 20-minute drive north on Route 100, visitors can tour this ice-cream factory (802-244-TOUR) and taste mouthwatering samples.

Snow Tube Park: a night-lit snow tube run on the Easy Rider Trail is open from 6 to 8:30 P.M. daily.

Discounts and Deals

Visit early or late season or in the last three weeks in January to take advantage of Discovery Weeks, when a five-day package of skiing, lodging, and a few extras is discounted.

Sugarbush is part of the American Skiing Company and offers lift ticket discounts through its Magnificent 7 card (800-543-2SKI), which is good for skiing at Sunday River (see page 250), Sugarloaf (see page 245), Sugarbush (see pge 225), Killington (see page 193), Mount Snow/Haystack (see page 198), and Attitash Bear Peak (see page 233).

New Hampshire

Attitash Bear Peak

Address: Route 302, P.O. Box 308, Bartlett, New Hampshire 03812

Telephone: 800-223-SNOW (central reservations); 603-374-2368, 603-374-0946 (snow conditions)

Web site: http://www.attitash.com

Two interconnected ski mountains—Bear Peak and Attitash—offer glorious views of the Mount Washington Valley and New Hampshire's White mountains from their summits. More intimate than many of the other mountains in the East, they are particularly well-suited for older kids who want to maneuver on their own and for younger ones who appreciate a quieter ski setting. Perfectly groomed slopes and first-rate customer service have become trademarks. On-mountain hosts in maroon, blue, and gray jackets anticipate guests' needs.

Bear Peak has a small base lodge with a restaurant, a retail shop, and rental shop, but most guest services are concentrated at the Attitash base area, about a mile away, where you'll find slopeside lodging (both condos and a luxury hotel), restaurants, the ski school, and a child-care center. North Conway is the closest town—about ten miles away—with many restaurants and ski stores and an enormous and popular outlet center.

Families of all abilities enjoy Attitash Bear Peak. Absolute beginners learn to ski on a special wide hill, The Learning Center, until they are confident enough to move along to the other beginning terrain. Intermediates have an abundance of broad cruisers and tree skiing at Bear Peak and old-fashioned New England trails at Attitash. Since Bear Peak has the longest double-black-diamond run in the state, experts can work up their courage to try its precipitous pitch.

MOUNTAIN STATISTICS

Base elevation: 600 feet (both Attitash and Bear Peak)

Summit: 2,300 (Attitash); 2,100 (Bear Peak)

Vertical drop: 1,750 feet (Attitash); 1,450 (Bear Peak)

Skiable acres: 273

Annual average snowfall: 120 inches

Snowmaking: 245 acres (98% of the resort)

Season: early November into May

Lifts: 11 (1 high-speed quad, 1 quad, 3 triples, 4 doubles, 2 surface lifts)

Terrain: 20% beginner, 47% intermediate, 30% advanced

Lift tickets: adults $39, children 6 to 12 and seniors 65 to 70 $25, 71+ $7, 5 and under free.

FAMILY STATISTICS

Day care: Attitots Day Care, ages 6 months to 6 years, 603-374-9296

Children's lessons: ages 3 to 12

Medical: Memorial Hospital, North Conway NH 603-374-5461

Our favorite special event of the year is the Attitash Bear Peak Open, held every year in late March, in which teams of four skiers in silly costumes compete on a nine-hole golf course over the snow.

How to Get There

The closest airport is 70 miles away in Portland, Maine. Driving times: Boston, 2.5 hours (130 miles); New York City, 6 hours (325 miles); Hartford, 4 hours (235 miles).

Where to Stay

Expensive

The brand-new *Grand Summit Hotel* features deluxe condominiums in a ski-in-and-out location right off Bear Peak. Its on-site day care offers real convenience to parents of nonskiing children, and its arcade and game room appeal to the older kids. Amenities include a health club with a steam room and sauna, an outdoor heated pool, a whirlpool, and kitchenettes in some units. $125–439. Route 302 Bartlett, NH 0312; 888-554-1900, 603-374-1900.

Moderate

Attitash Mountain Village has hotel rooms, efficiencies that can sleep up to four people, and one-, two-, and three-bedroom condos all scattered throughout eleven different buildings. All guests can use the swimming pool, hot tub, sauna, and game room. A few of the buildings have a ski-in-and-out location and the rest are about a ½ mile away from the ski area. Hotel rooms $49–109. Condos $119–379. Route 302, Box 358, Bartlett, NH 03812-0358; 800-862-1600, 603-374-6500.

Wentworth Resort Hotel has a skating rink on the property and cross-country trails across the street. This 125-year-old establishment has been modernized but still has elegant touches from another era, such as canopy beds in the suites and clawfoot bathtubs in the rooms. The dining room serves full dinners and has a children's menu. More casual fare is served in the bar. Standard rooms, suites, and condominiums are available: Except in the condos, rates include breakfast and dinner. $149–400. Hotel Route 16, Carter Notch, Jackson, NH 03846; 603-383-9700.

Red Jacket Motor Hotel offers complimentary sleigh rides on Saturdays from 4 to 7 P.M. along with hot chocolate and hot cider. Its rooms come in a variety of configurations that are comfortable for families: Some have bunk beds in an alcove off the main bedroom, several have lofts, and there are two-bedroom townhouses if you want extra space. The common room has a fireplace and puzzles for kids to put together. The hotel also has a game room, indoor swimming pool, sauna, and Jacuzzi. Cross-country skiing and snowmobiling are nearby. Weekend entertainment is offered in the lounge. $115–255. Route 16, P.O. Box 2000, North Conway, NH 03860; 603-356-5411.

Budget
Country Inn at Bartlett is a traditional country bed-and-breakfast establishment two miles from the mountain. Families find the cottages most comfortable. They come in a variety of floor plans, some with kitchenettes, others with bunk beds or trundle beds, but all have fireplaces. In addition, the Inn offers guests use of a game room, an outdoor hot tub, and access to cross-country trails. Per person charges: $37–64. Route 302, Bartlett, NH 03812; 800-212-2353, 603-374-2353.

Eagle Mountain House, about a ten-minute drive from Attitash and some of the other downhill resorts in the Washington Valley, is a historic hotel that is part of the 146-kilometer, cross-country Jackson Trail Network. Rooms have two double beds, and suites have a queen-size bed in the bedroom and a queen-size sleeper sofa in the living room. Both dining facilities—a casual tavern and a more formal dining room—have children's menus, and a game room has pool, Ping-Pong, and video games. $59–139. Carter Notch Road, Jackson, NH 03846; 603-383-9111.

Children's Ski School
Children ages 3 to 5 take Tiny Turn private lessons to familiarize them with moving across the snow in skis and boots. Perfect Kids, for 4- to 6-year-olds, is a group clinic with full-and half-day programs. This age group begins and ends the day with playtime at the day-care center. Adventure Kids, for ages 7 to 12, has separate headquarters with a lunch room. This group receives a total of four hours of skiing instruction with a supervised lunch in between. Miniriders, for 7- to 12-year-olds, offers snowboard lessons using the Perfect Turn technique. The ski-rental shop is next door to both facilities.

Day Care
Attitots Day Care (603-374-9296) is for children 6 months to 6 years who enjoy bright and cheerful playrooms filled with games, toys, and fun activities. A nutritious lunch is provided, and a two-hour minimum stay is required. Reservations are a must for children under age 1. The program

operates from a two-story facility. Children age 3 to 6 who plan to take a lesson (see above) stay downstairs where there is a changing area and a play area with games, arts and crafts, and puzzles. Upstairs, one room is for babies 6 to 11 months, and another provides play space for 1-, 2-, and young 3-year-olds.

Kids' Night Out for 5- to 12-year-olds takes place every Saturday from 6 to 9 P.M. It includes dinner, ice cream, and entertainment such as games, sleigh rides, parties, and Karaoke.

Snowboarding

Reckoning Snowboard Park at Bear Peak has a half pipe, tabletops, spines, jumps, and hits. The resort has placed benches at the top of all lifts and provides plenty of snowboard-only racks at the base lodges.

Cross-Country Skiing

Jackson Ski Touring Center (P.O. Box 216, Jackson, NH 03846; 800-XC-SNOWS, 603-383-9355) is one of the most highly regarded cross-country centers in the East, with 64 trails covering 155 kilometers (94 kilometers of which are groomed trails) and spanning three river valleys. Trails pass by inns, pubs, delis, and restaurants. Most of the trails are groomed daily and there is snowmaking at the instruction area and on five kilometers of trails. Anything you need for kids is available.

Great Glen Trails (603-466-2333) in the Pinkham Notch area has 37 kilometers of terrain, some with snowmaking, children's lessons, and skis and trailers.

Other Activities

Snowmobiling: Bartlett Rentals (603-374-6039) rents snowmobiles. Trails head out in the National Forest next door.

Snowshoe Tours: for both groups and individuals are available through guest services. Local naturalists lead families through the woods pointing out animal tracks and other winter features in the forest. 603-374-2368.

Deals and Discounts

Attitash offers packages midweek, and savings early and late season.

Inquire about the convenient and novel ticketing system called Smart Ticket. It allows you to pay by the vertical foot if you want to ski just a few runs. The points are good for two years and it can be shared by various family members.

Attitash Bear Peak is part of the American Skiing Company and offers lift-ticket discounts through its Magnificent 7 card (800-543-2SKI), which is good for skiing at Sunday River (see page 250), Sugarloaf/USA (see page 245), Sugarbush (see page 225), Killington, (see page 193) and Mount Snow/Haystack (see page 198).

Waterville Valley

Address: 1 Ski Area Road, Waterville Valley, Waterville, New Hampshire 03215
Telephone: 800-468-2553 (reservations), 603-236-8311
Web site: http://www.waterville. com

Waterville Valley is a self-contained resort village that offers action-packed all-inclusive winter family vacations. You can visit this ski resort à la carte, or you can buy a package called the Winter Unlimited Passport, which offers unrestricted downhill and cross-country skiing, ice skating, snowshoeing, and activities every night of the week.

Thanks to this program, Waterville Valley has become known as one of the best value family resorts of the East. All accommodations and businesses are situated around the Waterville Valley Town Square, whose classic Colonial-style buildings house restaurants, shops, a cross-country center, an ice rink, and lodgings. All accommodations are within 1 ½ miles of the Square, and frequent shuttle buses circle the property and take guests to the slopes, located two miles from the Town Square.

Because the ski area and resort center are off the main road and at the end of the route, Waterville's compact layout and secluded location make it a safe place for older kids to get around by themselves. There is no lodging and little development at the ski resort because it sits in the heart of the White Mountain National Forest, a protected wilderness area. The cross-country and snowshoe trails that start at the Town Square run through miles and miles of this undisturbed pristine wilderness.

MOUNTAIN STATISTICS
Base elevation: 1,815 feet
Summit: 3,835 feet
Vertical drop: 2,020 feet
Skiable acres: 255
Annual average snowfall: 140 inches
Snowmaking: 96%
Night skiing: none
Season: early November through late April
Lifts: 11 (2 high-speed quads, 2 triples, 3 doubles, 4 surface lifts)
Terrain: 20% beginner, 60% intermediate, 20% advanced
Lift tickets: adult $45, young adult 13 to 19 $35, children 6 to 12 $32, under 6 free.

FAMILY STATISTICS
Day care: Waterville Valley Child Care, ages 6 months to 4 years; 603-236-8311, ext. 3196
Children's lessons: Children's Ski School, ages 3 to 12 603-236-8311 ext. 3136
Baby-sitting: Waterville Valley Town Recreation Department publishes a list of baby-sitters, 603-236-4695
Medical: Spear Memorial Hospital in Plymouth, 603-536-1120

Rated "Best in the East" for snowboard parks by *Snow Country* magazine, Waterville Valley's snowboard features range from expert-only hits and jumps to a meticulously groomed half pipe and beginner's parks on mild and gentle terrain. The ski acreage is small, only 255 acres, but it includes terrain for skiers of all abilities, including advanced: Waterville Valley has hosted several World Cup races. When you've skied enough for the week, you can try the 60 miles of cross-county trails, more than half of which are groomed.

Families can purchase the Passport anytime during the season, but if they do so during one of the 13 Winter Escapade weeks, they get a lot more bang for their buck. The package still includes unlimited skiing, skating, and snowshoeing, but many extra events and activities have been planned during the day and every night of the week. Expect fireworks displays, magic shows, rides on the groomers (the monster trucks that groom the snow), presentations about animals by the New Hampshire Museum of Science, and all kinds of special activities for children. Upon check-in, guests get a Passport necklace that contains entry tickets and days and times of all activities that week. It couldn't be simpler.

How to Get There

Boston's Logan International Airport is served by United, USAir, Continental, and Delta. Driving times: Boston, 2 hours (130 miles); New York City, 6 hours (325 miles); Montréal, 3.5 hours (225 miles).

Where to Stay

Expensive

Mountain Sun Condominiums are quite deluxe and spacious and have been situated to make the most of a sunny exposure. Built on three floors, the ground floor has a kitchen, a living room with a double fireplace, and a dining room; the second floor has two bedrooms, and the third floor is a master bedroom with a private bath and Jacuzzi. $135–$290. Tecumseh Road, Waterville, NH 03215; 800-468-2553, 603-236-4101.

Moderate

Golden Eagle Lodge has comfortable two-room suites that can accommodate small families. Kitchenettes allow you to fix a quick snack and the location, right across from the Town Square, can't be beat. $78-249. P.O. Box 495, Waterville Valley, NH 03215; 888-70-EAGLE, 603-236-4600.

Black Bear Lodge has attractive condominiums in a variety of shapes and sizes. The most deluxe units can sleep up to six, and have a full kitchen and dining and living areas. All guests have use of the pool and Jacuzzi, and there is daily maid service. Children stay free in their parents' room. $75–$229. 3 Village Road, Waterville Valley, NH 03215; 800-349-2327.

Snowy Owl Inn is a quaint country inn with cozy common rooms for enjoying a good book or playing a board game. Rates include breakfast and afternoon wine and cheese. Standard rooms have two double beds, and larger rooms have a loft area with twin beds. Guests will enjoy the indoor pool and Jacuzzi. $65–190. Village Road, P.O. Box 379, Waterville Valley, NH 03215; 800-766-9969, 603-236-8383.

Budget
Silver Fox Inn has standard rooms with two double beds or one queen-size bed. Breakfast is included in the rates, and wine and cheese is served to guests every afternoon. Children under 12 stay free in their parents' room. $49–59. Snows Brook Rd., Waterville Valley, NH 03215; 800-486-2553, 603-236-8325.

Children's Ski School
SKIwee kids ages 3 to 5 receive game-based ski instruction and indoor play time. Mountain Cadets, ages 6 to 8, receive more intensive instruction, but still spend some time indoors for rest and snacks. Mountain Scouts are 9- to 12-year-olds who spend most of their time skiing. Snowboard lessons and rental equipment are available for kids as young as 5. Beginners learn in the fenced Kinderpark, a gently sloped area served by a rope tow.

Teen holiday camps include lessons and daily activities on the slopes and continue into the evening with snowshoeing, ice skating, cross-country ski tours with headlamps, and other activities. 603-236-8311, ext. 3136.

Day Care
Waterville Valley Child Care (603-236-8311, ext. 3196) at the ski-area base lodge entertains children from 6 months to 4 years with arts and crafts, a supervised lunch, and indoor and outdoor play. A separate area for infants has rocking chairs and a quiet nap room, and toddlers and preschoolers enjoy all kinds of toys, games, and activities. You can reserve by the hour, half day, or full day.

Teens
A Teen Adventure Club for 13-to 18-year-olds is offered during holiday weeks and special periods throughout the year. Teens ski with seasoned pros and stay with the same group and instructor for their entire stay. At night, programs include ice skating, basketball, cross-country ski and snow-shoe tours with headlamps, bonfires, and dances.

Snowboarding

Snowboard features and alpine parks are scattered throughout the resort. The Boneyard is an advanced-level park with hits, jumps, tabletops, quarter pipes, and gaps. The half pipe is called the Wicked Ditch of the East. The minipark Snowonder is a scaled-down version of the bigger parks meant for beginners and little kids on Valley Run. Boardwalk is a snowboard park with hits and rolls. Park Place has even more features.

"Minipark Jams" start at the top of Snowonder and are offered several times during the year for younger teens. Participants ride through the park and gather later for a raffle. Registration is free.

Cross-Country Skiing

Base Camp Cross Country Center (603-236-4666) has 70 kilometers of groomed trails and an additional 35 kilometers of backcountry trails through the heart of the White Mountain National Forest. Lessons and ski rentals are available for kids and adults. The Kid Power program is a two-hour lesson for 6- to 12-year-olds with instruction, ski games, races, and obstacle courses. Guided moonlight tours and family tours take place throughout the season. Trails start right at the Town Square.

Other Activities

Old-fashioned horse-drawn *sleigh rides* depart from Base Camp Adventure Center in Town Square (603-236-4666). Hour-long rides go around the valley floor (not included in the ski package).

An *indoor ice-skating rink* (603-236-4813) is next to the Town Square. Skate rentals are available.

All sizes of *snowshoes* can be rented at the Base Camp Adventure Center (603-236-4666), and guided walks are available, including moonlight tours, nature walks, and family programs.

All guests can use the **White Mountain Athletic Center** facilities (Route 49, 603-236-8303) free of charge: indoor squash and tennis courts, aerobics classes, a swimming pool, hot tubs, a weight room, and massage services.

Deals and Discounts

When you buy the Winter Unlimited Passport you can participate in the Winter Escapade program over certain weeks of the winter, usually mid-December through mid-March. Early-and late-season packages are less expensive but have fewer evening activities and special events.

Maine

Sugarloaf/USA

Address: RR 1 Box 5000, Carrabassett Valley, Maine 04947

Telephone: 800-THE-LOAF (on-mountain reservations), 800-THE-AREA (off-mountain reservations), 207-237-2000 (information)

Web site: http://www.sugarloaf.com

Sugarloaf, in the western corner of Maine, is far enough from major metropolitan areas that long lift lines are rarely a problem, even on weekends. It's a great place for families, attracting a mix of ages and interests, as there are excellent facilities for snowboarding, downhill skiing, and cross-country skiing all in the same area. Since Sugarloaf is one of the northernmost resorts in the United States, the snow falls early and the ski season runs well into May. Sugarloaf is the only resort in the East that has a summit above the treeline, which makes for great skiing but cold and windy conditions in the heart of winter.

The resort's base village is compact and convenient. This is condo country, and restaurants, a grocery store, and after-ski activities are concentrated just steps from your lodging. If you're on a budget and have a car, forego the higher prices of ski-in-and-out lodging and stay in one of the small villages nearby.

Children's programs are scheduled six nights a week from December to April, with special activities for kids ages 5 to 12 such as board games, movies, crafts, Karaoke, and tubing. Many ski areas offer teen programs only during holiday periods, but Sugarloaf keeps teens busy for the entire season. Teens 13 to 18 have their own teen club and special movie nights. Three special children's fes-

MOUNTAIN STATISTICS
Base elevation: 1,400 feet
Summit: 4,237 feet
Vertical drop: 2,820 feet
Skiable acres: 1,400
Annual average snowfall: 194 inches
Snowmaking: 490 acres
Night skiing: none
Season: late October through May
Lifts: 14 (4 high-speed quads, 1 triple, 8 doubles, 1 surface lift)
Terrain: 28% beginner, 32% intermediate, 40% advanced
Lift tickets: adult $49, teens 13 to 18 $42, juniors 6 to 12 and seniors over 65 $29, under 6 free.

FAMILY STATISTICS
Day care: Sugarloaf/USA Child Care Center, 6 weeks to 5 years, 207-237-6924
Children's lessons: ages 3 to 12, 207-237-6947
Baby-sitting: A private caregiver list is available through guest services, 800-843-5623
Medical: Farmington Hospital, 207-778-6031

tivals are planned throughout the season, with a special package deal and loads of activities.

Not just one but four stuffed fuzzy mascots—Amos the Moose, Pierre Dubois the Lumberjack, Leon the Yellow-Nosed Vole, and Blueberry the Bigelow Bear—ski with the kids around the mountain. A special kids-only alpine playground called Moose Alley has a secret entrance leading into a gladed area off a beginner's trail. Turns are so tight and obstacles to duck under are so low that adults attempting to sneak in will find themselves in big trouble.

To describe Sugarloaf as "snowboard friendly" is putting it mildly. Boarders consider "The Loaf" one of the best snowboard areas in the East. Endless diversions and half pipes (the longest in the country), cut to perfection by legendary pipe dragon driver/artist Crazy Eddy Michaud, keeps the snowboard parks and features constantly changing. Many professional ski-patrol members cruise the mountain on snowboards.

How to Get There

Portland Airport is 2½ hours from Sugarloaf, and Bangor International Airport is two hours away. Once you're at the resort you won't need a car (unless you're staying in a town nearby), as free shuttle buses travel around the resort every 15 minutes. Driving times: Boston, 4 hours (220 miles); Montréal, 4.5 hours (210 miles); New York, 8 hours (430 miles); Portland, 2.5 hours (120 miles).

Where to Stay

Accommodations are clustered in three areas, with the greatest number of options around the resort and other possibilities fourteen miles south in the town of Kingfield and seven miles north in the village of Stratton. If you're on a budget and have a car, look for lodging away from the base.

Expensive

Sugarloaf/USA Condominiums. Nearly half of the 900 condominiums and townhouse units at Sugarloaf are available for families to rent. They range in size from studios to six-bedroom places, and many are ski-in-and-out. All are available through Sugarloaf Mountain Corporation, RR 1, Box 5000, Carrabasset Valley, ME 04947; 800-THE-LOAF, 207-237-2000. Two of the most popular with families are Gondola Village and the Bigelows Condominiums.

If your children are small and will be visiting the day-care center, choose the Gondola Village condos near the Whiffletree lift, so you can take your kids to day care without even having to walk outside. Select from hotel-style rooms and larger one-and two-bedroom units with full kitchens that can accommodate up to six people. Thursday and Saturday night baby-sitting is available as a bonus from 6 to 9 P.M. $152–277.

Large families wanting deluxe accommodations should consider the **Bigelows Condominiums,** the most spacious and luxurious of the condos on the mountain, which are all five-bedroom units that can sleep up to 14. They're ideal for two or three families who want to share a unit, as there are two living areas and two kitchen areas (one is a kitchenette) so you won't get in one another's way. You can ski down a short trail to the lifts, but will need to walk or ride back up. $431–560. RRI, Box 5000, Carrabasset Valley, ME 04947; 800-THE-LOAF, 207-237-2000.

The Sugarloaf Mountain Hotel (http://www.sugarloafhotel.com) has regular hotel rooms and one- and two-bedroom suites that have queen-size beds, a sleeper sofa, microwaves, and minirefrigerators. Best of all, the lifts are just a few feet away. For after-ski relaxation there's a sauna, steam rooms, and hot tubs. $165–225. RR 1 Box 2299, Carrabassett Valley, ME 04947-9730; 800-527-9879 (reservations), 207-237-2222 (other calls).

Moderate

The Inn on Winter's Hill in Kingfield is a historic hotel with a dinner-only restaurant. Cross-country ski trails and snowmobiling are right out the back door. Rooms have two double beds or are partitioned with one queen-size and one double bed. There's a swimming pool, health club, and lounge with video games, a pool table, and TV. Plan on having your own car, as this property is a 15-minute drive to the lift, and shuttle service is not available. $50–85. RR 1 Box 1272, Kingfield, ME 04947; 800-233-WNTR, 207-265-5421.

The Sugarloaf Inn has a family-friendly restaurant in-house, and your lodging includes passes to the Sugarloaf Sports and Fitness Club, which has an indoor pool/price Mountainside Road, c/o Sugarloaf RR#1 Box 5000 Carrabassett Valley, ME 04947; 800-THE-LOAF.

Budget

Spillover Motel has very plain but clean standard rooms with two double beds in each. Extra people (more than two) cost $5 each, but there is no charge for a rollaway bed. The motel is seven miles from the lifts and you'll need your own car, as no shuttle is available. $58–68. Route 27, P.O. Box 427, Stratton, ME 04982; 207-246-6571.

Herbert Hotel is a historic lodging in Kingfield, about 20 minutes from the slopes. Its rooms and suites can accommodate two to six people. The dinner restaurant on the premises has a children's menu. $49–149. Main Street Kingfield, ME 04947; 800-THE-HERB, 207-265-2000.

Children's Ski School

The Mountain Magic program for children ages 3 to 6 incoporates the Perfect Turn method of teaching into the lessons. The full-day sessions include lunch, equipment, and all-day supervision. Half-day programs are available, too.

Mountain Adventures, for ages 7 to 12, receive both ski and snowboard instruction. Coaching is available for all levels, from absolute beginners to mountain-mogul skiers. 207-237-6947.

A regular teen program for 13- to 16-year-olds offers coaching from a ski pro and a fun time skiing and boarding with peers. Kids who come up to ski on a regular weekend basis can participate in a variety of other programs, including one where teens ski with the same coach every single weekend.

Day Care

Sugarloaf/USA Child Care Center (207-237-6924) offers full-day care for infants as young as 6 weeks and children up to age 5. Infants have their own separate room, as do toddlers. Nursing mothers are given beepers so they can be summoned as their babies need them. A preschool-like program for kids ages 2 ½ and up offers singing, crafts, and storytime. Children age 3 can receive a ski lesson if their parents wish (see above).

Teens

The Avalanche Teen Club is open nightly with a soft-drink bar, snacks, video games, air hockey, DJs and VJs on certain nights, movies (including ski movies) shown on a big-screen TV, and a big lounge area where teens can hang out.

Snowboarding

One of the largest half pipes in the country, 500 feet long and 30 feet wide with 12-foot-high walls, gives boarders the chance to perfect their skills. Small snowboard parks are situated all over the mountain, each a little different from the others; skiers are welcome to try them.

Cross-Country Skiing

Sugarloaf Touring Center (207-237-6830) has a base lodge with a restaurant, rental shop, and ski school. Trails include 85 kilometers of snow-covered forests, fields, and meadows. A few of the trails are lighted for night skiing.

Other Activities

Dogsled rides: 207-246-4461.

A night-lit *ice-skating rink* is found at the Sugarloaf Touring Center (207-237-6830). Skate rentals are available.

Snowshoeing is available at the Sugarloaf Touring Center (207-237-6830).

Sugarloaf Sports and Fitness Club (207-237-6946) has a pool, indoor and outdoor hot tubs, a steam room, a sauna, and an indoor climbing wall.

Western Maine Children's Museum (207-235-2211) is a small hands-on museum best for younger kids. Some of the exhibits include wildlife and Native American– and environmental-awareness displays. Kids can crawl inside a teepee or take an imaginary ride in a real Sugarloaf gondola car. A collection of furs let them experience what a real fox or beaver feels like. Open Saturday, Sunday, and Monday.

Deals and Discounts

Visit Sugarloaf during Children's Weekend in early December or one of the Children's Festival Weeks in January, February, or March (call for specific dates). Participants receive a minimum of 50 percent off ski tickets, ski rentals, and child care for kids age 12 and under when you book a stay of three nights or more.

Low-priced lodging packages in late or early season include lift tickets, lodging, lessons, and admission to the health club. For information, call 800-THE-AREA.

Sugarloaf is part of the American Skiing Company and offers lift ticket discounts through its Magnificent 7 card (800-543-2SKI), which is good for skiing at Sunday River (see page 250), Sugarbush (see pge 225), Killington (see page 193), Mount Snow (see page 198), and Attitash Bear Peak (see page 233).

Sunday River Ski Resort

Address: P.O. Box 450, Bethel, Maine 04217

Telephone: 800-543-2SKI (reservations), 207-824-3000 (information)

Web site: http://www.sundayriver.com

Whether the kids are snowplowing while Mom and Dad carve their signatures into fresh powder or the other way around, Sunday River keeps everybody happy. A safe beginner's bowl provides gently sloping terrain, and dozens of leisurely intermediate trails and challenging expert runs are spread over eight mountain peaks. A separate snowboard park and dozens of snowboard features are scattered throughout the 654 acres. When nature doesn't make fresh powder, state-of-the-art snowmaking machines supply it, covering 92 percent of the terrain. Sunday River's man-made snow is the angel food cake of the ski world—light, dry, and fluffy. Its quality is so remarkable that the "recipe" has been trademarked and sold to other ski areas.

You can ski or walk to slopeside lodgings of condominiums, two luxury hotels, or dormitory-style accommodations. Families with small children will find the condos in the South Ridge area most desirable because of their proximity to the children's ski facilities and beginner slopes. The Brookside units, closer to nighttime activities in the White Cap base that houses the teen club, a night-lit half pipe, and ice-skating rink, are better for families with older children. Accommodations in the village of Bethel are 10 to 15 percent cheaper than those on the mountain.

The 3,200-foot Children's Center serves as the base for daytime chil-

MOUNTAIN STATISTICS

Base elevation: 800 feet
Summit: 3,140 feet
Vertical drop: 2,340 feet
Skiable acres: 654
Annual average snowfall: 155 inches
Snowmaking: 92%
Night skiing: yes
Season: early October to late May
Lifts: 17 (4 high-speed quads, 5 quads, 4 triples, 2 doubles, 2 surface lifts)
Terrain: 25% beginner, 35% intermediate, 40% advanced
Lift tickets: adults $47, children 6 to 12 $29, under 6 free.

FAMILY STATISTICS

Day care: ages 6 weeks to 6 years, South Ridge Center (207-824-3000), The Summit Hotel and Conference Center (207-824-3500) and the Jordan Grand Hotel (207-824-5807)
Children's lessons: Perfect Kids, ages 3 to 18, 800-543-2SKI
Baby-sitting: A list of evening baby-sitters is available from the Welcome Center Desk 207-824-5146 and the Summit Hotel 207-824-3506.
Medical: Bethel Area Health Center, 207-824-2193

dren's programs. Outdoor ice skating and horse-drawn sleigh rides are available daily, and a torchlight parade and fireworks display take place at least once a week.

Nite Cap, Sunday River's new nighttime entertainment center at the Whitecape base lodge, has a 350-foot night-lit half pipe with music playing in the background. Snowboarders select whatever they want to hear, and the sound is played in the half pipe area of the mountain. The lighted ice-skating rink, special teen center, restaurant, nightclub, and video arcade keep older kids and parents happy and busy all season long.

How to Get There

Portland International Airport is a 90-minute drive by car. Boston's International Airport is three hours away by car.

Driving times: Boston, 3 hours (180 miles); Montréal, 3.5 hours (160 miles); New York City, 7 hours (350 miles); Portland, 1.5 hours (80 miles).

A complimentary trolley service makes stops throughout the resort complex at the base lodges, restaurants, and all on-mountain lodging properties.

Where to Stay

Expensive

The Summit Hotel and Conference Center is Sunday River's premiere hotel and the largest slopeside hotel in the East. On-site child care makes it a good choice for families with young kids who don't plan to ski. Accommodations range from spacious rooms with two queen-size beds to two-bedroom suites. Most units have kitchens and dining areas. Concierge services take care of any needs guests might have, and there's an outdoor heated pool, Jacuzzi, and ski storage. Room service is also available. $109-590. Sunday River Skiway Road, P.O. Box 450, Bethel, ME 04217; 800-543-2754, 207-824-3500.

The Jordan Grand Hotel and Crown Club, Sunday River's newest luxury hotel, located in the heart of Jordan Bowl, giving guests excellent ski-in-and-out options. The hotel has a child-care center, as well as a health club, arcade, spa, and two restaurants. 800-543-2754, 207-824-5807.

The Bethel Inn & Country Club, seven miles from the ski area and in the middle of the hamlet of Bethel, has traditional inn rooms in an elegant Colonial three-story mansion built in 1913, along with much newer townhouses. Each of the 42 townhouses has a full kitchen, fireplace, two bedrooms, two full baths, and a washer and dryer. The inn is known as a cross-country center, offering 40 kilometers of groomed trails. Family movies are shown in the conference room (sometimes during the dinner hour to give parents a break), and the restaurant has a children's menu. Recreational facilities include a library, game room, outdoor pool, hot tub, and sauna. Kids under 12 stay free in their parents' room, and breakfast and dinner are included in the rates if you stay in the inn. $198–238. Broad Street, P.O. Box 49, Bethel, ME 04217; 800-654-0125, 207-824-2282/6035.

Moderate

North Peak Condos can sleep up to six in their two-bedroom units. They're conveniently located at the base of the Perfect Turn Express high-speed quad on North Peak and adjacent to the South Ridge area. Very popular with families, the condos feature fireplaces, a heated outdoor pool, sauna, and laundry facilities. $205–390. Sunday River Access Road, P.O. Box 450, Bethel, ME 04217; 800-543-2754.

White Cap Condominiums have one- or three-bedroom units and access to a heated outdoor pool and sauna, a club room, and laundry facilities. Its location adjacent to the Road Runner trail, which runs to White Cap base, and its nonstop teen programs make it a good choice for families with older kids. $135–520. Sunday River Access Road, P.O. Box 450, Bethel ME 04217; 800-543-2754.

The Brookside Condominiums are also popular for families with older kids. Their one- and two-bedrooms units, complete with kitchens and gas fireplaces, are right next to the White Cap base. An outdoor heated pool and sauna are on-site. $195–420. Sunday River Access Road, P.O. Box 450, Bethel, ME 04217; 800-543-2754.

Budget

The Bethel River Motel has a variety of well-priced units such as two-bedroom condominiums, efficiencies, a 3-bedroom house, and hotel rooms with one queen or two double beds. Hotel $40–$80; condos $80–195, house $90–289. Route 2, West Bethel, ME 04286; 207-836-3575.

Snowcap Inn has simple rooms with two queen beds. Guests can enjoy an outdoor Jacuzzi and can relax in front of the three fireplaces in the lounge area. $89–150. Sunday River Skiway, Bethel, ME 04217; 800-543-2754, 207-824-7669.

Children's Ski School

Sunday River's "Perfect Kids" ski-school program (800-543-2SKI) offers coaching for children age 3 to 18. All sessions group children according to age and ability level. Full and half days are available, and the program has its own rental shop adjacent to the beginners' terrain.

Within Perfect Kids are specialized programs for various ages groups: Tiny Turns for children 3 to 4 offers an hour of private coaching; children are taken out of the day-care center for their lessons. Mogul Mites is for children 4 to 6, and Mogul Meisters is for 7- to 12-years-olds. Clinics in snowboarding are offered for kids 7 and up.

Day Care

Three licensed day-care centers, at the South Ridge Center, the Summit Hotel and Conference Center, and the Jordan Grand Hotel, care for children from 6 weeks to 6 years. At the South Ridge Center, infants 6 weeks to 18 months have their own separate space. When they're steady on their feet they can move into the toddler room. Preschoolers 3 years and older can attend the short one-on-one ski lesson (additional charge), offered through the Tiny Turn program (see above). The Center has an area called the River House for kids age 3 and over that can pick up the overflow during peak holiday periods. Situated just across the street, it's one big room divided in half, with a lunchroom. All children enjoy games, arts and crafts, circle time, and snow play. Reservations are recommended.

Day care at the Summit Hotel and Jordan Grand Hotel is more limited and is largely reserved for hotel guests.

Teens

The MTV Club (More Terrain and Vertical) operates throughout the year for skiers, and the Black and Blue crew for snowboarders. Both programs offer instruction and include a special "back-of-the-house" sessions for teens interested in learning how the ski resort operates.

Snowboarding

The main boarding attraction at Sunday River is a competition half pipe groomed by a pipe dragon, the specialized pipe-grooming implement that can create ultra high, ultra steep, and ultra smooth walls. The resort's main snowboard park is by the half pipe, but there are eight terrain parks all over the mountain. "Phat" features rolls and a big air jump, and "Spinal Tap" is a long spine of snow that is popular with skiers as well.

Cross-Country Skiing

Sunday River Cross Country Ski Center is a half mile from the Sunday River ski area. Forty kilometers of groomed trails lead through the forest to picnic spots and a covered bridge. Ski rentals include children's sizes, and there are lessons for all ages and abilities and decorated children's trails. R.F.D. 2, Box 1688, Bethel, ME 04217; 207-824-2410.

Bethel Inn & Country Club has 40 miles of groomed trails, many heavily wooded, along with ski lessons, children's equipment, and pulkes. Broad Street, P.O. Box 49, Bethel, ME 04217; 800-654-0125, 207-824-2175.

At **Carter's Farm and Cross-Country Ski Centers**, 25 kilometers of trails lead through the foothills of western Maine with vistas of the Presidential Range. Ski rentals include children's sizes and pulkes, and there is one lift, lessons, a ski patrol, and narrow tracks made just for children. 420 Main Street, RR1 Box 710 (Route 26), Oxford, ME 04270; 207-539-4848.

Telemark Inn (207-836-2703), ten miles from Bethel, offers 22 kilometers of groomed trails. The property is also known for its beautifully restored Adirondack-style lodge filled with antiques and a lovely restaurant. R.F.D. #2, Box 800, Bethel ME, 04217.

Other Activities

Ice skating at the base of White Cap, is open from 8 A.M. to 10 P.M. and is lit at night. Ice skating is free, and skate rentals are available at the White Cap base lodge.

Mahoosuc Guide Service of Maine (207-824-2073) offers a variety of dog-sled tours.

Norland Living History Center (207-897-4366) gives visitors a glimpse of life in this part of the country in times past.

Snowmobiling rides travel through hundreds of miles of trails around the area. For information, call Sun Valley Sports (207-824-SLED).

Deals and Discounts

Sunday River has quite a few Ski and Stay packages that offer savings throughout the season. Call 800-543-2SKI or 207-824-3000 for details.

If you plan to ski for more than a week each season, get an Edge Card. It's a frequent skier, direct-to-lift access card which allows you to earn points toward free lift tickets and other deals at Sunday River or any of its affiliated resorts. Another bargain is the Magnificent 7 card, which allows you to purchase seven lifts tickets at a discount, good for any of the affiliated resorts which include Attitash Bear Peak (see page 233), Sugarloaf/ USA (see page 245), Killington (see page 193), Sugarbush (see page 225), and Mount Snow/Haystack (see page 198).

CANADA

The East

Mont-Sainte-Anne

Address: Case Postale 400, Beaupre, Québec, Canada G0A 1E0
Telephone: 800-463-1568 (lodging), 418-827-4561
Web site: http://www.mont-sainte-anne.com

Just twenty miles east of Québec City, the mountain called Mont-Sainte-Anne rises dramatically over the St. Lawrence River. On a clear day the views from the top are breathtaking: The wide swath of river, the extended sweep of snowy plains, and Québec City in the far-off distance. Most visitors stay in lodging at the base of the mountain or in nearby villages, but there are several hotels in downtown Québec City that offer ski packages with a skier shuttle to the slopes.

In addition to its reputation as a solid downhill skiers' mountain, this resort area is popular with snowboarders and cross-country skiers. Host of the Snowboard World Cup since 1993, the resort purposefully placed its snowboard park under a night-lit chairlift so guests could enjoy the spectacle of boarders catching big air.

The cross-country trail network and extensive base lodge make Mont-Sainte-Anne the biggest cross-country ski center in Canada. Hotels and condos offer both downhill and Nordic ski packages.

The Children's Centre offers one-stop shopping, with everything in one building at the base of the mountain. But the best part of Mont-Sainte-Anne is that you feel a world away from the United States. Much of the population speaks French, and the food customs are definitely Québecois. The Sugar Shack, right on the slopes, sells maple-sugar candy for a quick pick-up if you tire. The sugar syrup is boiled on the spot, poured into

MOUNTAIN STATISTICS
Base elevation: 575 feet
Summit: 2,625 feet
Vertical drop: 2,050 feet
Skiable acres: 400
Annual average snowfall: 180 inches
Snowmaking: 85% (340 acres)
Night skiing: Tuesday through Sunday from 3 to 7 P.M.
Season: mid-November to the end of April
Lifts: 12 (1 8-person gondola, 2 high-speed quads, 1 regular quad, 1 triple, 2 doubles, 5 surface lifts)
Terrain: 22% beginner, 48% intermediate, 20% advanced, 10% extreme
Lift tickets: adults $38 CN ($28 U.S.), children 7 to 13 $24 CN ($17 U.S.), seniors 65-69 $29 CN ($21 U.S.), Children 6 and under and seniors 70 and over free. Tax not included.

FAMILY STATISTICS
Day care: Children's Center, age 6 months to 10 years, 418-827-4561.
Children's lessons: 418-827-4561
Baby-sitting: Individual hotels keep lists of names and phone numbers.
Medical: Sainte-Anne de Beaupres Hospital, 418-827-3726

the snow to cool, and passed out to eager young guests. Family Weeks in March have delightful activities throughout the week.

How to Get There
Québec City International Airport has flights from many cities in the U.S. and Canada. Montréal is 180 miles away; Albany, 395 miles; New York City, 574 miles; Boston, 400 miles.

Where to Stay
Expensive
Château Mont-Sainte-Anne is so close to the gondola it doesn't even count the distance in feet, only in steps: 42. All rooms and suites have kitchenettes, and the recreational amenities are impressive: an indoor and outdoor pool, a game room, theater, ice skating, tobogganing, and a health club. (central reservations). $95–250. 500 Boulevard Beaupres, Beaupres, Québec GOA 1EO; 800-463-1568, 418-827-5211.

Moderate
Val des Neiges, at the foot of the mountain, has 75 studios with kitchens and 60 two-bedroom condos with kitchens and washer/dryers. It has the best-equipped fitness center in the region as well as indoor badminton, a video arcade, an ice-skating rink, and billiards. $75–200. 2013 Val des Neiges Street, Beaupres, Québec, GOA 1EO; 800-463-1568, 418-827-5721.

Le Château Frontenac in the heart of Old Québec offers skier shuttles to Mont-Sainte-Anne as well as to the airport. There's an indoor swimming pool, health spa, massage services, and restaurants on-site. $89–200. 1 Des Carrieres, Québec City, Québec Z1R 4P5; 800-463-1568 (central reservations).

Children's Ski School
All services for children, including lessons, ski rentals, registration, and day care, are located in the Mont-Sainte-Anne Children's Centre. The kids' ski school program, called Kinderski, sticks to its philosophy that the best way for children to learn to ski is by having fun, and instructions are presented in a game-like format. Lessons start at age 2 ½ and are available for kids through the age of 10. The day begins and ends with indoor warmup exercises, games, and singing. Kids take a break for lunch and lessons continue into the afternoon.

Day Care

The Mont-Sainte-Anne Children's Centre, right at the base of the mountain by the gondola, takes care of little ones from age 6 months to 10 years. Babies and toddlers 6 to 18 months have a special nursery area and a separate nap room. A larger playroom accommodates children age 19 months to 10 years. Kids enjoy arts and crafts, games, puppetry, music, fantasy and dress up play, and movies while they're inside, and sledding, skating, and sleigh riding when they're outside. Parents can bring food for their children or arrange a hot lunch from the cafeteria. All children have a rest time/quiet time after lunch. The rooms for both the day care and the ski school surround an atrium where registration, ski rentals, and a small theater are found.

Teens

The Youth Camp packages offer five days of lift tickets and four days of group lessons.

Snowboarding

A snowboard park lit for night skiing gives Mont-Sainte-Anne its ranking as a top spot for boarders. The park, open to skiers, too, starts with an 80-meter half pipe and then runs through various features: a "freecarve" slalom course, a series of small rolls, several tabletops, quarter pipes, and a big roll with two big jumps followed by a last jump over waves. A recently purchased pipe dragon cuts and smooths the half pipe to perfection.

Cross-Country Skiing

Mont-Saint-Anne has the most extensive cross-country network in Canada. With 225 kilometers, its variety of trails include skating tracks and a ski patrol. The center has its own ski schools, lessons (including children's), and an enormous waxing room and shop. You can even trek to wilderness camps equipped with bunks, stoves, and firewood. There is a special trail that starts at the alpine ski area base parking lot, and leads to the cross-country base, about 7 kilometers away.

Other Activities

Dog sledding adventures are some of the most interesting anywhere: A special program for kids takes 4- to 13-year-olds on an educational introductory ride. An overnight program gives visitors a taste of the lives of the *coureurs des bois* as you head into the forest to a special encampment. Here you'll see how they take care of the dogs, after which you can enjoy a hot meal and views of the Northern Lights before retiring to a heated tent for the night. After breakfast the next morning you harness the dogs and head back. 418-827-2227.

Ice skating: An Olympic-size skating rink is at the base of the lifts. It's lit for night skating. Skate rentals are available. (418-827-3708).

Paragliding Gliders take off from the summit of the ski area and soar slowly to the bottom of the mountain, enjoying breathtaking views of the St. Lawrence River and islands below. The minimum age is 16; 418-824-5383.

Quebec City Region Ski Museum (418-827-5279) inside the base lodge, has exhibits of old skis and equipment, trophies, photos, an original gondola car, and information about the history of skiing in the region.

Sleigh Rides: On busy weekends and holiday periods, sleighs pull skiers from the parking lot to the gondola. One hour-sleigh rides can also be arranged.

Snowmobiling: Trails at the base of the mountain take you to a major provincial trail network. Snowmobile Rental Center, 418-827-8478, S.M. Sport, 418-826-0343 or Laurentides Sports Services, 418-827-8478.

Snowshoeing rentals (and three snowshoeing loop trails) are available at both Mont-Sainte-Anne and at the Mont-Sainte-Anne Cross-Country Center. Rentals 418-827-3708.

Deals and Discounts
Novices can ski two of the beginners' lifts for free.

❄ Mont Tremblant

Address: 3005 Chemin Principal, Mont Tremblant, Québec,
Canada J0T 1Z0

Telephone: 800-461-8711 (resort information and lodging), 800-567-6760 (reginal reservations), 819-681-2000.

Web site: http://www.tremblant.ca

Just north of New England in southern Québec, Mont Tremblant (Trembling Mountain) was given its name by the Algon-quin Indians who, witnessing cascades of rocks and water tumbling down its face every spring, feared they had offended the spirit of the mountain. Now the mountain trembles with the gleeful shouts of snowboarders and skiers who zigzag down its face. When they reach the base, they can tumble into any number of French-style patisseries, grab a café au lait, and ride a sophisticated high-speed lift back up for another run.

First built as a ski resort in 1939, Mont Tremblant ran into some difficulty until it was purchased by Intrawest, the owners of Whistler Resort and Copper Mountain Resort. An infusion of cash and the choice of sensitive architects created a picturesque base village reminiscent of a charming Swiss alpine town, but with a French-Canadian flair. Cobblestones pave the main Place St. Bernard, where kids can line up during sugar season for *tire d'erable*, maple syrup poured in ribbons on the snow to harden and be rolled onto a lollipop stick. The colors of the resort are bright and cheerful, buildings are trimmed with bay windows, and shop and restaurant signs appear from a different era where

MOUNTAIN STATISTICS
Base elevation: 870 feet
Summit: 3,001 feet
Vertical drop: 2,131 feet
Skiable acres: 500
Annual average snowfall: 144 inches
Snowmaking: 375 acres
Night snowboarding: Wednesday and
  Saturday, 6:30 to 9 P.M.
Season: mid November to late May
Lifts: 11 (1 6-passenger high-speed
  gondola, 5 high-speed quads, 1
  regular quad, 3 triples, 1 surface
  lift)
Terrain: 20% beginner, 45%
  intermediate, 25% advanced, 10%
  expert
Lift tickets: adults $43 CN ($30 U.S.)
  youth 13 to 17 and seniors 65+
  $33 CN ($23 U.S.) children 6 to 12
  $22 CN ($15 U.S.).

FAMILY STATISTICS
Day care: Mother Nature's Day Care,
  ages 1 to 6, 800-461-8711, 819-
  681-3000, ext. 5666
Children's lessons: Kidz Club, ages 3 to
  12, 888-ECOLE-SKI, 819-681-3000
  ext. 5666
Baby-sitting: Lists are available through
  the individual hotels
Medical: Laurentian Medical Center, 819-
  324-4000

hand-painting and -carving were de rigueur. Most lodging is scattered around the base area.

The ski experience has been well-thought out, too, and Mont Tremblant's lifts are fast and efficient. Its children's ski school and day-care facilities are in one central spot right next to the beginner's lift. Day-care scheduling is unusually flexible here, as parents can opt for as little as one hour of care or as long as one day. Cellular phones are available for parents' peace of mind when they leave their kids. On weekends, parents get the night off with Children Âprès Ski, a special kids' evening for 1- to 12-year-olds with entertainment and dinner.

How to Get There

Montréal has the closest major airports: Dorval and Mirabel both have skier shuttles from the airport directly to resort properties. Local shuttles run from 7 A.M. to 11 P.M.

Where to Stay

Expensive

Club Tremblant's deluxe and spacious condominiums are popular with families. Located on the shore of Lac Tremblant across from the mountain (about 2 miles) the club has a free shuttle to the lifts. Condos come in one-, two-, and three-bedroom units, with and without lofts. All feature fully equipped kitchens and washer/dryers. There's an indoor pool, a sauna, a whirlpool, and a game room. The club's restaurant serves a buffet breakfast and French cuisine for dinner. $260-370 CN. 121 Cuttle Street, Mont Tremblant, Québec, Canada J0T 1Z0; 800-567-8341, 819-425-2731.

Chateau Mont Tremblant is a brand-new Canadian Pacific Hotel built in the tradition of the grand mountain ski lodges in Banff and Whistler. Standard hotel rooms are available, but families will be most comfortable in the one- and two-bedroom suites that have kitchenettes and extra amenities. There's an indoor heated pool, saunas, Jacuzzis, a small gym, and a game room in this ski-in-and-out property. $145–505 CN. 3045 Rue Principale, Mont Tremblant, Québec, Canada J0T 1Z0; 819-681-7000.

Marriott Residence Inn is a ski-in-and-out property reminiscent of a French-Canadian manor house. Its suites are studios, one-bedroom, two-bedroom, and one- and two-bedroom loft units. All are equipped with a full kitchen or kitchenette, fireplaces, balconies, and fresh, modern furnishings. The family restaurant has a kids' menu, and the rates include a deluxe complimentary continental breakfast. $115–275 CN. 170 Chemin Curé Deslauriers, Mont Tremblant, Québec, Canada J0T 1Z0; 888-272-4000, 819-272-4000.

Sun Star Properties manages a number of different condominiums in the Tremblant Resort Village. Most are within walking distance of the lifts, and range in size from studios to four-bedroom units. Prices vary, depending on the number of people the unit can accommodate. 2001 Principal Street, Mont Tremblant Village, Québec, Canada J0T 1Z0; 819-425-8681.

Moderate
Suites Tremblant, at the base of the ski mountain, has a variety of rooms ranging from standard hotel rooms to two-bedroom condominiums with a loft. Many family packages are available. $69-316 CN. 305 Chemin Principal, Mont Tremblant, Québec, Canada J0T 1Z0; 800-461-8711.

Budget
Condolets and Apparthotel feature one-bedroom units that can sleep up to four people in two twin beds and a futon couch. There's a small but fully outfitted kitchen and a freestanding fireplace/woodstove. Most condos are ski-in-and-out, making these a good buy for budget-conscious families. $105-140 CN. 3005 Chemin Principal, Mont Tremblant, Québec, Canada J0T 1Z0; 800-461-8711, 819-681-2000.

Children's Ski School
Kidz Club (888-ECOLE-SKI) offers ski lessons for children ages 3 to 12 and snowboarding lessons for ages 6 to 12. Classes are arranged according to age (3 to 6; 7 to 8; 9 to 12) and further divided by ability. Both full- and half-day programs are available. The rental shop for children is within the Kidz Club building. Classes range in size from four to nine kids per instructor. Teens take classes out of the other ski school next door in the Johannsen Building.

Day Care
Mother Nature's Daycare on the first floor of the Kidz Club building provides day-long activities for children between the ages of 1 and 6. Babies have their own room with cribs, rockers, and age-appropriate toys. Four other toy-filled playrooms house the rest of the age groups. Your child will get plenty of fresh air, since outdoor play is offered in the morning and

afternoon. All enjoy arts and crafts, puppets, games, a hot lunch, and a rest period. Cell phones are available for parents to carry so they can call in and check on their children.

Teens

Teen Ski and Snowboard Weeks are for visitors who stay a minimum of four days. Teens ski together as a group with an instructor, receiving a two-hour lesson in the morning and a one-and-a-half hour lesson in the afternoon. Individuals can choose to eat with the group or with their parents, meeting up again for the afternoon session. Skiers get the chance to try the funny short skis called "Bigfoots" sometime during the week.

Snowboarding

Mont Tremblant's snowboard park won an award for best snowboard park in Quebéc. Designed by snowboarders, it features big-air jumps, ramps, quarter pipes, and rails.

Five casual snowboard events are offered throughout the season: Participants are scored as they board through the park on creativity, imagination, and form. Another casual contest to see who can get the "biggest air" is open to anyone who wishes to participate.

Cross-Country Skiing

Parc Mont Tremblant (819-425-5588) has 90 kilometers of groomed trails, lessons, and rentals. Tracks of varying distances and difficulty start at the base of the mountain and loop around the golf course, across the river, and through the woods.

Other Activities

Aqua Club, (800-461-8711) an indoor water park designed as a Laurentian lake, has 3 pools, rope swings into the water, a small beach area for the kids, whirlpools, and a gym.

Dog sledding behind a team of four huskies; 819-681-3000, ext. 6642.

One-hour horse-drawn sleigh rides go through the village and into nearby forests (819-681-3000, ext. 6642).

Ice skating on Lac Miroir: skate rentals are available at the lake next to Vieux Tremblant.

Snowmobiling: Trips leave from the Place St. Bernard (819-681-4535) and head into the mountains. A nighttime trip under the stars and a daily trip up above the treeline are available.

Snowshoeing trips take you through the Laurentian forest with a biologist on a two hour deer-observation tour. 819-681-3000, ext. 6642.

Deals and Discounts

The cleverly titled "Forget the Books" package is an alluring deal for families and a great buy that wraps six days of skiing, five nights of accommodations, and 14 hours of ski lessons for the kids into one low-priced package. Other early-season packages, including an early Christmas ski week, can save you money.

Discounted lift tickets are available to guests staying at resort lodging.

The West

❄ Whistler Resort

Address: 4010 Whistler Way, Whistler, BC, Canada V0N 1B4
Telephone: 800-944-7853 (information and central reservations),
604-932-2394 (activity and information center)
Web sites: http://www.whistler-resort.com., http://www. whistler-mountain.com, and http://www.blackcomb.com

The two monumental mountains of Whistler and Blackcomb stand side by side and together offer visitors more vertical and more skiing than any other resort in North America. The mountains ski as separate yet linked entities, each having a little something different, and a lot, such as superior grooming and numerous high-speed lifts, in common. All this and a convenient purpose-built pedestrian base village with most parking tucked away in underground garages has made Whistler Resort, as the entire area is known, first among American skiers for the last five years.

The majority of accommodations, shops, and restaurants are found at the base of Whistler mountain, but Blackcomb's base has a deluxe hotel and slopeside ski-in-and-out condominiums. The two base areas are a four-minute walk apart. Together they offer more ski in and out accommodations than any other ski resort in North America. Skiers who are staying at the base of Whistler and want to sample Blackcomb's terrain can board a gondola that whisks them to Blackcomb's mid-mountain area. Guests staying at Blackcomb who want to ski Whistler mountain can take a lift up and ski across any of the well-marked trails. One lift ticket allows you to ski both mountains.

**MOUNTAIN STATISTICS—
WHISTLER MOUNTAIN**
Base elevation: 2,140 feet
Summit: 7,160 feet
Vertical drop: 5,020 feet
Skiable acres: 3,657
Average annual snowfall: 360 inches
Snowmaking: 150 acres
Night skiing: None
Season: late November through April
Lifts: 13 (2 gondolas, 3 high-speed
    quads, 3 triples, 1 double, 4 surface
    lifts).
Terrain: 20% beginner, 55%
    intermediate, 25% expert
Lift Tickets: adult $55 CN ($41 U.S.),
    youth 13 to 18 $44 CN ($33 U.S.)
    children 7 to 12 $25 CN ($19 U.S.)
    under 7 free

Both base areas have a children's (and adults') ski school that offers top quality skiing and snowboarding instruction. Some kind of supervised children's program is available at one of the two base areas every late afternoon or evening of the ski season.

The resort is located in the coast range outside of Vancouver, which means they receive the mild weather patterns brought down by the warm Japanese current, resulting in snow conditions that can vary from fluffy dry powder to thick, heavy oatmeal. The fleet of grooming machines that smoothes the runs nightly guarantees a very reliable firm, satiny finish to both mountains, no matter what the weather. Fog can occasionally obscure parts of the lower mountain.

Both mountains have wide open bowls, meandering through-the-trees runs, and precipitous steeps. Lift lines are short thanks to the numerous high-speed lifts, and the quantity of skiable terrain insures that there is always an uncrowded run somewhere on the mountain, even over peak holiday periods.

How to Get There

Vancouver International Airport is two hours south of Whistler Resort. The city of Vancouver is 75 miles (about 1 ½ hours) south.

Where to Stay

Expensive

Delta Whistler Resort (http.//www.delta-whistler.com.) is in the heart of the Whistler Village and is one of the most deluxe full-service hotels at the Whistler base. The hotel contains restaurants, bars, shops, and art galleries and is just steps from the gondolas to Whistler and Blackcomb mountains. Rooms have two double or queen beds; suites contain a variety of bed and room configurations and often have small kitchens, fireplaces, and balconies. Guests may use the heated outdoor pool, indoor and outdoor whirlpools, tennis courts, massage therapy, on-site ski rentals, and ski valet. Kids under 18 stay free in their parents' room and children age 6 and under eat free off the kid's menu in one of the restaurants. $335–1,200 CN. 4050 Whistler Way, Whistler B.C. VON 1BO; 800-268-1133 (Canada) or 800-877-1133 (USA), 604-932-1982.

Chateau Whistler Resort is a luxury resort hotel right at the base of the Blackcomb mountain. It's a stunning ski-in-and-out property built to look like an elegant old chateau but with modern elegance and refined amenities. Hotel rooms have one queen bed or two double beds and some have connecting doors. If you're feeling flush, choose one of the spacious Junior Suites which have a king-size bed, sitting area with sofa bed, and French doors separating rooms. One- or two-bedroom family suites are also available. A health club on the premises has spa services, and there is a swimming pool, an outdoor whirlpool tub, a sauna, and steam rooms. Children under 18 stay free in their parents' room. $260–950 CN. 4599 Chateau Boulevard, Whistler, B.C., Canada VON 1B4; 800-441-1414, 604-938-8000.

Timberline Lodge has 42 luxurious condominiums ranging in size from studios to one bedroom loft units. All have a full kitchen, hairdryers, and fireplaces. The complex has a heated outdoor pool, hot tub, and sauna, plus a fireside lounge, laundry facilities, and ski lockers. $225–390 CN. 4122 Village Green, Whistler, BC, Canada VON 1B4; 802-253-8582.

Mountainside Lodge offers ski-in-and-out lodging, about 100 yards above the lifts at the Blackcomb Mountain base. Studio lofts are best for families, accommodating four to six people with their own private sauna, full kitchen, fireplace, and Jacuzzi. There's a pool, hot tub, sauna, restaurant with kids' menu, and laundry facilities. Kids under six and rollaways are free. Extra person charge: $35. $180–400 CN. 4417 Sundial Place, Whistler, BC Canada VON 1B4. 800-667-2855 or 604-932-4511.

Moderate
Listel Whistler Hotel, about 100 yards from the ski lifts at the Whistler Mountain base, has standard hotel rooms and suites. It features an outdoor pool and Jacuzzi, restaurant, and bar. Standard rooms have two queen-size beds, and junior suites have one queen-size bed, a sofabed, and living area. Many of the rooms have a small refrigerator. Kids 16 and under are free in their parents' room. $199–249 CN. 4121 Village Green, Whistler, BC, Canada VON 1B0; 800-663-5472, 604-932-1133.

Crystal Lodge is steps away from the high-speed gondolas of both Blackcomb and Whistler mountains. Standard rooms have two double beds, but studios offer families a full kitchen and fireplace. Even more spacious studio lofts have two queen-size beds upstairs and a kitchen and living room downstairs. The lodge has an outdoor pool, indoor and outdoor whirlpools, steam room, guests' laundry, and ski storage. $195–270 CN. 800-667-3363, 604-932-2221.

Budget
The Hostel has one family room available with one double and two single beds for only $44–60 CN for four people. The guest kitchen on the premises and dining room are open 24 hours a day. 5678 Alta Lake Road, P.O. Box 128, Whistler, BC, Canada VON 1B0; 604-932-5492.

Children's Ski School
Whistler Mountain
Children age 18 months and older are enrolled in ski school although little ones spend their time playing in the snow, often on skis, and the rest

MOUNTAIN STATISTICS— BLACKCOMB MOUNTAIN

Base elevation: 2,214 feet
Summit: 7,494 feet
Vertical drop: 5,280 feet
Skiable acres: 3,344 acres
Annual average snowfall: 360 inches
Snowmaking: 330 acres
Night skiing: yes, on one small chair
  lift Wednesdays and Saturdays until
  9 P.M. Snowboarding lessons are
  offered at night as well.
Season: mid-November to May with
  summer skiing and boarding on
  Blackcomb's Horstman Glacier mid-
  June to mid-August
Lifts: 16 (1 gondola, 7 high-speed
  quads, 2 triples, 7 surface lifts)
Terrain: 15% beginner, 55%
  intermediate, 30% expert
Lift Tickets: adults $55 CN ($41 U.S.),
  youth 13 to 18 $44 CN ($33 U.S.),
  kids 7 to 12 $25 CN ($19 U.S.),
  under 7 free.

FAMILY STATISTICS

Daycare: Whistler (18 months and up
  as part of the ski school) 604-932-
  3434, Blackcomb 18 months and up
  604-938-7748
Children's Lessons: Whistler 888-588-
  3434, 604-932-3434, Blackcomb
  604-938-7748
Baby-sitting: The Nanny Network, 604-
  938-2823 or Tiny Tots
  604-938-9699
Baby gear: Baby's Away rents cribs,
  high chairs, car seats, strollers, toys,
  etc., 604-932-4844.
Medical: Whistler Medical Centre, 604-
  932-4911

indoors at the Children's Learning Centre. A program for children ages 5 to 12 are headquartered at the Children's Learning Centre at Olympic Station, one-third of the way up the Whistler Village Gondola. Kids meet their instructors at the base of Whistler Mountain, and then head up on the gondola to the new facility that includes a cafeteria and playrooms for tiny skiers. Little Riders snowboard lessons are offered for children ages 5 and 6; Young Riders snowboard lessons are offered for children age 6 to 12.

Blackcomb Mountain

The Kids Camp program at Blackcomb is for children who are toilet trained. Mini Merlins, for 4 to 6 year olds, gives kids four hours of ski time and time inside resting and playing or eating in a restful play room that is separate from the older kids. Children from 5 to 7 years olds can take L'il Rippers snowboarding classes. All beginners get to use the Magic Carpet Lift (800-766-0449).

Children 7 to 12 years participate in Super Kids ski programs or the Junior Jibbers Snowboarding classes if they are 8 to 12 years of age.

The Summit Club and Ride Tribe are for 13- to 17-year-old skiers and boarders. Groups are formed by age ability level.

Day Care

Two late afternoon/evening programs take place at both base areas: Kids' Night Out is offered Tuesday and Thursday in Whistler and Blackcomb, offering children a supervised evening of games, crafts, activities, and dinner. On one night it takes place in Whistler, the other in Blackcomb. Blackcomb's locations allows kids to participate in night sledding. Kids' Après programs at both base areas offer supervised activities for kids age 5 to 12 on Monday, Wednesday, and Friday of certain weeks from 3:30 to 5:30, just enough time for parents to select their own après ski activity.

Whistler Mountain

There is no official day-care-only program at the Whistler base, but the ski school program for children ages 18 months to 36 months has a strong day-care component. Children begin in the base area's Children's Centre where they play and enjoy various activities. They go up the gondola with an instructor and their skis to the Children's Learning Centre where they participate in snow play on skis. There are several rooms in the Children's Learning Centre just for this younger age group. If your child is younger or doesn't want to ski, contact the Nanny Network at 604-938-2823.

Blackcomb Mountain

Wee Wizards are kids 18 months to 3 years who have a program that includes indoor and outdoor activities. Children 18 months to 2½ don't ski but children over 2½ enjoy a short introduction to skiing during their day. Wee Wizards Plus is for ages 3 and up who enjoy various indoor and outdoor activities as well. There is a separate safe snowplay area for these children. The ski school also uses this facility for their younger children, but different age groups have their own rooms.

Snowboarding

Whistler Mountain

A competition half pipe at the top of the green chair is groomed nightly. Whistler's Terrain Park begins just below the half pipe and has table tops, kickers, a quarter pipe, spines, and banded turns, all groomed nightly.

Blackcomb Mountain

Kokanee Terrain Park has recently been increased to 16 acres in size and has quarter pipes, table tops, jumps, and hits, accompanied by a hot sound system and the nearby Snack Shack to feed those hungry appetites. Blackcomb's Fate Half Pipe, above the Solar Coaster Chair, is groomed regularly by the resort's pipe dragon.

Teens

Blackcomb's Summit Club has programs for skiers and riders ages 13 to 16. Whistler's Freeski and Freeriders programs are for intermediate to advanced skiers, and for all levels of riders age 12 to 16. Participants learn to ski and board in powder, bumps, steeps, and gates.

Cross-Country Skiing

The Valley Trail is a paved trail that serves as a bike and roller blade track during summer that is groomed in winter and used as a cross-country trail. The loops that go around scenic Lost Lake are lit for night skiing. Cross-country lessons can be arranged through the ticket booth (604-932-6436) at the beginning of the Lost Lake Trail System, which consists of 30 kilometers of trails. Equipment can be rented at Wild Willys (604-938-8036) in Whistler Village and The Escape Route (604-938-3228) which is closer to the ticket booth. A cozy log hut perched on shore of Lost Lake allows an indoor rest stop along the way. Cross-country ski trail maps and rental equipment information are also available at the Whistler Activity and Information Center.

Other Activities

Ice Skating: The arena at the Meadow Park Sports Center, about six kilometers north of the town center has an NHL-sized ice surface. Admission includes use of the swimming pool. 604-938-7275.

Indoor Rock Climbing: Stone Wall Whistler Rock Gym (a little way from the village) at Function Junction. 604-938-9858.

Meadow Parks Sports Center has ice skating, a swimming pool just for kids, a lap pool, fitness facility, and squash courts. Off Highway 99 in Alpine Meadows. 604-938-PARK.

Mountain World is a 20,000 square foot virtual entertainment center in the Whistler Conference center that has virtual reality video games, and ski, snowboard, and other sports simulators. Parents must accompany their children.

Movie Theater in the Whistler Conference Centre shows movies twice nightly. Often the early show is suitable for families. 604-932-2422.

Sleigh rides on Blackcomb take guests up to a lookout above the lights of Whistler village followed by a hot chocolate stop at a warming hut. 604-932-7631 or 604-894-6601.

Snowmobile Tours: Explore the forests and fields during the day or evening for one to three hours. Some tours include dinner. Canadian Snowmobile Adventures, 604-938-1616.

Snowshoe tours explore the mountains and valley. Select from a nature tour, fondue tour, après ski tour or custom excursions. Canadian Snowshoe Adventures, 604-932-0647.

Deals and Discounts

Early and late season value packages (November 21-December 18 and April 5 to April 25) for 3, 5, or 7 nights are an excellent buy. Check the central reservation number in the spring because there are often last-minute, late-season, low-priced deals. 880-WHISTLER.

Lake Louise

Address: P.O Box 5, Lake Louise, Alberta, Canada TOL 1EO
Telephone: 800-258-7669 (reservations) 403-522-3555
(information)
Web site: http://www.skilouise.com

Set in a location of breathtaking beauty, skiers at Lake Louise are rewarded with dramatic views of the lake, the majestic Canadian Rocky Mountains, and Victoria Glacier from the top of many of the ski area's chair lifts. The resort sits in the corner of Banff National Park, a enormous wonderland of soaring vistas and craggy peaks where grizzly bears still wander about in the summer. The town of Banff, 35 miles away, is a popular stop for visitors who want to take in the scenery both summer and winter. Guests who stay in Banff drive or take a shuttle to the ski area, but there are plenty of excellent lodging options in Lake Louise. Because the region is a popular summer tourist destination, lodging prices actually drop in the winter. That, plus lift ticket prices that seem a throwback to several decades ago, make Lake Louise a particularly good buy for families.

The skiing is spread over four faces—each facing a different direction—of three separate mountains, offering a whopping 4,000 lift-served acres. Another 3,000 unpatrolled acres are available to skiers to explore. Every chairlift has at least one green or easy run down, allowing families of all abilities to ride up together and meet again at the bottom. Intermediates have any number of possibilities, but should plan at least one run down Meadowlark, an intermediate trail that meanders through the forest for a 3,000-foot, 3-mile

MOUNTAIN STATISTICS
Base elevation: 5,400 feet
Summit: 8,650 feet
Vertical rise: 3,250 feet
Skiable acres: 4,000
Annual average snowfall: 144 inches
Snowmaking: 40% of mountain (1,600 acres)
Night skiing: none
Season: early November to mid-May
Lifts: 11 (2 high-speed quads, 1 quad, 2 triples, 3 doubles, 3 surface lifts).
Terrain: 25% beginner, 45% intermediate, 30% expert
Lift tickets: adults $46 CN ($34 U.S.), children 12 ands under $15 CN ($11 U.S.), Student 13–17 with valid ID, or college students up to 25 with a valid ID and seniors over 65 $36 CN ($27 U.S.) under 6 free.

FAMILY STATISTICS
Licensed Daycare: 18 days to five years 403-522-3555
Children's Lessons: Kinderski ages 3 and 4, Kid Ski ages 5 to 11 403-522-1333
Baby-sitting: Individual hotels have lists of sitters for their guests
Medical: Mineral Springs Hospital in Banff, 403-762-2222

descent. The back bowls are home to some fiercely steep black diamond pitches including some precipitous double black diamond trails. Newcomers should link up with a volunteer guide, called "Ski Friends of Lake Louise," who offer free tours of the area's lifts, trails, and hidden delights.

Lake Louise's location right on the continental divide provides dry and fluffy powder snow, but the sunny south-facing slopes are targeted with snowmaking machines anyway (Lake Louise has the biggest snowmaking operation in Canada) to make sure there is plenty of the right white stuff. The region can suffer from blasts of freezing Arctic air in December and January and is colder than many other Western resorts at this time. It's best to plan to a ski trip after February 15 to avoid unseasonably cold weather.

Lake Louise has something for all ages and abilities, from babies needing day care to boarders needing to perfect their half-pipe technique. Cross-country skiers are rewarded with 60 kilometers of trails that crisscross through the scenic National Park.

If your children are school age or older, don't miss the popular Torchlight Dinner and Ski. The evening starts at 4 P.M. mid-mountain at the White Horn Lodge with appetizers and drinks followed by a full hot dinner buffet. Live entertainment provides music, and many people actually dance a bit in their ski boots, not an easy feat. When dinner is over the guided torchlight ski down begins. Each skier gets his or her own headlamp and follows the ski pros (who carry the torches) down a beginner trail to the bottom. A complimentary bus service is offered to return Lake Louise guests to their lodgings. The slope is groomed while guests are eating dinner so there is always reliably smooth, fresh corduroy to ski on. A plethora of other activities, such as ice skating and sleigh rides, are available as well.

There are no ski-in-ski-out lodgings due to the environmental restrictions placed on the ski area by Banff National Park, but a number of attractive hotels and lodges are a five-minute shuttle ride away.

How to Get There

Lake Louise, about 115 miles west of Calgary, is a two hour drive from Calgary's International Airport. The resort is 35 miles west of Banff.

Where to Stay

Expensive

Chateau Lake Louise, built in the grand manner of one of the old railway lodges, is one of two premiere lodgings in Lake Louise. Standard rooms come in a variety of configurations with two queen beds, a king and a single, and many different suites with sofa hideaways. Some rooms can contain a rollaway (no extra charge). Many of its 515 rooms look across the lake to stunning Victoria Glacier cutting a path through the surrounding mountain peaks; the other rooms (which cost slightly less) look out upon the mountains. Three dining rooms and various delis, an ice cream shop, bars, and gift shops are found in the Chateau. The Chateau is the center for much of the recreational activities in Lake Louise, such as cross-country skiing and ice skating, right out the door. A supervised complimentary children's program in the Children's Play Center for kids over the age of 2 is offered during the ski season on Fridays from 3 to 9 P.M., Saturday 7:30 A.M. to 9:30 P.M., and Sunday 7:30 A.M. to 2:30 P.M. Extended hours are offered over holidays. $175–480 CN. Lake Louise, Alberta Canada T0L 1E0; 800-828-7447, 403-522-3511.

The Post Hotel, another elegant lodge and a member of the prestigious hotel group Relais and Chateau, is more like a posh log country home. The original log building now houses the renowned Post Hotel restaurant, the finest dining establishment in the National Park. There are three different types of family suites available—some with kitchenettes and fireplaces—along with standard rooms that have two double beds. Guests enjoy the use of a library, a lounge, a pub, and an indoor swimming pool, whirlpool, and steam room. A complimentary shuttle takes guests to the ski area 5 minutes away. $150–375 CN. Lake Louise, Alberta Canada T0L 1E0; 800-661-1586, 403-522-3834.

Moderate
Lake Louise Inn

All rooms at this comfortable inn have at least two double beds, and children under the age of 16 are always free in their parents' room. Larger families will be most comfortable in the family lodge unit that can accommodate up to six or a superior loft which can accommodate eight. Both larger units have kitchens and fireplaces. Four eateries including a pizzeria are on the premises, along with an indoor swimming pool and whirlpool. The Inn provides a free shuttle to the slopes. Kids night out takes place once a week from 6 to 9 P.M. for children 4 to 10 years old. $70–240 CN. P.O. Box 209, Lake Louise, Alberta, Canada T0L 1E0; 800-661-9237, 403-522-3791.

Deer Lodge is just a few minutes walk from Lake Louise. First built as a teahouse in 1921, it began adding on guest rooms in 1925 and now has a total of 73 rooms. Rooms do not have televisions and only a few have telephones, but there are two lounges, one with a TV, the other with a lovely large stone fireplace. Rooms come in a variety of configurations, with a double and two single beds being one of the most popular with families. Guests can use the outdoor rooftop hot tub, sauna, dining room (open for dinner), and lounge (open for breakfast, lunch, and dinner). $110–180 CN. 109 Lake Louise Drive, Lake Louise, Alberta, Canada TOL 1EO; 403-522-3991.

Children's Ski School

The Kinder Ski Program for ages 3 and 4 comes in several plans: one-hour lessons allow you to drop in for a short introduction to skiing. Supervised day care can also be arranged that is combined with a one-hour lesson or two one-hour lessons (book through the day care).

Kid Ski for ages 5 to 11 offers classes for 8 different groups of skiing abilities. Kids learn skiing skills through fun and games. Morning-only, afternoon-only, and full-day programs are available. A hot lunch can be added on to any plan for a small additional charge. The ski school has its own seating area for meals and children's videos are shown during the lunch hour, especially during cold season.

Children especially enjoy the beginner-area terrain park which has a ski tunnel, whoop de doos (a series of bumps), and little jumps. 403-522-1333.

Day Care

The Day Care Center is brand new and has a special nursery area for children 18 days to 18 months. Toddlers have their own play area as do children ages 3 to 6. Hot meals are provided daily. There are many bright and colorful toys plus arts and crafts activities and outdoor play. Pre-school age children can take a one-hour lesson as part of their day. Reservations are required for children 18 months and under. 403-522-3555.

Teens

The Mountain Adventure Program for kids ages 12 to 16 is a chance for teens to ski with others their own age in a supervised setting. It's a combination of a fun ski experience and a ski class.

Snowboarding

Lake Louise is the host of the Alberta Snowboard Championships. The resort's half pipe and snowboard terrain park, about a kilometer long, is mid-mountain and features tabletop jumps, rollers, and various hits and jumps. Freeriders also enjoy Lake Louise for its natural jumps and steeps.

Cross-Country Skiing

The cross-country trail network in the national park consists of about 60 kilometers of groomed trails. Three different ski rental shops in the Lake

Louise area can get you started if you don't have your own equipment: **Chateau Louise** (403-522-3511) is the main center of activity for cross-country skiing in the area, offering rental skis, rental clothing, and lessons. Several trails, including a good one for children and beginners called the Shoreline Trail, start from the Chateau. Cross-country skiing rentals are also available at the **mountain base** where another trail loop starts and at **Wilson Mountain Sports** (403-522-3636) in the village.

Skoki Backcountry Lodge, about a three hour and seven mile trip through the forest and open meadows is an historical lodge built in the 30's by the Canadian Ski Club. Families with older kids who are intermediate skiers might enjoy an overnight stay in the middle of the backcountry. 403-522-3555.

Other Activities

Calgary Flames Hockey Games: If your timing is right, you can hop on a bus and head to the Olympic Saddledome in Calgary to watch the Calgary Flames in a home game. Snowtime 403-762-0745.

Dog Sled Tours: Tour the Rockies behind a friendly husky dog team. Choose from a 35-minute trip, a half-day trip, a full-day tour, and an overnight tour. 403-522-3532.

Ice Skating: Chateau Lake Louise is the center of ice skating on the lake open daily from 2 to 4 and 7 to 9 P.M. with complimentary hot chocolate, music, and a bonfire. Skate rentals are available. 403-522-3511.

Sleigh rides: Sleigh rides under the stars are offered nightly. 403-522-3511 ext. 1210.

Snowmobiling: Challenge Snowmobile Tours offer introductory tours, full-day, or multi-day tours. 800-892-3492.

Snowshoeing: Rentals are available at Wilson Mountain Sports who can advise you on where to snowshoe. 403-522-3636.

Deals and Discounts

Beginner learn-to-ski and snowboard packages include half-day lesson, ski equipment, and lift ticket for the surface lifts and are a very good value. The Stay and Ski at Louise packages offered early and late season are very low priced.

SKI RESORTS BY REGION

Ski Resorts by Region

Vermont

Wyoming

GENERAL INDEX

General Index